Resistance in Indian Documentary Film

POLITICAL CINEMAS
Series Editor: David Archibald

Political Cinemas publishes books which offer new insights into how film and film culture have both shaped and responded to the crises through which we have lived, and how they might positively influence the ones we are moving into.

Titles in the series include:

Looking Beyond Neoliberalism: French and Francophone Belgian Cinema and the Crisis
Martin O'Shaughnessy

Tracking Loach: Politics | Practices | Production
David Archibald

Resistance in Indian Documentary Film: Aesthetics, Culture and Practice
Edited by Shweta Kishore and Kunal Ray

Resistance in Indian Documentary Film

Aesthetics, Culture and Practice

Edited by Shweta Kishore and Kunal Ray

EDINBURGH
University Press

Edinburgh University Press is one of the leading university presses in the UK. We publish academic books and journals in our selected subject areas across the humanities and social sciences, combining cutting-edge scholarship with high editorial and production values to produce academic works of lasting importance. For more information visit our website: edinburghuniversitypress.com

© editorial matter and organisation Shweta Kishore and Kunal Ray, 2024, 2025
© the chapters their several authors 2024, 2025

Grateful acknowledgement is made to the sources listed in the List of Illustrations for permission to reproduce material previously published elsewhere. Every effort has been made to trace the copyright holders, but if any have been inadvertently overlooked, the publisher will be pleased to make the necessary arrangements at the first opportunity.

Edinburgh University Press Ltd
13 Infirmary Street
Edinburgh EH1 1LT

First published in hardback by Edinburgh University Press 2024

Typeset in 12 on 14pt Arno Pro by
Cheshire Typesetting Ltd, Cuddington, Cheshire

A CIP record for this book is available from the British Library

ISBN 978 1 3995 2566 4 (hardback)
ISBN 978 1 3995 2567 1 (paperback)
ISBN 978 1 3995 2568 8 (webready PDF)
ISBN 978 1 3995 2569 5 (epub)

The right of Shweta Kishore and Kunal Ray to be identified as the editors of this work has been asserted in accordance with the Copyright, Designs and Patents Act 1988, and the Copyright and Related Rights Regulations 2003 (SI No. 2498).

Contents

List of Figures vii
Notes on Contributors viii
List of Abbreviations xiii

Introduction: Resistance in the digitised present 1
Shweta Kishore and Kunal Ray

Part I Critical perspectives on documentary aesthetics and form

1. The corporeality of homelessness in *Cities of Sleep*: Social aesthetics and an unreliable narrator 27
   Shweta Kishore

2. 'Canine spaces': Kolkata's slum dogs 47
   Veena Hariharan

3. 'Threadbearing': Journeys with our subjects and our documentary narratives 66
   Anjali Monteiro and K. P. Jayasankar

Part II Representation of lived experience

4. Personal is political: Documentary and intimacy 83
   Shabnam Sukhdev

5. Making films from and about the margins 92
   Lipika Singh Darai

6. Against all odds: A filmmaker's quest to make films in Northeast India 100
   Haobam Paban Kumar

7. Experiencing and representing conflict: Encounters of a Kashmiri filmmaker 109
   Raja Shabir Khan

8. Documentary and oppositional Bahujan agency 114
   Jyoti Nisha

Part III Resistance in practice

9. Curating documentary film and video art in a museum: Reflections from *Loss and Transience* 127
   Rashmi Devi Sawhney and Lucía Imaz King

10. Working with time: Editing the documentary 148
    Sameera Jain

11. Cultural documentary: Dialogues between aesthetics and society 165
    Ein Lall

12. The politics of image-making 174
    R. V. Ramani

13. Two starting points: The sonic in my films 182
    Yashaswini

14. Conversations, confusions, confessions: Living with and working in cinema 189
    Anupama Srinivasan

15. About critique: Indian media and documentary cinema 197
    Kunal Ray and Mochish K. S.

Epilogue: On building documentary cultures of resistance 211
An interview with K. P. Jayasankar and Anjali Monteiro

Films Cited 223
Index 225

List of Figures

5.1 Still from *Dragonfly and Snake* (2014). The film appears as a split screen with two different images running on each half of the screen, visualising a conversation between the filmmaker and her great-aunt. Picture courtesy of author. 94
6.1 Still from *AFSPA 1958* (2005). Picture courtesy of author. 101
9.1 Detail, painting from the series *Each Night Put Kashmir in Your Dreams* by Nilima Sheikh, featured in the documentary *The Garden of Forgotten Snow* (2017) by Avijit Mukul Kishore. Image courtesy of Nilima Sheikh. 134
9.2 Ranbir Kaleka, still from *Forest* (2009). Image reproduction courtesy of artist. 138
9.3 Installation view of *Loss and Transience* at the Hong-gah Museum, Taipei, Taiwan, 2021. Image courtesy of Hong-gah Museum. Photo credit Hsiang-Ling Huang. 141
10.1 *Sudhamayee* (*Laced with the Nectar of Life*, 2019) by Megha Acharya (student film from the course Creative Documentary, New Delhi). Picture courtesy of author. 150
10.2 The accident filmed from a balcony in *Mera Apna Sheher* (2011). Picture courtesy of author. 153
10.3 Still from *A Quiet Little Entry* (2010) by Uma Chakravarti. Picture courtesy of author. 154
12.1 Still from *My Camera and Tsunami* (2011). Picture courtesy of author. 179
13.1 Still frame of a 35mm celluloid film strip used to make *kyatketis*, from *That Cloud Never Left* (2019). Picture courtesy of author. 185
14.1 A rough attempt at a diagrammatic representation of the filmmaking and exhibition process. 193

Notes on Contributors

Shweta Kishore lectures in Screen and Media at RMIT (Royal Melbourne Institute of Technology) University. Her core research focuses on Indian documentary, documentary ethics, feminist film, documentary film practice, co-constructed documentary and film festivals. She is the author of *Indian documentary film and filmmakers: Independence in practice* (2018, Edinburgh University Press). Her research has appeared in *Third Text, Bioscope, Camera Obscura, Feminist Media Studies, Studies in Documentary Film* and *Senses of Cinema*. Kishore is a documentary practitioner and in 2019 curated Artist Cinema: Documentary from Vietnam at the Kochi Muziris Biennale, India.

Kunal Ray is an academic and leading culture critic. He teaches Literary and Cultural Studies at FLAME University, Pune. His writings on art and culture in India regularly appear in *The Hindu, The Indian Express* and *Hindustan Times*, among other publications. He has co-edited *Shabd aur Sangeet: Unravelling song-text in India* (2019). He is also the co-founder and co-editor of *On Eating: A Multilingual Journal of Food and Eating*.

Anjali Monteiro and **K. P. Jayasankar** are retired Professors of the School of Media and Cultural Studies, Tata Institute of Social Sciences, Mumbai. Their documentary films, which have been screened around the world, have won thirty-three national and international awards. They research and write in the broad areas of censorship, documentary film and Media and Cultural Studies and have contributed to scholarly journals and edited volumes. Their publications include *A fly in the curry: Independent documentary film in India* (2016), which has won a Special Mention for the best book on cinema at the 2016 National Film Awards; together with

Amit S. Rai, the edited volume *DigiNaka: Subaltern politics and digital media in post-capitalist India* (2020); and together with Faiz Ullah, the edited volume *Many voices, many worlds: Critical perspectives on community media in India* (2021).

Anupama Srinivasan is a Delhi-based filmmaker, film educator and curator. An alumna of Harvard University and the Film and Television Institute of India, she has been making documentaries for over twenty years, often shooting and editing her own work. *Flickering Lights* and *Nocturnes*, two of the latest feature documentaries that she co-directed, premiered and won awards at IDFA and Sundance. Anupama served as Director of the IAWRT Asian Women's Film Festival for three years (2013–15) and of the Peace Builders International Film Festival in 2016.

Ein Lall is a documentary filmmaker and video artist who works from New Delhi and Colombo. Focussing on women in the arts, she interweaves the documentary format with creative imagination, using dance and music to suggest subliminal motifs in the work of women artists. Lall has made short-films on educational and activist subjects for the Goethe Institute, Jagori, UNICEF and INTACH. She has created multi-channel video installations for dance and theatre performances at the National School of Drama, New Delhi; Haus der Kulturen der Welt, Berlin; and Japan Foundation, Tokyo.

Haobam Paban Kumar is a prominent voice from the restive northeastern state of Manipur, India, dabbling in both non-fiction and fiction storytelling. His film *AFSPA 1958* was awarded the Golden Lotus for the Best Documentary at the 56th National Film Awards 2008. *A Cry in The Dark* is another film screened at the 31st Toronto Film Festival 2006 and MOMA New York 2007. After a decade of documentary filmmaking, he made his critically acclaimed feature film *Loktak Lairembee* (*Lady of the Lake*) which featured at the 67th Berlin Film Festival 2017 and New Currents, 21st Busan International Film Festival 2016.

Jyoti Nisha is an academic, writer, screenwriter and filmmaker with a focus on cinema, gaze, caste, gender and media. She has fifteen years of experience in print, radio and television. Her article 'Indian cinema and the Bahujan spectatorship' is credited with conceptualising a theory that opposes the popular culture's casteist male gaze and stereotypical representation of the marginalised. She has directed, produced and crowd-funded the feature-length documentary film, *Dr. B. R. Ambedkar: Now & Then* in collaboration with Pa Ranjith's Neelam Productions. Her writing has also appeared in *AlJazeera, Economic & Political Weekly, The Verve Magazine, The Times of India, The Indian Express* and *NDTV*.

Lipika Singh Darai is a film director and editor based in Bhubaneswar, Odisha. She has a specialisation in Sound Recording and Design from the Film and Television Institute of India. Between 2010 and 2017, she received four National Film Awards – two in direction, two in sound recording and narration of a film. She hails from the Ho indigenous community of the Mayurbhanj district in Odisha. Her recent documentary *Night and Fear* had its world premiere in the Ammodo Tiger Short Competition section at the International Film Festival Rotterdam 2023.

Lucía Imaz King's research and practice fall into three strands. The first pertains to her work as a practitioner in drawing, painting and video installation artworks. The second concerns her engagement as a researcher of artists' moving image. Following a period of residency in India in the 2000s, Lucía acquired a PhD from SOAS Centre for Media and Film (University of London), specialising in the creative methodologies of South Asian artists, filmmakers and experimental documentary filmmakers, including the transnational distribution contexts of their works (1990s to the present). Thirdly, she is a curator of artists' moving image and, in 2014, she founded VisionMix, an artist-led professional network of artists, filmmakers and curators that operates transnationally, with many of its associate members based in India.

Mochish K. S. holds a PhD in Media and Cultural Studies from the Tata Institute of Social Sciences, Mumbai. His doctoral research analyses the role of Malayalam newspapers in land struggles and movements in Kerala between 1930 and 2008. His areas of academic interest include media histories, media and public action and political communication. Mochish teaches at FLAME University, Pune.

Raja Shabir Khan is a documentary filmmaker hailing from Kashmir. He is widely recognized for his works that showcase the beauty and struggles of his homeland. Shabir's filmmaking has earned numerous accolades, including a National Award, and has led him to collaborate with some of the world's leading broadcasters, such as NHK (Japan), MediaCorp (Singapore), KBS (South Korea) and Aljazeera Documentary (Doha). Shabir's documentaries have not only brought attention to Kashmiri culture but also shed light on the complex political and social issues of the region.

Rashmi Devi Sawhney is Associate Arts Professor of Film and New Media at New York University, Abu Dhabi. She is co-founder, with Lucía Imaz King, of VisionMix (www.visionmix.info), an international network for creative practice and research. She writes on cinema and the visual arts in South Asia. She is editor of journal issues on Women at Work: The Cultural and Creative Industries (2019); South Asian Science Fiction and Fantasy (2015), and co-editor of South Asian Artists' Film and Video (2018). Her book, The Vanishing Point: Moving Images After Video, was published in 2022.

R. V. Ramani is a leading Indian documentary filmmaker. With more than thirty independent films to his credit, he has established a unique style of his own, making impressionistic subjective documentaries exploring various aspects of expression. His film *Oh, That's Bhanu* was awarded the 68th National Award for best direction, and his films are frequently featured in collections of experimental Indian documentary. He regularly conducts filmmaking workshops and has collaborated on many films as a cinematographer.

Sameera Jain edits and directs films and is involved with diverse aspects of filmmaking practice. Her work has been exhibited widely, and she is an active participant in film juries and curriculum design. Jain teaches and mentors at several platforms and institutions, including her alma mater, the Film and Television Institute of India (FTII). She has a sustained interest in structuring pedagogic practice which pushes the boundaries of the documentary form and interrogates accepted codes around it. Since 2013, she has served as Course Director for the course Creative Documentary, SACAC (Sri Aurobindo Centre for Arts and Communication), New Delhi.

Shabnam Sukhdev is an Indo-Canadian filmmaker and educator with an MFA in Film Production from York University and a post-graduate diploma in Cinema from the Film and Television Institute of India, Pune. Driven by a strong social conscience, her work focuses on core issues of identity and culture, feminism and sexuality, migration and mental health. *The Last Adieu* is an intimate account of her relationship with her father, which captures the spirit of documentary filmmaker S. Sukhdev as it traces the Indian documentary film movement of the 1960s and 1970s. She is currently pursuing doctoral research at York University.

Veena Hariharan is Associate Professor of Cinema Studies at the School of Arts and Aesthetics, Jawaharlal Nehru University. Her essays and articles on documentary, non-fiction cinema and the environment have appeared in anthologies and journals. She is currently Alexander von Humboldt Fellow at the Goethe University, Frankfurt, where she is working on her project on human/non-human entanglements in cinema and new media. Her book *Embers of reason: Contemporary Indian documentary and the secular imagination* is forthcoming.

Yashaswini works with film and sound. She developed a special interest in sound and its narrative potentiality while making her album 'man in the eye' with her friend Jackie Ford. Her film *That Cloud Never Left* premiered at the International Film Festival of Rotterdam 2019.

List of Abbreviations

AFSPA – Armed Forces Special Power Act
BMRCL – Bangalore Metro Rail Corporation Limited
CBC – Canadian Broadcasting Corporation
CD – Compact Disc
CSDS – Centre for the Study of Developing Societies
DCP – Digital Cinema Package
DV Cam – Digital Video Camera
DVD – Digital Versatile Disc
FD – Films Division
FTII – Film and Television Institute of India
HD – High-Definition
HDV – High-Definition Video
HIV – Human Immunodeficiency Virus
IAS – Indian Administrative Service
IAWRT – International Association of Women in Radio and Television
IDSFFK – International Documentary and Short Film Festival of Kerala
IFFI – International Film Festival of India
ISI – Inter-Services Intelligence
ISO – International Organisation for Standardisation
LGBTQ – Lesbian Gay Bisexual Transgender Queer
LOC – Line of Control
MAMI – Mumbai Academy of Moving Image
MMB – Max Mueller Bhavan
MIFF – Mumbai International Film Festival
NBA – Narmada Bachao Andolan
NFDC – National Film Development Corporation
NGO – Non-governmental organisation

OTT – Over the Top
PARI – People's Archive of Rural India
PSBT – Public Service Broadcasting Trust
SIM – Subscriber Identity Module
SRFTI – Satyajit Ray Film and Television Institute of India
TISS – Tata Institute of Social Sciences
TV – Television
VFX – Visual Effects
VHS – Video Home System

Introduction

Resistance in the digitised present

Shweta Kishore and Kunal Ray

Documentary film in India faces an interesting contradiction. While its expression and practice remain unique, varied and mutable, its broader understanding and discourse foreground communicative functions of bringing change through education, information and the influencing of opinions. This can be explained partly by the historical development of independent documentary as a practice forged in opposition to a centralised regime of media production and distribution, aimed at building nationalist sentiments in the post-independence phase of nation-building. Reacting to the nationalistic and propagandist impulse of this phase of government documentary filmmaking, the independent movement that broke ground in the mid-1970s sought a public forum to represent perspectives and histories marginalised in state discourse. Scholars have focussed on the themes, issues and voices that constitute histories of resistance in this cinema (Jayasankar and Monteiro 2015; Kishore 2018) but less is known about contemporary modes and aesthetics of resistance where, on the one hand, not much has changed in relation to documentary's cultural outsider status, while on the other, the aesthetic and production landscape of contemporary documentary is alive with new voices, technologies, spaces and methods. Partially and expectedly, this is a response to changes in political, economic, social and environmental conditions, even as new audio-visual technologies, spaces of production and exhibition, and transnational flows of culture act to transform the forms, meanings and functions of documentary. As global media industries and cultures transform, the local contexts of majoritarian political discourse, globalising cultural meanings, rising social inequalities, tightening media regulatory mechanisms and variable access to digital technologies extend and produce new structures of power, inequality and forms of marginalisation against which practitioners identify contemporary languages and practices of resistance.

From the standpoint of representation, a commitment to diverse perspectives and their potential to challenge fixed subject positions distinguishes documentary in a congested media landscape. With 869 private television channels, more than 50 per cent of the Indian population is part of the television universe; as scholars argue, media in general and television in particular have become an essential instrument of nationalism under the current Modi government (Rajagopal 2016; Chopra 2019). The category of patriotism and nationalism are reorganised within a homogenous national community of Indians, even as minority voices of dissent and interrogation are overwhelmed or purposefully delegitimised in mainstream media. Public discourse on national identity in India, observes Rajagopal (2016), demonstrates alliances between commercial media and the state. The Indian government deregulated broadcasting in 1995, which many believed would deliver freedom of opinion and choice based on healthy competition amongst media outlets. On the contrary, the expansion of media outlets has narrowed channels of dissent, as commercial media has replaced the powerful propagandist role of state broadcasting.

The renewed focus on the contours of resistance and how documentary may 'alter the world' (Nichols 1991, 3) is prompted by shifts in the socio-cultural and technological landscape of documentary production and circulation. In India, this takes on a particular potency in the context of (a) filmmakers' artistic and social commitments to representing voice as a political objective and (b) the chronic lack of financial and institutional support for documentary cinema in which digital technology presents both opportunities and constraints at the levels of expression and practice. At the outset, the critique of digital technology usages reveals the construction of 'digital collectivities' or strengthening modes of religion-based subjectification in India (Bhatia 2021). Digital infrastructures and tools mediate virtual realms where religious communities and individuals define their associations based on religious subjectivities, interwoven with political agendas and actions. Within their digital usage, people increasingly base their political conduct and aspirations on a common religious subjectivity.

Yet, as sites of struggle, diverse actors, individuals, groups, communities and organisations mobilise digital technologies to intervene in the social and political domains (Carpentier 2011, 120). The proliferation of digital tools for recording and dissemination, particularly mobile phones, access to internet-based communication – including, among others, social media apps, YouTube, Facebook, Snapchat and Instagram – and web-based file sharing, video-editing and web-hosting services have expanded access to modes and technologies of self-representation, media practice and film culture. Digital technology's contradictory and uneven effects produce competing potentials for hegemonic and democratic forms of communication, participation and formation of publics. In socially embedded engagements, cultural producers from the social margins embrace a political conceptualisation of media representation by mobilising digital media affordances for functions of self-representation, social commentary and sharing of information.[1] Filmmaking collectives and individual filmmakers mobilise their experiences of caste and religious discrimination to produce media for self-defined needs and goals. Therefore, an evident pushback against upper-class and, frequently, upper-caste spokespersons including documentary filmmakers can be seen to take shape. Arguably, this does not mean that the digital empowerment discourse is without limitations, but, to the extent that this is indicative of the democratisation of media technology, what the digital proliferates are new forms of media participation producing distinct expressions, subjectivities and publics that act as discursive formations in constructing documentary's notion of the political in the digitised present. With shifts in globalised and localised forms and expressions of power, the tools and spaces of resistance are occupied by a more diverse range of actors for whom resistance is grounded in lived experience and struggle. These present new possibilities for the definition and discourse of documentary by focusing attention on the diversity of languages and expressions that filmmakers and practitioners devise, adapt and transform to contest the forms of oppression which they face personally and as part of a community or collective, both socially and as media subjects.

To this purpose, this collection draws together contributions by scholars and practitioners, including filmmakers, curators, educators and critics. Documentary practitioners relate first-person accounts about how they approach media technology that illustrate individual understandings and functions of the documentary form. In *Rethinking Documentary* (2008), Austin and De Jong combine documentary scholarship and practice for related objectives that reflect the 'manifold practices and objects' which may be grouped under the category of documentary. Solicited based on open-ended questions about key concerns underpinning individual practice, the practitioner accounts in this volume yield an enormously rich understanding of how individuals interpret cultural forms and technologies for the expression of individual and community goals. These multiple perspectives speak to the intersecting social locations of individuals on criteria such as identity, community grouping, experience and competencies, and they model how Film Studies can move beyond critique to provide concrete resources for the organisation of resistance as social practice. In this respect, we hope to 'co-construct' our conclusions through methodologies that bypass the positioning of practitioners in academic research either as informants in data-gathering or as authors who become known through textual expression, or whose accounts are presented as description, or generalised as a representative category (Horner 2016, 8). Instead, the subjectivist methodologies in this volume attempt to produce localised knowledge about power structures, practices and discourses against which individuals organise audio-visual resistance and the ways in which this expands the concept of documentary resistance in historically situated ways.

Theorising resistance in documentary

Documentary film has historically aligned with resistance towards the hegemonic tendencies of state and social institutions, by taking a position and point of view to enter public debate. Documentary's counter-hegemonic modes engage the historical world by 'shaping its photographic record' from a 'distinct perspective' to become 'one voice amongst many' in an arena of discursive contestation (Nichols 2010, 37). Documentary's address to the viewer is as a citizen, a putative participant in the public sphere, theoretically a space of rational debate, discussion and deliberation. However, as Chanan (2007, 38) points out, the public sphere is a field of overlapping interests and 'constant skirmishes' between political parties and interests battling between different strategies of debate and communication. Documentary often takes the position of 'a sniper' challenging the conventions of what is debated and how it is debated. Documentary intervenes in social processes not only by attacking the discursive construction of issues, but also by granting the means to speakers and voices to represent oppositional perspectives. As Kluge et al. (1981, 212) state, the expansion of the existing public sphere involves 'carrying one piece of information to another place in society', thus establishing 'lines of communication' that are 'just as important as direct action, the immediate on-the-spot struggle'. An expanded or alternate public sphere in contrast to the one created by mass media such as television and private interests, according to Kluge, acknowledges the existence of ideological exclusions which rule out genuine debate and representation in the public sphere. The work of the documentary then is to contribute to the construction of a community in which people are able to identify what they 'have in common with other people' as the basis of an alternative public sphere (213). For Kluge et al., documentary's oppositional location in relation to cultures of mass media and entertainment is based on a political-economic analysis linking signification to social conditions of media production. In these discussions, resistance is interlinked with documentary's public address as a communicative medium whose authenticity is tied to its location beyond industrial capitalist modes of production and to the representation of issues excluded or suppressed from public discussion.

This theorisation is crucial to the configuration of resistance in Indian documentary, both in terms of its political charge as well as its relation to dominant systems and structures of authority and representation. From an Adornian perspective, culture needs criticism as an integral component of its very existence, since culture 'is only true when implicitly critical' (Adorno 1967 [1983], 22). For documentary, the reluctance to be considered as part of a culture industry, with its implications of social domination and rational instrumentality, is integral to its position of resistance. The political perspective towards culture as a field of struggle, between competing values and interests, encompasses both historical forms of resistance towards which Indian documentary aligns with other resistant actions and cultural forms, as well as resistance towards its own systemisation as a vehicle for hegemonic or didactic forms of knowledge. Therefore, dissent and critique while seemingly existing in the world of artistic discourse are crucial foundations of resistance within Indian documentary film. Public speech and documentary narratives take aim at hegemonic regimes of capital, class, gender, caste and the like, which dominate cultural production, thereby keeping documentary alert to its appropriation by mainstream consensual relations between culture, capital and power.

John Corner's (2009) conceptualisation of politics in documentary is particularly useful to situate the definition of resistance in this volume. Politics may point towards a *sphere or designated space* in which politics is visible, obvious and direct; however, as a *level or dimension*, politics is intertwined with areas of everyday life. The revealing of this non-self-evident layer vitally offers the possibility of portraying the hidden politicality of the world, which we take for granted by politicising its givenness and self-evident nature. Opening up the analysis of *how* documentaries represent (not only *what* they represent), this approach brings aesthetics into focus as an area of critical meaning, more than just style or artistic flourish. In this relation, aesthetic is a critical space where questions of form refer to rules and instruments of legitimisation that ultimately act to establish and contest hierarchies, categories and definitions. Following Rancierian thought, politics appears not so much as a pre-existing set of issues, but rather 'revolves around what is seen and what can be said about it, around who has the ability to see and the talent to speak, around the properties of spaces and the possibilities of time' (Rancière 2006, 13). By focusing attention on the form or enunciation of a statement, the position of the enunciator and the context of the enunciation, analysis retains all the possibilities of examining politics in the organisation of documentary aesthetics and practice, as well as its social relations.

In a powerful statement against the constriction of politics to a function of story or narrative, Lebow and Juhasz (2021) draw on Rancierian politics when defining the diverse functions of documentary to 'intervene in perceptual and sensible reckonings – how the social world is perceived and understood'. Rancière's notion of 'dissensus' connects the political and the aesthetic: 'A dissensus is not a conflict of interests, opinions, or values; it is a division inserted in "common sense": a dispute over what is given and about the frame within which we see something as given' (Rancière 2010, 69). For Rancière, 'consensus' constricts politics to authoritarian norms of 'the police', the distribution of society into groups, positions and functions, and an aesthetic division between the sayable and the unsayable, the audible and the inaudible. In documentary, consensus is equally undesirable. In their manifesto, Juhasz and Lebow (2021) offer the clearest yet most open conceptualisation of documentary resistance, stating that, while 'cinema can provide one remedy for the human need to create causal sense, it can also resist, embellish, complicate, or mirror this lack'. Resisting closure or consensus are films that 'run outside of structures of capitalist accumulation, subjective pleasure, ease, or comfort, or even a desire for rational sense'. Resistance to consensus in documentary politics must acknowledge the plurality and heterogeneity of documentary languages and associations to expand beyond causal and representational notions of politics. In this sense, this volume takes up documentary forms that, instead of advocating for a political issue, uncover a sphere of politicality where varied modes of engagement include the creative use of unreliability, performance, emotion, pleasure, memory, personal experience, Adivasi (indigenous) creation mythology and non-human presence, which collectively resist consensus over documentary's rhetorical strategies of verisimilitude, factuality and its distance from the 'distracting shadow play of fiction' (Nichols 1991, 4).

Placing films in context, in this volume we analyse how documentary processes reflect and resist historic and semiotic orders through interventions ranging from critically expressive strategies to concrete practices. The categories of subject and power and familiar binaries of dominance and submission are complicated by discursive constructions of subject, power and resistance. Rather than a genuine collapse of power hierarchies and social divisions, these shifts require ways of seeing and understanding that re-examine how resistance in documentary encompasses diverse forms, voices and expressions. This volume is an attempt to explore these aesthetic and subjective multiplicities which contest unitary and instrumentalist narratives of identity, capital and culture that have historically existed but whose categorising functions have gained further momentum in India. To this end, the volume offers an expanded and contemporary reflection on the meaning of resistance, so as to consider how in taking a position documentary film enters social debate and challenges accepted orders of genre, form and technique – thus configuring resistance as both historical and symbolic practice. This requires an expansive consideration of how films are made, circulated and exhibited, particularly in historical contexts where documentary cinema has evolved outside defined institutional spaces or studios, in ways that in themselves offer a potent statement of resistance against the systematisation and institutional obligations attributed to cultural production. Therefore, in this collection, politics is intertwined across symbolic and historical realms, across the signified and the signifier, across the filmmaker's textual presence and her historical body, and in the multitude of relations, networks and sites where documentary film is created, exhibited, discussed, argued over, taught, archived, curated and sensed. The 'impact of documentary' is therefore not delimited by the projection of an issue, but in the messy 'doing' of documentary, as it attempts unique aesthetic vocabularies and establishes different relations of viewing and participation that challenge the practices of 'making' and 'doing' of arts and culture. Important among this is the need to challenge the systemisation of documentary's political impulse, by rethinking the elements of politics in documentary, its aesthetic regimes, its modes of address, its spaces of intervention, as well as the public and private forms of engagements it forms with people.

Resistance in Indian documentary

Scholarly work on the historical development of independent documentary in India has flourished in recent years (Wolf 2013; Sarkar and Wolf 2012; Jayasankar and Monteiro 2015; Battaglia 2017; Kishore 2018;

James and Venkatesan 2021); therefore, this account (rather than mapping this history) coheres around a resistant history of this practice. Extending beyond representational issues or textual positions, what comes across is a set of approaches, decisions and actions through which film practitioners resist the ideological positioning of culture in relation to market functions and as an instrumental form of communication to legitimise institutional relations of power.

Textual resistance: Voice, subjectivity and ethics

Scholars apply three primary frameworks to analyse the subject-matter and aesthetic politics of documentary's resistant positions in India: 'committed cinema' aimed at altering historical social relations (Waugh 2011 [1990]); documentary resistance against patriarchal social and aesthetic norms which steer a representational turn towards the 'subject' in Indian documentary (Vohra 2011; Gadihoke 2012); and resistance against 'statist imaginaries' and representations of nation and culture against which documentary intervenes politically and aesthetically (Jayasankar and Monteiro 2015). Each frames, resistance in terms of documentary's discursive roles of representing, reinterpreting, critiquing and contesting the expression and effects of power in the public domain, with the objective of altering social relations and relations of speech and visibility.

Taking relatively early documentary from the 1970s and 1980s as its subject, 'committed cinema' references left-wing, dissident and activist film that declared solidarity with radical socio-political transformation, in the form of immediate localised action, or by analysing issues and causes confronting ordinary people, workers, minorities and the disenfranchised (Waugh 1986). Drawing on the emancipatory politics of Third Cinema and post-colonial theory, as a politics of culture, resistance in independent documentary emerges against the 'paralysing grip' of the dominant 'top-down' Griersonian organisation of the state-run Films Division (Waugh 2011, 242). Ideological resistance against state-sponsored cultural production erupted during the state of emergency imposed by Prime Minister Indira Gandhi (1975–77), provoking 'dissident voices to part fully from governmental patronage' (Wolf 2013, 366). Independent documentary 'cast off' the 'inherited baggage' of centralised film production and distribution and its mass public address, or 'official worship', as termed by Anand Patwardhan (2015), towards an alternative, non-institutional form of filmmaking that instead of building consent sought to critique, interrogate and examine constructions of nation, citizen and state.

Films produced by the state film board or Films Division have been widely critiqued for their Griersonian aesthetics, or a 'state gaze' and 'sound' that collapsed rich and heterogenous cultures, histories and identities into discourses of nationhood and national citizenship (Roy 2007; Deprez 2013). The statist aesthetic of the nation was voiced in 'a voice from nowhere', alternating between an anglicised baritone or Sanskritised Hindi, both of which failed to capture the diversity and functionality of expressions and cultures contained in the linguistic communication of ordinary people (Roy 2007, 57). Against this, in independent films such as *Voices from Baliapal*, Waugh (2011, 252) identifies a different mode of political voice in the aesthetic of collective speech and oral culture, or 'first-person plural'. Waugh's analysis of voice and sound in independent documentary as an audible expression of committed politics discloses an aesthetic rebuttal to what Roy terms the 'policyspeak' of FD films. If mise-en-scène remains a site where one can read social relations, the diverse relations of speaking in independent documentary testify to resistance against the vocal assertion of nation-state and its incompatibility with diverse beliefs, values and identities of its heterogeneous population.

Extending Waugh's framing of commitment, the early films of filmmaker Anand Patwardhan reveal a uniquely localised adaptation of Third Cinema to represent local socio-political conflicts and struggles for the rights and guarantees promised by a democratic state (Hanlon 2015; Kishore 2016). *Waves of Revolution* and *Prisoners of Conscience* document the suspension of democratic liberties and the resulting mass political dissent during the state of emergency and aesthetically draw on languages of collective protest, including protest songs and poetry. Both films bring into the public domain the voices of those officially denounced as traitors on account of their participation in the protest movement, while offering broader political analysis of the events against Gandhian histories of non-violent resistance and non-cooperation as forms of protests.

Materially, too, the personal connection between the filmmaker and the represented historical world ties this filmmaking practice to the principles of Third Cinema. In contrast to the determinedly detached relationship between the filmmaker and the film participants of Direct Cinema, Patwardhan's practice intersects with the rhetorical questions posed by García Espinosa (1979, 25) in 'For an Imperfect Cinema'; there, he asks: 'Why protect oneself and seek recognition as a (revolutionary, it must be understood) political and scientific worker, yet not be prepared to run the same risks'. Patwardhan's filmmaking – which has interrogated hegemonies of nationalism, caste discrimination and religious fascism

– is inseparable from his political activities in the social world (Kishore 2016).² Encompassing a pointed analysis of ideology and structural relations of power, the intersection of artistic and social objectives of independent filmmakers extends beyond textual responses. Instead, filmmakers utilise documentary for the construction of social relationships and action in people's movements for resources and rights. During the 1980s, the framing of documentary beyond institutional functions fundamentally challenged cultural and social binaries – between culture and everyday life, between audience and participant, between artist and activist – thus laying the foundations for an independent non-institutional, self-organised practice. Grounded in personal political participation, documentary representation attained meaning in relation to dissent against social inequalities and ideologies of patriarchy, social discrimination and nationalist groupings.

The political context of student movements and the women's movements in the late 1970s and early 1980s mediated the rise of feminist filmmakers and collective forms of filmmaking. The Delhi-based Mediastorm founded in 1985, comprising six film school graduates, was the first such all-women collective to use video for the collective authoring of documentary. Mediastorm member and film scholar Shohini Ghosh (2018) recalls a broader interrogation of documentary ethics and representational politics, such as the notion that 'the indexical bond to the referent was no longer adequate' to corelate documentary image with historical truth. Urgent self-critique at this juncture was to steer a turn towards subjective documentary modes and aesthetics that extended resistance to representational critique. Self-reflection on the ethics of documentary representation and the distribution of power between filmmaker, subject and spectator connect this moment to international discourses of feminist documentary. Reflecting on this period, Sabeena Gadihoke (2012, 145) notes that, 'as in the West, the turn to more open forms of first-person filming emerged out of identity politics and the feminist and queer movements in particular'. Hence, to the extent that films such as *Hidden Story* not only address patriarchal oppression, but also in terms of their narrative, they reflexively interrogate documentary ethics by featuring the negotiation between the distinct social and cultural positions of the city-based filmmaker and rural women film-subjects. The presence of the filmmaker persona rubbed up against established notions of authority in documentary, which meant that these interventions were dismissed as self-absorbed conceits of middle-class filmmakers (Gadihoke 2012). In response, filmmakers argued that these practices contained the possibility to forge alliances across social differences to uncover shared erasures and interiorities.

In 1991, economic liberalisation in India was accompanied by the entry of satellite networks, cable channels and the further commercialisation of national broadcaster, Doordarshan. The ideology of liberalisation promised the introduction of market reforms and unhindered economic growth; however, in actuality the reforms aggravated class inequality as the state shifted from its welfare functions to protect market and business interests (Rajagopal 2001, 35). In a burgeoning media economy, documentary filmmakers identified critical oppositional relations between independent film and the institutional settings and functions of market and state. In their manifesto, in a politically trenchant section titled 'Beyond delivering audiences to advertisers', FIFV, an association of independent film- and video-makers, stated: 'Independent filmmaking is an attitude […] It represents a desire to make and see films that are free from commercial and propagandist imperatives' (1996, 13). Art critic Geeta Kapur (2008) identifies a 'cultural conjuncture' between art and documentary during this period that sharpened documentary resistance against an ascendant rightwing proto-fascist politics connected with the expansion of a neoliberal consumer society. A fundamental churning in the Indian art scene, including documentary, was led by shifts towards a more consciously unstable, volatile and radical artist subjectivity (Kapur 2008, 37). Importantly, while belonging to the class of national elite wielding cultural and social capital, filmmakers 'supported the more contestatory values' of a democratic polity and took a position on contested issues, notes Kapur (2008, 37). As filmmaker Saba Dewan (quoted in Singh 2019) recalls, …

> As students we had all the filmmakers at that time, from Anand Patwardhan to Deepa Dhanraj coming and showing their work. I remember genuinely feeling charged because I was a part of student politics through my undergraduate years, and here was a medium to protest injustice in new ways, to expose the hidden realities. That is the kind of filmmaking I gravitated to in the early period of my career.

Framed by values of democratic dissent, filmmakers often formed alliances with people's movements to assume positions of concerned citizen, social commentator, investigator, participant and inquirer. These roles were to later attract reflection and critique, expanding the terrain of resistance into more self-reflexive and interrogatory territory.

In the post-liberalisation phase of economic reorganisation, historical connections between working-class politics, radical movements and leftwing activism seemed to loosen, and the identity and author position of the 'revolutionary' filmmaker came under sustained scrutiny. In an essay titled 'Dotting the i: The politics of self-less-ness in Indian documentary practice', filmmaker Paromita Vohra (2011) critiques Indian documentary's enunciating positions, ethics and representational politics. In Vohra's contention, political films of the 1980s and 1990s submerge the self of the filmmaker in a discourse of self-lessness or a desire to be 'the voice of the people' (48). Injecting a semiotic dimension to resistance, Vohra and others interrogated the collapse of the authoring self of the filmmaker into revolutionary or spokesperson, categories whose socially conscious persona refracted questions of subjectivity and power. In a turn mediated by feminist aesthetics and practice, filmmakers such as Vohra, Madhusree Datta and Saba Dewan adopted self-reflexive positions, allowing the filmmaker and film-subject to navigate power equations and thereby releasing the subject from merely performing as proof of argument (Wolf 2013). In documentary films from the 2000s, Vohra observes a 're-examination of modes of power in conversation/interview, the idea of oral histories, a comfort with personal viewpoints and approaches' (49). Instead of performing as educator or legislator in films such as *7 Islands and a Metro*, *Saacha*, *Jashn e Azaadi* and *A Season Outside*, the filmmaker features as an inquirer or provocateur problematising the stability of social truths and official narratives of nation and citizenship, as well as their screen representation.

More recent scholarship locates dissent in the contestation of dominant and exclusionary narratives of nation, caste, gender and shifting forms of marginalities (Jayasankar and Monteiro 2015). What remains consistent in the theorisation of committed cinema is the central focus on documentary's charge of interceding in the public sphere, albeit with greater attention to the complex modes and styles that produce critical and reflexive forms of spectator engagement. Drawing on the Foucauldian separation between signifier and signified, or the problem of a recursive 'similitude relayed indefinitely', the relation between truth and representation is problematised (Jayasankar and Monteiro 2015, 71). Therefore, resistance exceeds political representation to include the appreciation of the practices of poetic and artistic filmmakers, such as Mani Kaul, who foreground expressive, experimental and often non-verbocentric approaches to image and sound.

Resistance in practice: Audience and industry

The centring of documentary film practice and ethics in the relationship between the self and the world forms a significant departure from standardised notions of culture, cultural producer and cultural production in the context of capital-intensive and highly regulated contemporary media ecologies. Importantly, the study of practice makes tangible the interpretation of rules and norms in the form of observable performance, showing how these may be interpreted or resisted through embodiment in publicly accessible activity (Rouse 2000, 504). Admittedly, a diverse, kaleidoscopic and mobile field of practices – fundamental to the resistant and politically independent position of this practice – is an artisanal mode of production (Kishore 2018). An artisanal approach can be delineated on the basis of the subject-positionality or Self of the cultural producer or filmmaker; a symbolically autonomous producer who, while situated within socio-historical conditions and systems of patronage, endeavours to retain cultural authority or their 'own direction at all stages' of production (Williams 1981, 45). A central goal for Indian filmmakers, artistic autonomy is based on a conceptualisation of art practice alternative to neoliberal consumption-driven, capital-intensive, professionalised and standardised modes of media production (Kishore 2018). As the 'commodity image' of capitalist production transfers the profit motive onto cultural forms, artisanal production contests the logics and patterns of perception that fix culture into commodity form.

Distinguishing itself from other authorised non-fiction media such as current affairs reportage, journalism, or information production, the cultural and formal dimensions of Indian documentary based on content (politically radical, socially and/or culturally radical), form (aesthetic varieties of presentation), distributive use (alternative sites of distribution) and transformed social relations (de-professionalisation, improvisation, cooperative organisation) mark independent practice closer to Atton's (2001) conceptualisation of 'alternative media'. Featured in this collection, and more broadly, a vast range of films resist industrial production frameworks around content, format or genres, distribution and evaluation, thus depicting an alternative terrain and philosophy of media practice. Contemporary Indian documentary addresses a wide range of functions (for example, consciousness-raising, interrogation of historical or social forms of authority, documentation of community or individual experience, portrayal of social phenomenon, aesthetic critique of art and media forms), takes diverse aesthetic approaches (performance, reflexivity, non-indexical image and sound relations, unreliable narrator, associative, experimental, expository), localises technologies (consumer-grade or semi-professional digital technology, small-scale, improvised, adapted) and diverse circulation approaches (mobile screenings, digital and online, non-traditional screening spaces, reflective curation, anti-copyright) and transforms social relations (individual filmmaking, cooperative practices, audience participation, education and training).

To apprehend the ways in which documentary resists systemisation or categorisation, it is useful to consider Benjamin's (1970) discussion of art and activism centring on the concept of 'technique'. The political positionality of the artist and artwork is expressed in the 'progress or in regression of literary technique' or the relation between social context and the conceptualisation of technique, according to Benjamin. Benjamin's concept of political technique refers to a practice that stretches into the social world, rather than being a purely artistic set of functions. In the context of resistance in Indian documentary, 'technique' often encompasses determined political position-taking, most productively illustrated in actions surrounding film censorship and documentary financing.

Public protest actions by documentary filmmakers form a visible sphere of resistance against the restrictions placed by both industrial valuation and state regulation of cultural production. Against the silencing of cultural dissent in the form of censorship regulations, filmmakers have led resistance by utilising both judicial means and coordinated physical protest in public spaces. A legacy of colonial governance, the censor certificate is mandatory for public and theatrical film screenings.[3] The power of the CBFC to ban films under state-defined criteria of 'public interest' has historically marginalised political documentary films by utilising a series of regulatory mechanisms effectively restricting film circulation through private, improvised and precarious methods and, thus, to limited audience communities. A further tightening of documentary's public performance is likely, as the recent Cinematograph (Amendment) Bill 2021 proposed by the Modi government seeks to strengthen existing censorship regimes.[4] Its potential to restrict documentary circulation is summed up by Patwardhan (quoted in Rappolt 2021):

> The new proposed bill is crazy – it allows the present right-wing government to remove clearances that were granted under previous governments. All of my work is endangered. Clearly this kind of law, while it pretends to protect 'public morality' and 'sensibility', is aimed at the human-rights-oriented films we made, films which somehow got through the system in the past, some bruised and some intact.

In what may seem like a counterpart to the theatrical suppression of documentary, the new Information Technology Rules 2021 (Intermediary Guidelines and Digital Media Ethics Code) specifically place regulations on internet platforms and channels, thereby effectively shrinking online spaces of documentary circulation.⁵ Rule 4(4) compels content filtering, requiring that providers review and pre-screen content and endeavour to deploy technology-based measures, including automated tools or other mechanisms, to 'proactively identify information' that has been forbidden under the 2021 Rules.⁶ Documentaries have come under direct scrutiny of the Examination Committee of India's Ministry of Electronics and Information Technology (MeITY). In 2022, following a legal complaint by the Government of India, Sandeep Ravindranath's *Anthem for Kashmir*, a nine-minute short-film on human rights violations in the Kashmir Valley was blocked by YouTube for viewers in India (American Kahani 2022).

Striving for political and cultural transformation that occurs through the flow of meanings, filmmakers rebut the logics of cultural regulation to emphasise film exhibition and the formation of publics (Kishore 2018). While film practitioners agree with a mechanism for dating and classifying films, arbitrary actions to censor films have resulted in 'collective acts' of resistance grounded in democratic values of free and open debate. The formation of Vikalp (an alternative) Film Festival in Mumbai in 2004 offers a potent example of conscious and intentional resistance against the exercise of state power (Wolf 2015; Monteiro and Jayasankar 2015; Deprez 2014; Kishore 2016). Formed in response to the unofficial censorship of political films at the government-sponsored Mumbai International Film Festival, the moment contains remarkable models of citizen resistance. By inviting 'filmmakers and citizens to get together to find creative and positive ways to resist censorship', Vikalp also signifies a collapse of reified categories of cultural producer and consumer (Jayasankar and Monteiro 2016, 206).

Alongside censorship and exhibition, fundraising exerts discursive and tangible influence on the ideological and social relations of documentary practice. The effects of neoliberal capitalism on culture, cultural production and cultural producers are well-documented (Mcguigan 2016; Kapur and Wagner 2011). The reorganisation of media industries and symbolic regimes following economic liberalisation continues to define social relations, subjectivities, culture and citizenship through the primary means of consumption. In recent years, documentary has been drawn into corporatised systems of funding, production and circulation, thus re-positioning its social impulse under industry discourses of 'social change', 'high-impact' and 'issues-focused' films. Streaming video on demand (SVOD) which has surfaced in discussions of documentary theory and practice is a crucial factor reshaping documentary form, culture and audience relationships

(Glick 2021). The rise of SVOD services is transforming documentary financing and exhibition, particularly in countries where public service and network television have been absent or minor players in the documentary landscape. Questions, however, emerge in relation to the nature of these transformations; for example, studies on Netflix note a regional investment disparity, with Western Europe receiving a larger share of documentary investment outside of the US, even as English continues to dominate the first official language of Netflix documentaries (Iordache et al. 2023). Thematically, while politics, society and culture dominate, these topics relate directly to social and topical discussions in the Western World (Iordache et al. 2023), and the majority follow a house style defined by character-driven narratives, high production values and the expository impulse of television journalism (Glick 2020). Character-driven narratives certainly dominate Netflix Original documentaries in India, with four of the five titles – *Ladies First* (2018), *Rooting for Roona* (2020), *Searching for Sheela* (2021) and *The Elephant Whisperers* (2022) – released between 2018 and 2023, following the trials and tribulations of persons facing obstacles in the achievement of a goal.

From one perspective, institutional interest promotes larger production budgets, attracts theatrical and network exhibition, and ultimately invites diverse national and global audiences. Yet, serious concerns underlie the relative dominance of institutional funding when tied to the objectives of box office success or measurable social impact and its effects on artistic expression and documentary's critical relation to culture, society and institutions. Social change as a discourse appears to be tightly contoured formally and socially. In formal terms, demands for engaging storytelling and compelling character arcs exemplify institutional investments in documentary (Lebow and Juhasz 2021), while socially, discourses favouring quantifiable measures of social impact derived from market research principles appear troubling (Winston, Vanstone and Chi 2017).

Many Indian filmmakers' express ambivalence towards international funding regimes which they consider a top-down imposition of discursive and instrumental frameworks on filmic themes, aesthetics and representation (Vohra [in Nathan 2015], Patwardhan 2015). Standing firm in her position as an independent filmmaker, Vohra outlines fundamental tensions between art, self and material well-being, which filmmakers navigate in their political stance towards film financing: 'An artist should produce work that is rich with their own voice and that will lead to other work that will pay him or her. I'm not dying of poverty. I'm not rich. If I want to be an artist, I have to know that I'm not going to be rich' (Vohra 2014). Resisting the international funding refrain of the 'story is king' (Lebow and Juhasz 2021), individual interpretations of documentary form in relation to aesthetics, duration, themes and format constitute a feature of Indian documentary, enumerating diverse artistic expressions encompassed in the concept of 'documentary'.

Chapter structure

Part I: Critical perspectives on documentary aesthetics and form

This section explores aesthetic strategies and documentary rhetoric that move beyond documentary's legislative function as a discourse of objectivity to create diverse forms of spectator engagement. The essays emphasise documentary's capacity to disperse meaning and create more reflective and participatory forms of spectator engagement, in contrast to its dominant mode of political analysis in Indian documentary – a form of 'emergency communication' consisting of evidentiary usage of image and sound and legislative speaking positions (Rajagopal and Vohra 2012). Moving beyond the representation of an existing political reality, the essays identify political meaning in the aesthetic treatment of social reality to bring forth a critique of instrumental notions of the political in social documentary.

In *Cities of Sleep*, Kishore examines the sensory representation of homelessness felt by the body of homeless individuals, a 'social aesthetics' produced in interactions between the social and corporeal environment of the street. In contrast to an analytical approach towards homeless individuals as a category or representative group, a sensory approach, Kishore argues, engages emotions and senses which attempt to collapse the distance between the spectator, the represented subject and a world 'out there'. In her chapter on *Pariah Dog*, Hariharan analyses the construction of canine space as an ethical alternative to the representations of a contested urban spatiality between non-human and human subjects and bodies. *Pariah Dog*, she argues, creates an imaginative geography of human-animal entanglements against human-centric representations of urban space. Taking up the presence of the filmmaker in documentary, Jayasankar and Monteiro reflect on the ethics of documentary authorship based on their film practice spanning three decades. Interrogating theirrole as 'outsiders' brings fundamental shifts in how both filmmakers position themselves in ways that integrate questions about their own identities into the filmic narrative. Bridging the symbolic distance between subject and author, the performative figure of the 'sutradhar' or 'puller of threads', derived from Indian dramatic traditions, allows the authors to critique and interrogate their authorial role to decentre purely epistephilic objectives.

Part II: Representation of lived experience

The essays in this section, written by film practitioners, examine documentary as a form of expression that lives in the relation between an individual and their historical existence to connect documentary practice to lived experience, perceptions and desires. Critiquing documentary's gaze towards the 'other', as well as documentary's relation between filmmaker and the represented, Shabnam Sukhdev foregrounds the subjective interests of documentary-makers. Sukhdev focuses on personal considerations when filmmaking is not so much about representing universal or historical truths but a struggle to find a language to represent lived experience and to translate questions into visual form. In their essays, Raja Shabir Khan, Lipika Singh Darai, Jyoti Nisha and Haobam Paban Kumar address the nature of subjectivity that they invest in documentary. The authors discuss how they make choices about media practice and ethics that reflect a conscious choice to 'speak' with the documentary form from their marginal locations in response to social and historical conditions. Focusing on her Adivasi roots, Darai recounts her struggles as a woman filmmaker in Odisha to make films about her land and her people, while responding to 'othering' representations of tribal groups and practices in popular media. Haobam Paban Kumar shifts the focus to his location in the Northeast of India and to the way in which fiction and non-fiction imaginations and vocabularies blur in his films about the place and its people. Khan discusses his subjective motivation for making documentaries in Kashmir, as well as the personal, institutional and psychological challenges involved in making films in the context of ongoing political conflict and the dominating presence of Indian armed troops. Drawing on her own experience of viewing popular cinema as a Dalit woman, Jyoti Nisha writes about the creation of an Oppositional Bahujan Agency through documentary cinema, which rests on the radical politics of Dalit intellectual and activist Dr Bhimrao Ambedkar. What comes across in these essays is a spectrum of techniques that refer to the conditions in which the films are made; these include issues of social discrimination, censorship and political unrest. In the absence of prescribed industrial formats, the aesthetic approaches, techniques and vocabularies demonstrate a dynamic relation between the self, documentary and society when created by people outside institutional and industrial contexts.

Part III: Resistance in practice

Exploring resistance as an organisational mode of practice offers the possibility of re-placing documentary as a social practice whose aesthetic and rhetorical forms are always in a state of mutuality with the world surrounding the text. The essays in the final section focus on the ways in which practitioners approach technologies, collaborations, institutions and industries as a phenomenon to be interpreted, critiqued, reworked and remodelled, in ways that underscore the ideological grounds of these entities and how social conditions enable and disable forms of cultural uses and functions. Examining the practice and theory behind modes of 'political curation' of documentary film, Sawhney and King discuss their curatorial approach towards an exhibition of Indian non-fiction and documentary film at the Hong Gah Museum in Taiwan to argue for a collaborative politics of trans-locationality in documentary exhibition. In her chapter, Sameera Jain draws on her film-editing practice to reflect on the conceptual and aesthetic principles that attend to the formal properties of the image, thus extricating it from its conventional framing as evidence or argumentation. Ein Lall, in her essay, focuses on the genre of art documentary and how a critique of 'object'-focused art documentary underpins her distinct socially-embedded approach to representing art and the artist. Examining the politics of the image from the perspective of documentary cinematography, Ramani discusses questions that frame his visual language and offers possibilities to challenge hierarchies imposed by visual technologies and institutional formats. Yashaswini draws attention to the experimental use of sound in her films that challenges a traditional visual-driven evidentiary approach of synchronised looking and hearing in Indian documentary film. Srinivasan interrogates the cultural and aesthetic tensions surrounding European- and US-based funding of documentary cinema in India. She identifies questions that may prompt a re-framing of filmmaking and film festival curation and, subsequently, the creation of new knowledge in such contexts. In the concluding chapter, Ray and Mochish address the lack of documentary film criticism in popular media to understand the perceptions of documentary among mainstream media producers and its effects on the development of documentary culture. Bringing attention to contemporary debates on SVOD and the foundational work of creating documentary cultures of resistance, in the epilogue Anjali Monteiro and K. P. Jayasankar outline a methodology combining scholarship, practice and education.

Focusing on the concrete material terrain in which film cultures are located and sustained, these chapters provide rich and critical accounts of the constraints that confront documentary in India and of the strategies that reimagine and rework these limits from outside industry positions. Ultimately, these moves reveal how vigorous documentary culture is created through a tense dialectics of regulatory power and tactical resistance. Common to all these essays is an analysis of how filmmakers and practitioners navigate social context in order to carve out spaces to show, teach, make, discuss and critique documentary. To the extent that these actions construct a critical and reflexive documentary presence in the public domain, they also introduce the element of discursivity in what seem to be absolute, closed and fixed structures, therefore demonstrating the means to resist the dominance of instrumentalist ideologies in cultural production.

Notes

1 It is worth mentioning *Chalchitra Abhiyan*, an Uttar Pradesh-based digital media collective comprised entirely of producers from Dalit and religious minority groups who respond to the under-representation of these communities in media industries and representation. For more information, see Kishore 2023. Dalit Camera is a YouTube channel that has become a platform to represent and express the history and effects of discrimination against Dalit communities; see Kumar 2016.
2 The rushes from Patwardhan's *Bombay, Our City* were used as evidence by the People's Union for Civil Liberties to successfully obtain a temporary reprieve against slum demolitions. The filmmaker continued to participate in anti-demolition movements after the completion of the film. In February 1986, nearly two years after the release of the film, Patwardhan courted arrest with 150 slum residents against the demolition of dwellings in the Sanjay Gandhi Nagar slum. Later, in May 1986, he joined a hunger strike with three slum residents to demand alternative land allocation.
3 The British Government passed the Cinematograph Act in India in 1918 and, with the establishment of Censor Boards in major Indian cities, colonial era beliefs of governance – which considered the colonised masses as irrational or 'a volatile diversity perpetually on the brink of combustion' – continue to form the basis for a paternalistic discourse of culture, placing the state and its institutions as the final arbiter of viewing cultures and practices (Mazzarella 2013, 16).
4 Its two key proposals include legislation to give the central government 'revisionary

powers', thereby enabling it 'to order recertification of an already certified film. And in a curtailment of the constitutional right of filmmakers, the independent appellate body or the Film Censorship Appellate Tribunal (FCAT) has been dissolved, effectively forcing filmmakers to approach the judiciary in what are likely to be expensive and protracted legal trials' (Gulati 2021). In 2023, certain clauses relating to the revisionary powers of the government of India were removed, but the initial draft indicates the authoritarian intention and approach of the government towards cultural dissent.
5 The amended rules are hosted on the website of the Ministry of Electronics and IT, available at https://egazette.nic.in/WriteReadData/2022/239919.pdf. These amendments are particularly threatening, as filmmakers use digital circulation to counter legitimate and illegitimate forms of censorship. For example, in June 2017, following the official non-certification of the three documentaries *In the Shade of Fallen Chinar* (2016), *The Unbearable Being of Lightness* (2016) and *March March March* (2017) at the International Documentary and Short Film Festival Kerala, the filmmakers responded by sharing the films online via YouTube and Vimeo.
6 Wide-ranging criteria forbid content comprising 'any information which is prohibited by any law', specifically laws for the protection of 'the sovereignty and integrity of India; security of the State; friendly relations with foreign States; public order; decency or morality' (Freedom House 2021).

Works cited

Adorno, T. W. (1983). *Prisms*. Cambridge: MIT Press.
American Kahani (2022). Ban on short film 'Anthem for Kashmir' is Indian Government's attempt to cover up real picture, says filmmaker. *American Kahani*. https://americankahani.com/business/ban-on-short-film-anthem-for-kashmir-is-indian-governments-attempt-to-cover-up-real-picture-says-filmmaker [accessed 12 October 2022].
Atton, C. (2001). *Alternative media*. London: Sage Publications.
Austin, T., and de Jong, W. (eds). (2008). *Rethinking documentary: New perspectives and practices*. Maidenhead: McGraw-Hill International.
Battaglia, G. (2017). *Documentary film in India: An anthropological history*. Oxon: Routledge.
Benjamin, W. (1970). The author as producer. *New Left Review*, 62, 83–96.
Bhatia, K. V. (2021). Religious subjectivities and digital collectivities on social networking sites in India. *Studies in Indian Politics*, 9(1), 21–36.
Carpentier, N. (2011). *Media and participation: A site of ideological-democratic struggle*. Chicago: Intellect.
Chanan, M. (2007). *Politics of documentary*. London: British Film Institute.
Chopra, R. (2019). *The Virtual Hindu Rashtra: Saffron Nationalism and New Media*. New Delhi: Harper Collins India.
Corner, J. (2009). Documenting the political: Some issues. *Studies in Documentary Film*, 3(2), 113–29.

Deprez, C. (2013). The Films Division of India, 1948–1964: The early days and the influence of the British documentary film tradition. *Film History*, 25(3), 149–73.

Espinosa, J. G. (1979). 'For an imperfect cinema'. *Jump Cut: A Review of Contemporary Media*, 20, 24–26.

Forum for Independent Film and Video. (1996). *A vision for television*. New Delhi: FIFV.

Freedom House (2021). 'Country overview: India'. *Freedom House*. https://freedomhouse.org/country/india/freedom-net/2021 [accessed 10 October 2022).

Gadihoke, S. (2012). Secrets and inner voices: The self and subjectivity in contemporary Indian documentary. In A. Lebow (ed.), *The cinema of me: The self and subjectivity in first person documentary*, 144–57. New York: Columbia University Press.

Ghosh, S. (2018). A way of being in the world: Shohini Ghosh in conversation with Ravi Vasudevan [Interview]. *The Free Library*. https://www.thefreelibrary.com [accessed 5 April 2022].

Glick. J. (2021). Platform politics: Netflix, the media industries, and the value of reality. *World Records*, 5(5), 59–76.

Gulati, S. (2021). Super censorship of cinema? *Economic and Political Weekly*, 56(31). https://www.epw.in/journal/2021/31/comment/super-censorship-cinema.html [accessed 1 December 2023].

Hanlon, D. (2015). Making waves: Anand Patwardhan, Latin America, and the invention of Indian Third Cinema. *Wide Screen*, 5(1), 1–24.

Horner, Lindsey, K. (2016). Co-constructing research: A critical literature review. *AHRC*. https://connected-communities.org/index.php/project_resources/co-constructing-research-a-critical-literature-review [accessed 3 January 2022].

Iordache, C., Raats, T., and Mombaerts, S. (2023). The Netflix original documentary explained: Global investment patterns in documentary films and series. *Studies in Documentary Film*, 17(2), 151–71.

James, R., and Venkatesan, S. (2021). *India Retold: Dialogues with Independent Documentary Filmmakers in India*. New York: Bloomsbury Academic.

Jayasankar, K. P., and Monteiro, A. (2015). *A fly in the curry: Independent documentary film in India*. New Delhi: Sage Publications India.

Kapur, G. (2008). A cultural conjuncture: Art into documentary. In T. Smith, O. Okwui Enwezor and N. Condee (eds), *Antimonies of art and culture: Modernity, postmodernity, contemporaneity*, 30–59. Durham: Duke University Press.

Kapur, J., and Wagner, K. B. (eds) (2011). *Neoliberalism and global cinema: Capital, culture, and Marxist critique*. New York: Routledge.

Kishore, S. (2023). Re-framing documentary's victims: Documentary and collective victimhood at Indian media collective Chalchitra Abhiyan. *Studies in Documentary Film*, 17, 14–31.

Kishore, S. (2018). *Indian Documentary Film and Filmmakers: Independence in Practice*. Edinburgh: Edinburgh University Press.

Kishore, S. (2016). Participation, poetry and song: Anand Patwardhan and New Latin American cinema. *Jump Cut: A Review of Contemporary Media*, 57. https://www.ejumpcut.org/archive/jc57.2016/-KishoreIndiaDoc/index.html [accessed 23 November 2023].

Kluge, A., Levin, T. Y., and Hansen, M. B. (1981). On film and the public sphere. *New German Critique, 24/25*, 206–20.

Kumar, C. (2016). Dalit Camera: Through untouchable eyes. *IRA International Journal of Education and Multidisciplinary Studies, 3*(1), 2455–2526.

Lebow, A., and Juhasz, A. (2021). Beyond story. *World Records, 5*(5), 9–13.

Mazzarella, W. (2013). *Censorium: Cinema and the open edge of mass publicity*. Durham: Duke University Press.

McGuigan, J. (2016). *Neoliberal culture*. Basingstoke: Palgrave Macmillan.

Nathan, A. (2015). And I make documentaries. *The Hindu*. https://www.thehindu.com/features/friday-review/and-i-make-documentaries-paromita-vohra/article7061461.ece [accessed 3 November 2023].

Nichols, B. (2010). *Introduction to documentary* (2nd ed.). Bloomington: Indiana University Press.

Nichols, B. (1991). *Representing reality: Issues and concepts in documentary*. Bloomington: Indiana University Press.

Patwardhan, A. (2015). Interview by Georgia Korossi [Interview]. *British Film Institute*. http://www.bfi.org.uk/news-opinion/bfi-news/earth-vision-interview-anand-patwardhan [accessed 3 November 2023].

Rajagopal, A. (2016). The counterrevolution will be televised: On the current crisis of Indian universities. *Los Angeles Review of Books*. https://www.lareviewofbooks.org/article/counterrevolution-will-televised-current-crisis-indian-universities/ [accessed 1 November 2022].

Rajagopal, A. (2001). *Politics after television: Hindu nationalism and the reshaping of the public in India*. Cambridge: Cambridge University Press.

Rajagopal, A., and Vohra, P. (2012). On the aesthetics and ideology of the Indian documentary film: A conversation. *BioScope: South Asian Screen Studies, 3*(1), 7–20.

Rancière, J. (2010). *Dissensus: On Politics and Aesthetics*. London: Bloomsbury.

Rancière, J. (2006). *The politics of aesthetics*. New York: Continuum.

Rappolt, M. (2021). 'All of my work is endangered': Anand Patwardhan on the future of documentary films in India. *Art Review*. https://artreview.com/all-of-my-work-is-endangered-anand-patwardhan-on-the-future-of-documentary-films-in-india/ [accessed 12 August 2022].

Rouse, J. (2000). Practice theory. *Handbook of the Philosophy of Science, 15*, 499–540.

Roy, S. (2007). *Beyond belief: India and the politics of postcolonial nationalism*. Durham: Duke University Press.

Sarkar, B., and Wolf, N. (2012). Editorial. *BioScope: South Asian Screen Studies, 3*(1), 1–6.

Singh, H. (2019). We had a sense that we couldn't dismiss them [Interview with Saba Dewan]. *Fountain Ink*. https://fountainink.in/qna/039we-had-a-sense-that-we-couldn039t-dismiss-them039 [accessed 10 April 2022].

Vohra, P. (2011). Dotting the I: The politics of self-less-ness in Indian documentary practice. *South Asian Popular Culture, 9*(1), 43–53.

Waugh, T. (2011). *Right to play oneself: Looking back on documentary film*. Minneapolis: University of Minnesota Press.

Waugh, T. (ed.) (1986). *Show us life: Towards a history and aesthetics of the committed documentary*. Metuchen and New York: Scarecrow Press.

Williams, R. (1981). *The Sociology of Culture*. London: Fontana.
Winston, B., Vanstone, G., and Chi, W. (2017). *The act of documenting: Documentary film in the 21st century*. London: Bloomsbury Publishing.
Wolf, N. (2013). Foundations, movements, and dissonant images: Documentary film and its ambivalent relations to the nation state. In K. M. Gokulsing and W. Dissanayake (eds), *Routledge handbook of Indian Cinemas*, 360–74. Oxon: Routledge.

Part I:

Critical perspectives on documentary aesthetics and form

1

The corporeality of homelessness in *Cities of Sleep*: Social aesthetics and an unreliable narrator

Shweta Kishore

How can documentary film overcome 'engagement at a distance' to perceptively express urban experience? Modern cities offer filmmakers a dense terrain to examine the spatialisation of ideology and power inscribed in architectural forms, everyday practices, social relations and ultimately the body of urban inhabitants. The relationship between cities and cinema is a highly productive space of scholarship where scholars examine the aesthetic and historical representation of cities in cinema (Beattie 2008; Koeck and Roberts 2010; Birdsall 2014; Álvarez 2015), as well as the space of the city, institutions and urban formations in which cinema is located and consumed (Fitzmaurice and Shiel 2011; Dutta, Kaushik and Shivkumar 2013). Indian documentary cinema has a rich history of representing the spatial politics of urban settings, often highlighting perspectives and voices absent from narratives and discourses that celebrate urbanisation as a symbol of national development and modernisation. Films such as *Bombay Our City* (1985), *The City Beautiful* (2003), *My Own City* (2011), *When Four Friends Meet* (2001), *Vertical City* (2011), *Saacha* (2001), *7 Islands and a Metro* (2006), *Jari Mari* (2001) and *Quarter no 4/11* (2011) address rising inequalities resulting from a particularly Asian form of urbanisation in which the 'developmental state' in conjunction with neoliberal forces continues to define, regulate and discipline space, bodies and experience (Brosius and Schilbach 2016).[1] Far from being a neutral framework, urban space is shown to produce a spatial politics that actively organises publics, socialises subjects, refracting and mediating bodies and identities in complex social arrangements.

Cities of Sleep

In this essay, I examine the sensory aesthetic of *Cities of Sleep* (dir. Shaunak Sen, 2015) and its engagement with place, the body and lived experience in portraying homelessness and its oppressive urban form, as experienced by its two protagonists in the city of New Delhi.[2] Focusing on the struggle for sleep and the organisation of urban sleep cultures, director Shaunak Sen is interested in creating a human-centred ethnography of the 'social and political exertions on offer at night'. Rather than an abstract scientific examination of sleep 'through the lens of psychoanalysis or "biomedical discourse"', this aim propels the examination of an urban condition, its relation to the social production of the body and subjectivity of homeless urban sleepers' (Ramnath 2015). Reviewers note that the film's 'intent humanistic gaze' captures the 'fretful delirium of the nocturnal environments inhabited by homeless migrants in the city of Delhi' (Sahdev 2016; Klaus 2016). The film's sensory approach towards urban space draws attention to Benjamin's concept of phantasmagoria. In the nineteenth-century city, the combination of economics and technology produced commodity cultures based in illusory visual representations that 'alter(ed) human consciousness' through a 'flooding of the senses' (Buck-Morss 1992, 22). In the twenty-first century, the urban phantasmagoria of Delhi is a hypermediated world of digital and virtual media technologies creating an architecture of spectacle characterised by affect and immersion. In *Cities of Sleep* (hereafter COS), blending commodity and media cultures, Delhi's congested neighbourhoods, chiaroscurist lit streets, motorised traffic, mobile phone screens and an acousmatic soundtrack of Bollywood music and twenty-four-hour television produce a phantasmagoric nocturnal environment. Reality and technology blur the perception of each, blending in spaces such as cinema halls. As Ranjeet, one of the two filmic protagonists and video hall owner, observes, 'I love those films in which I fall asleep. In my dream state, the film and the dream become mixed, and I love waking up from sleep in a cinema hall. I feel safe. In the cinema we don't only watch films, it is a home where people come, watch films, rest and relax' [translation mine].

Sen's portrayal of the lived experience of two individuals, Shakeel and Ranjeet, traverses a sensory realm evoking an affective engagement with urban norms, authority systems and practices that structure the life stories, bodies and identities of both. Sen's choice of a sensory approach should be read against an aesthetic critique of Indian documentary and documentary more broadly, particularly its historic reliance on evidentiary audiovisual argumentation and filmmaker-led discourses of authority (Rajagopal and Vohra 2012; Sharma 2015). As if to address this, rather than engaging purely analytical constructions, COS encourages an experiential consideration of homelessness as a bodily condition felt by the skin, the flesh, the muscles, the psyche and the Self. In this respect, the film represents an attempt to re-engage us with the much-criticised 'victim' of documentary cinema, by evoking more than rational thought or sympathetic reasoning. In this essay, I make two arguments relating to modes of spectatorial engagement in *Cities of Sleep* (COS). First, I argue that, in responding to the shifting spatiality of social life, the sensuous body functions as a primary means to convey urbanisms translated into effect, sensation and behaviour that invite bodily connections with documentary's traditional outsiders and victims. Political meaning, therefore, I contend, derives not so much from 'epistephilia' or engagement in the 'pleasure in knowing', but from the act of feeling, sensing and perceiving, which attempts to collapse our distance from a represented subject and world 'out there' (Nichols 1991, 178). Relying less on the verifiable value of historical evidence or documentary transparency, textual aesthetics arouse engagement in the form of sensory pleasure, empathy and participation. Extending my attention to representation, next, I argue that, by dismantling unified subjectivities of on-screen subjects', the film challenges audience expectations of a stable self and subjectivity in documentary representation. Instead, subjectivities are shown to respond to social experience, modes of inhabiting and everyday encounters, revealing a terrain of power relations experienced corporeally and emotionally in contemporary cities.

Cities of Sleep draws useful connections between subjectivity and social and historical environments and practices, in line with David MacDougall's (2005) conceptualisation of social aesthetics. Instead of signifying an essential or interior property, the concept negotiates the visual representation of the human body and subjectivity together with sensory environments, social location and community membership. Concerned with everyday formal expressions, social interactions and bodily behaviours, social aesthetics recognize the perception of culturally patterned responses produced in socio-cultural environments as a form of knowledge about the world (2005, 98). In COS, embodied expressions respond to the invisible ordering elements or aesthetics of situated forms of power and structural norms. The assemblage of tangible and intangible factors includes local authority systems – for example, government officials, community workers, local mafia, security and surveillance; laws and regulations, weather and environment; infrastructure (or lack thereof) such as government night shelters, water supply and public toilets; structural factors such as social class, religion, language group and gender; and finally, filmmaker presence and the filmmaking process. Each of these elements produce modes of bodily expression the meaning of which may be approached through an exploration of sense and experience. MacDougall (2015) observes: 'Films act upon us through our vision and hearing, but our responses are by no means limited to just these two of Aristotle's five original senses. And what a film does not evoke directly we tend to create for ourselves, out of our own past experiences of touch, taste, and smell'.

Social aesthetics brings into play more than a singular feature of environments such as socio-economic or cultural properties. Instead, by examining distinct parts of a whole, a complex of properties is felt and received. I will discuss three aesthetic expressions of environmental contingency that solidify as bodily behaviours, psychical responses and subject positions; an 'exposed' city bared to environmental vagaries; an 'unsettled' city lacking the necessities of human habitation; and a 'restricted' city where social identity determines access. Each is encountered as a condition of insecure housing, thus isolating the politics and culture of a particular experience of homelessness from the multiple possibilities of urban experience.

A bodily focus in Documentary and Urban Studies

The relation between the body and environment is a crucial visual methodology for MacDougall (2005) to study the relation between individuals and societies. Writing in the context of his Doon School film series (2000), MacDougall views places or human environments as constructions of human activities and human bodies which are constantly being acted upon by and acting upon structures and institutions. The sensory qualities of these environments, in this case an elite school and its disciplinary practices, become 'impressed upon one's consciousness' and expressed in the students' gestures, ritual or behaviour (2005, 111). Film assesses this relationship in two ways. First, despite its fragmented nature, the time-based properties of film are suited to access this complex interplay of vision, sound and tactility that constitute environments and experiences (2005, 54). Furthermore, by recovering expressive dimensions of human experience in particular settings, film makes it possible to better understand the ideological and cultural construction of places.

According to Nichols, 'to experience is to become involved' (1991, 194). The experience of a world not dependent on distance, objectivity or rationalism opens the way for 'empathetic involvement' or engagement with the other (194). MacDougall's focus on film as a sensory technology encoding verbal and non-verbal knowledge is particularly significant to identify an involved documentary spectatorship. Engagement with the 'other' also becomes possible through other aesthetic approaches that include performative and non-verbal means of dramatisation requiring participation and partaking. The corporeal dimensions of knowledge provide the counter to a detached bystander gaze or didactic verbal discourse in documentary, introducing a form of participatory engagement with the represented world. Resting on an affective understanding of the world and the 'other', empathy, identification and sensation may provoke political change by moving the spectator away from the status of observer to participant. Nichols states:

> The affective engagement of the viewer with social tensions and pleasures, conflicts and values move the viewer away from the status of observer to that of participant. Something is at stake. Namely, our very subjectivity within the social arena. The move beyond observation to experience coupled with understanding and interpretation, discovery and insight opens a space for contestation (194).

Contestations or social actions, as Nichols states, arise from an encounter with the text, a form of experience that results in a change in the perception of the viewer and thus potentially in the historical world. Reflecting on the relation between art and the world, Nichols argues that 'ideological struggle and political change follow from changes of habit that art, and the art of documentary, can provoke' (194). In mapping sensorial geographies of its marginalised protagonists, constructed equally through the cinematic rendering of performance, gesture and non-verbal expression as much as through subjective verbal reflections and commentary, COS evokes a realm of intersubjectivity that shapes our responses to the subjects and the social issues that they represent. On screen, subjects become known to us through tangible expressions or performance and the performative nature of documentary representation. As Bruzzi (2006, 10) argues, all documentaries are performative acts involving a 'multi-layered' exchange between subjects, filmmakers/apparatus and spectators. In COS, this condenses as aesthetic technique that includes repetition, durationality, montage and absences, in conjunction with rhetorical verbo-linguistic discourse which – rather than constructing purely informative, chronological, or causal accounts – privileges a philosophical and reflective subject-voice.

Bodily experience is one means of conceptualising the relationship between cities and human societies. The meaning of space in its expression of neighbourhoods, buildings and cities is not static but comes into existence, through spatial practice encompassing personal, cultural, historical, social and economic contexts, or as perceived symbols, according to Lefebvre (1991, 39). The re-placing of the body in space or the foregrounding of the role of the body in the constitution of the built environment opens up deeper ways of understanding human experience and the embodiment of space (Sen and Silverman 2014, 2). Sen and Silverman consider embodiment as a tangible and unconscious phenomenon. On the one hand, to embody something is to express and make perceptible something that may exist as an abstraction. On the other hand, embodiment entails the formation of human subjects through the experience of place. The phenomenology of the body demarcates space and place; human actions and sensory attachments such as memory and imagination transform space into place. Processes of self-construction and self-identification occur in concert with social contexts reproducing habits and bodily practices that lead to the reproduction of societies and social systems (Sen and Silverman 2014, 4). Insofar as the body is a sensory node, it makes visible symbolic underpinnings of place or the hidden political processes which grant meaning to places. Therefore, the study of individual behaviour and bodily processes articulates the effects of larger psychological, political, experiential and ideological contexts that are particular to places (Sen and Silverman 2014, 4).

Urban contestations and two neighbourhoods

The visual and historical terrain of COS can be read against the forms and discourses of urbanisation in India, in particular New Delhi where market-driven urbanisation has deepened socio-economic unevenness and spatialised inequality. Much like in the rest of the Global South, cities in India show intense signs of conflict entangled with the reproduction and transmutation associated with neoliberal forms of governance as well as global economic and cultural flows. Cinematically, a focus on the physical landscape is fundamental to the discussion of social aesthetics; as MacDougall suggests, 'rituals' and 'physical surroundings' create a social landscape and a sensory terrain reflected in bodily performance, behaviour and affective responses.

In this section, I outline the historical context of the two filmic locations, Old Delhi and the Yamuna Pushta area of Delhi, to illuminate their cultural and economic features, physical topographies and neoliberal discourses, the imprint of which features in the material conditions and struggles of both protagonists. About four kilometres apart on either side of the river Yamuna, both areas host large numbers of homeless dwellers who live in temporary settlements, shanties, or without any shelter at all. Both areas in large measure represent the effects of urban planning which in the post-independence Nehruvian imagination of a planned, modernised and socialist economy ignored the welfare and needs of migrants flooding into the city in the 1970s and 1980s to work as wage labourers in trading and manufacturing establishments and in informal menial jobs, such as construction workers or load carriers (Batra and Mehra 2008). With virtually no housing arrangements, the number of slums grew in Old and New Delhi and along the banks and flood plains of the river Yamuna. More recently, new models of economic and social organisation with the increased privatisation of land and the rising influence of bourgeois ideologies of consumption have followed neoliberal economic reform in the early 1990s, further intensifying spatial contestations and destabilising the claims of the poor to urban space.

Old Delhi

The Walled City of Old Delhi – its construction dates to the sixteenth-century Mughal rulers – comprises an area of about 8 square kilometres but an extremely high population density of approximately 35,000 people per 1 square kilometre, in contrast to the 9,700 people per 1 square kilometre in the capital region of Delhi (2020).[3] With a mixed-use land pattern, Old Delhi combines a high concentration of residential dwellings with commercial and small-scale manufacturing units. In Dupont's (2000) study of homelessness patterns in Old Delhi, a striking 96 per cent of homeless respondents were found to be migrants from rural agricultural areas who chose to come to Delhi to improve their employment and economic prospects. Dupont notes that most migrants, after an initial stay with family or acquaintances, were compelled to stay in pavement dwellings or sleep in night shelters which were shown to them by communities of workers in similar occupation types.

According to the study, homelessness in large part was found to be related to insecure employment and the uncertainty of earning a regular and fixed amount of income. Seasonal fluctuations in the demand for workers as well as irregular daily earning in occupations such as cycle rickshaw pulling, construction work and begging constituted a major obstacle in securing housing or a rental accommodation that requires a fixed expense which cannot be adjusted based on fluctuating earnings. Therefore, for those sleeping outdoors, a system of hiring beds and quilts on a nightly basis developed and continues, preferred by many on account of its flexibility. When earnings drop to zero, these daily expenses can also be reduced, particularly when weather conditions are favourable. With insufficient state welfare services, private entrepreneurs form part of a 'sleep mafia' that bargains with itinerants and labourers who require respite in Old Delhi (Gandhi 2016). In COS, Jamal's bed-hire enterprise depicts exploitative forms of patronage resulting from market-driven economies exploiting the vulnerable. Weather and changing seasons are another important variable in the sleeping patterns of homeless sleepers. For example, during the summer, preference is given to sleeping in open areas, on non-covered pavements, road dividers, or in parks; during the rainy season, verandas, night shelters, or sleeping areas protected with ground and overhead plastic sheeting are more in demand; and in winter preference is given to quilts for hire, night shelters and verandas. COS alerts us to these specific sensory criteria in the opening sequence, as Shakeel prepares to sleep on a road divider to avoid the summer scourge of mosquitoes, even as his search for a safe and secure space to sleep forms an ongoing existential struggle.

Yamuna Pushta

As New Delhi expanded during the 1980s, slums spread onto the western embankments and the flood plain of the River Yamuna, traditionally cultivated by peasant communities who held leasehold rights to the riverbed. During the Asian Games, 'Asiad '82', held in New Delhi, thousands of migrant workers employed in the construction of buildings and stadiums came to settle in the Yamuna Pushta (riverbank) which remains prone to flooding during the monsoons when the dry riverbed is quickly submerged by rising river waters. Most residents of Yamuna Pushta (neighbouring the Old Iron Bridge in COS) are daily wage workers – construction workers, rickshaw pullers, domestic workers and rag-pickers or recyclers (Batra and Mehra 2008). Over the decades, the initial shanties have been strengthened with brick and basic infrastructure, such as public water, taps, primary schools and dispensaries secured through the help of NGOs (Baviskar 2011). Although largely invisible to the wider public, the low-lying area has been transformed into a dense settlement of Delhi's under-class – a squalid, illegal, but nonetheless vibrant cultural world (Baviskar 2011). The slums, despite their shortcomings, have provided a degree of security to large numbers of people situated outside urban planning and policy frameworks. With locally organised non-formal educational and adult education centres, NGO-funded dispensaries, workers' committees and a functional economy, these slums – even if not the 'slums of hope', as note Batra and Mehra (2008) – are certainly not the 'slums of despair'.

Neoliberal contestations

With the shift to neoliberal economic policies in the early 1990s, cities such as New Delhi transformed as destinations and channels for the flow of capital, goods and people across national boundaries. The rise of a new consumptive Indian middle class has since inaugurated a host of new industries – IT, entertainment, personal care and leisure services – while increasing gentrification has sought to expand spaces for elitist consumption targeting sites of informal settlements and slums. Cities have witnessed an exacerbation of urban spatial conflicts through a re-worked capital-space equation that has globally integrated urban space into financial markets and intensified its commodification (Harvey 2008). In cities such as Delhi and Mumbai, for instance, public space continues to be transferred to private developers and re-designated for private functions such as commercial developments, industrial zones and gated residential communities, aspiring to the elite urbanism of Singapore and Shanghai. This leads to denser slum settlements or their destruction altogether, through state-supported 'slum removal' drives.

Much like in the developing world, in India a profound shift in urban politics and the way in which the poor are represented, governed and evaluated can be traced to shifts in urban development discourse from 'liveable cities' towards 'world-class cities' (Bhan 2009). In concrete terms, this is visible in the accelerated construction of infrastructure projects such as highways, tunnels, airports, wide roads and spaces for recreation. Urban geographer Gautam Bhan identifies two simultaneous impulses that have delegitimised the presence of the poor and homeless in this urban discourse. First, the neoliberal value of self-responsiblisation, or the responsibility of ensuring housing and access to services, is divested by the state or the elite to the poor themselves, with the market being the main intermediary for providing this facility. Able to separate themselves spatially in gated spaces, the elite no longer feel obliged to an imaginary community with the poor, and unequal housing is therefore accepted as an unavoidable part of a market society.

It is the second impulse, however, that speaks to a discourse justifying eviction of the poor from urban space rendering them homeless.

An ongoing process of 'aestheticisation' in Indian cities, suggests Bhan, has reduced the slum to an aesthetic problem based on its characterisation as filthy, poor and fragile. This approach flattens the urban poor and slums to an aesthetic problem, devoid of history, structure and subjecthood. The slum, therefore, becomes the index of all that is unwanted, and its removal in the form of eviction does not immediately cause concern for its human inhabitants, their lives and futures. For instance, both Old Delhi and Yamuna Pushta have witnessed 'beautification' drives implemented in a logic of 'cleaning up' in order to make the spaces available for purposes of commerce and leisure. Particularly in relation to Yamuna Pushta, local politicians mobilise the language of disgust and dirt to proclaim that the area is 'destroying our sacred heritage of the past and making the living conditions of the present chaotic and even polluting and corrupting our future', and therefore liable for slum clearance (The Hindu 2004). Batra and Mehra capture an underlying moral contradiction in this approach, which renders slum residents homeless within a rhetoric of 'cleaning up' the city, even as they are necessary for the functioning of the urban economy, including urban sanitation.

The exposed city

> Have you ever wondered why people sleep on (road) dividers during the summer? When cars pass by, the gush of wind prevents mosquitoes from biting. So, if you wish to save yourself from dengue or malaria in Delhi, sleep on the dividers (Shakeel, in *Cities of Sleep*).

Along with an estimated 150,000–200,000 other homeless persons who live on the streets, under fly-overs and bridges, in public parks and other common spaces, the migrant protagonists Shakeel and Ranjeet live without basic shelter in Delhi.[4] On Delhi's Eastern edge, Ranjeet lodges amidst the pylons of the Loha Pul/Iron Bridge, an inexorable artery transporting goods and labourers over the River Yamuna. Here, he runs a makeshift video hall the darkened surrounds of which seduce homeless labouring men to sleep.[5] Shakeel inhabits the densely populated Meena Bazaar settlement in the Walled City area of Old Delhi. When we see Shakeel, his physicality is immediately striking; his frailness, his shuffling gait, his worn-out overcoat and (when a beam of light reflects off his face) his facial disfigurement – or, as a reviewer notes, his 'sepulchral appearance' (Ramnath 2015). Shakeel's appearance evokes the physiognomic aspects of the face which is capable of a complexity of affect and emotional display. Drawing on Balázs' theory of the filmic face, Renov (2016, 4) believes that facial emotions often overtake capacities of language as a linear signifying system. Considering the face in combination with verbal testimony, Renov recognizes an intuitive understanding derived from human expression, which may not entirely replace language but access deeper feeling and emotion (Renov 2016, 6). Our primary means of engagement with Shakeel requires us to engage with his visage bringing an empathetic recognition of the additional hurdles in his struggle for survival as 'an outcast even in a space constituted of economic outcasts' (Sen, 2018; see also Dore 2018).

As an existential condition, homelessness places bodies in direct contact with natural and built environments, the tangible and intangible properties of which become known through sensory perception. In COS, the successful negotiation of these properties is vital in order to achieve a basic level of biological functionality. The (non-)availability of sleep in this socio-sensory environment and the struggle to achieve it form the tension which the protagonists attempt to overcome. We first meet Shakeel in Meena Bazaar on a wintry night. Cinematic tracking shots capture the saturated nocturnal sensorium of the commercial-residential locality, a blurred streetscape of out-of-focus lights, sundry objects, people, street stalls and stray animals. The aesthetic strategy foregrounds smaller pieces or parts of a whole which are not necessarily a survey of the locality's entirety but a visual assembly of various activities, spaces and fleeting encounters that express improvised and exposed forms of habitation. Distorted sounds of television, traffic, indeterminate shouting and vendors' cries impress perceptively the contrasting sonic urbanisms of the city. Repetition or the repeated presentation of an event serve to underline significant story information, and in COS they invoke a certain kind of pattern of everyday life. The recurring presence of a late-night tea stall where the homeless gather discloses precarious forms of community, as groups of homeless men congregate to eat, converse, or sleep.

The vivid rendering of local environmental conditions comprising extreme temperature, dust, fumes and mosquitoes opens a realm of sensations experienced by bodies unprotected by the structure of a dwelling. The textual enumeration of the temperature of '9 degrees' vivifies an abstract environmental condition with precise tactile awareness. The sensation of bodily threat in the unsound dwellings of this Old Delhi neighbourhood is affectively expressed through the portrayal of a powerful storm that hits the area. The physical impact of high-speed winds and rain on both improvised shelters and exposed human bodies is expressed as visual repetition and as focus on small but expressive details. Men are filmed in states of frantic activity as they rescue bedding, rush for cover and secure rickety shop stalls. Visualised in a state of turmoil – running, sheltering, huddling, crouching – the bodies speak of panic and confusion as they pull, stretch and tug at unprotected belongings. Numerous faces shelter under a small tarpaulin, crowded together, the camera at an awkward angle among them. On the wordless soundtrack, urgent but indistinct human cries mixed with wind and cracking thunder palpably communicate a sense of disquiet beyond language. As if amplifying the event's intensity, the camera suddenly breaks free of its harness, the accidental visual movement forming an indexical link to the event. The experience of presence in the profilmic moment is encoded in the accidental aesthetic of the image itself.

In the absence of a place to settle, homelessness becomes embodied in the forms of movement and activity that the body performs. The arrangement, appearance and movement of the body make 'macro-scale' social phenomenon visible at the 'micro-level of the individual body', states Kawash (1998, 326). For instance, Kawash observes that homeless persons are often in a perpetual state of movement, not because they are going somewhere, but because they have nowhere to go. Shakeel walks day and night, a ceaseless state of motion in everyday life as he searches for repose in a city with little unclaimed space. In recurring durational sequences, the camera positioned behind Shakeel follows him, uniting us with the direction and pace of the movement. The angle of view aligned with Shakeel's perspective indicates a spatial relation with the surroundings, while durationality draws emphasis to the activity's temporal dimensions. When Shakeel finally settles at a bus stop in New Delhi, he has walked several miles from Meena Bazaar across a swathe of urban terrains. Accompanying him visually to these multiple locations (car parks, metro stations), we apprehend his physical exhaustion in his bodily posture: his footsteps drag on the asphalt, his speech is tired. Connecting these bodily expressions with the temporality of the shot, our senses actively construct a whole where the depiction of Shakeel's body over time brings a subjective awareness of bodies as sensate, fleshy, material objects.

We find resonances between Shakeel and Baudelaire's flaneur, the ragpicker, instead of the bourgeois idler whose flânerie takes the form of a leisurely stroll. The rag-picker is the 'most provocative member of human history' for Benjamin; while living on society's margins, he collects the 'detritus of history' or those parts of the city which society wishes to discard, ignore, or hide (cited in Le Roy 2017, 127). The methods of the rag-picker, writes Le Roy, are at times like a 'detective' or like an 'archivist' undoing recognized historiographies (128). The rags that the rag-picker collects are the materials and experiences through which we may demystify the contemporary city, apprehend a different dimension or angle, since the 'rag picker moves across urban landscape but as a scavenger, collecting, rereading and rewriting its history' (Parsons 2000, 3). The urban space 'winks at the flaneur', and ordinary, mute, unremarkable topographies and signs speak of histories and geographies of the in/visible (Benjamin, cited in Le Roy 2017, 128). When Shakeel is in the car park, he is worried about security guards who might throw him out to protect the cars that belong to the city's elite. Through his sense of the geography of the city, we unlock a different orientation towards urban topography and its primary capitalist and spectacular logics. Shakeel's performative practice of walking reveals ordinary urban objects and architectural forms ignored in everyday rhythms of life – such as road dividers, bus stops, car parks and asphalt street surfaces that implement the logic of capital pervading urban practices.

An unsettled city

The visual portrayal of the Loha Pul settlement invites us to re-vision the city through embodied social practices. A mutually constitutive relationship between place and the body is shown to unfold in peripheral city spaces that remain invisible in popular representation. In cinematic terms, MacDougall uses the term 'landscape' to describe social environments which are conjunctions of the 'cultural and the natural' requiring, in addition to a capacity for evaluation, a 'sensitivity to the aesthetics of community life – to forms and resonances that are often as complexly interlaced as the rhymes and meanings of a poem' (2005, 96). The quotidian tussle between the needs and desires of human beings and the inhospitable physicality of the settlement beneath the bridge that inevitably emerge at this location destabilise easy categorisation of the people who inhabit this peripheral wasteland.

The cinematic language of juxtaposition and movement, as well as a mix of diegetic and non-diegetic sound design, fracture time and space into a multitude of disentangled impressions to affectively produce a montage relaying a discomforting awareness of how it might feel to inhabit the makeshift settlement. The overpowering industrial-mechanical behemoth entity of the bridge is filmed in slow-moving shots where extended temporality conveys a vast spatial scale; its vast vertical geometry and materiality of iron beams and concrete pillars starkly contrasts with the fragility of the bamboo-and-fabric constructions underneath. Once again, disassembled details such as the movement of objects in the breeze, patterns of light from passing trains, the sleeping form of a dog. A diegetic non-synchronous soundtrack of the sonic bass of overhead traffic and Bollywood music reverberate across the cavernous underside of the bridge, generating an impressionistic rather than indexical portrait of how the space might feel and sound. The social aesthetic of improvisation includes an unreliable supply of public services, like electricity, obtained through dangerously illegal means of tapping into overhead high-voltage power lines.

The local 'sleep cinema' provides a striking study of embodiment in this setting. Captured in ethnographic detail, the quotidian improvised video hall screens films to patrons lounging on the floor in varying states of alertness. Pieced together from fabric, bamboo, a television, a portable video player and precariously strung lights, for 10 rupees, patrons have the choice to watch three films or sleep for six hours, lulled by Bollywood film soundtracks and the ambient overhead bass.[6] The space functions as a space of repose; everyday life appears to slow down amidst darkened surroundings, as tired working bodies untangle and stretch on floor mattresses. Low-angle shots move the angle of view from a neutral eye level to a subjective placement in line with the floor where patrons sit or lie down. Through its visual representation of the sparse but restful cocoon, the sequence interrogates how leisure is configured by those located outside the economy of defined leisure spaces, such as movie theatres, nightclubs, or sports stadiums. We witness how, besides allowing the consumption of leisure activities, the nest-like space produces modes of embodied leisure captured in a series of close-up shots of men engaged in writing, thinking, dozing, dreaming and, ultimately, resting their bodies and minds. Depicting highly localised forms of use, the make-shift cinema at the base of the industrial artery conveys an individual relation with both place and cinema, which is expansive yet intimate and dreamlike. Moreover, performing discursive functions, located in one of the most marginal of city environments, the cinema transpires as a site that resists singular 'othering' readings of homelessness and the subjectivities of homeless individuals.

The restricted city

In this section, I return to the question of documentary meaning which evolves alongside the sensory interests of the film as a subjective re-consideration of physical reality and its documentary representation. By drawing attention to gaps, conflicts, contradictions and questions which remain unexplained in the diegesis, the film evokes the plenitude of the world outside of its representational horizon. In documentary, the historical and factual reliability of the narrative forms the foundation of the truth contract between the screen and the spectator. The authority of the narrator or story-teller is a function of their trustworthiness and authenticity, which filmmakers mobilise as a form of rhetoric when constructing representations of the world. Thus, the unreliability of the protagonists introduces a degree of doubt about narrative truth, indicative of subjective intercession between the historical world and its representation. By mounting distinctions between character narrators, cinematic narrators, or visual commentary and implied author or filmmaker, the construct of an unreliable narrator can draw attention to *how* a story is being told and *whose* perspectives is represented (Otway 2015). Ultimately, by drawing attention to the tenuous nature of 'documentary truth', the unreliable narrator encourages an active and possibly more evaluative mode of spectatorial engagement. Relatedly, the construct of an unreliable narrator points towards the contested issue of power imbalances in documentary representation:

> The documentary film narrator (whether the narrator is a character in the film, a voice of God outside the diegesis, the cinematic narrator, or even a representation of the implied author) is often in an extraordinary and sometimes problematic position of power over the audience. The construct of an unreliable narrator can help draw attention to the power embedded in layers of narration (Otway 2015, 8).

The reliability of Shakeel is put into question early in COS, and while this does not undermine his historical abjectness, it adds tonality to his subjectivity, eliciting complex spectator engagement beyond mere sympathy or emotional identification. Two specific scenes demand consideration. In the first, we see Shakeel walking alongside a busy road when he abruptly affects a limp to cut a compelling figure as a beggar. The scene cuts to shots of him begging at car windows and ends with Shakeel standing, now without a limp, by the roadside and counting his earnings. The cinematic narrator in this scene consists of audio and visual techniques. Most prominently, Shakeel's own philosophically reflective audio narration states: 'When you beg, you have fallen to the bottom; it is strangely peaceful because you can't fall any further'. On the visual register, in one single durational shot, the camera captures the staging of rejection as passengers roll up their windows when Shakeel approaches, only to roll them down once he moves on. The second scene of Shakeel's unreliability directly relates the existential struggle for sleep with the re-arranging of subjectivity. After a particularly difficult period in Delhi, on a train journey to his family home in Assam, Shakeel light-heartedly confesses that, while he is a Hindu, upon arrival in Delhi he chose to adopt a Muslim name. Shakeel's actions respond to his belief that, in Old Delhi's predominantly Muslim community, a Muslim identity improves the chances of securing resources. Astonishing as this information is, the narrative barely dwells on the revelation, dispersing its significance by cutting quickly to the next shot of Shakeel arriving at his hometown.

It is worth considering the information first in the context of *The Homeless Body*, where Samira Kawash (1998, 329) argues that the contours and functioning of a homeless body are not that of an original, 'natural' body, but one that is produced in specific negotiation with the contested and contingent environments that it inhabits. The condition of exclusion is marked on the body – the material, fleshy body which transpires as embodiment of the economic and spatial processes that secure certain subjects while rendering others like Shakeel as non-existent and excluded from urban citizenship as well as its rights and benefits.

In a critical context, however, the revelation itself and its treatment are indicative of a broader commitment to discursivity in the film. On the one hand, the scene's intimacy foregrounds an intersubjective domain where the filmmaker becomes a means of 'evoking' the subjective experience' of the subject in a 'cinema of proximity' comprising both visual and personal closeness with the filmed subject (MacDougall 2015, 5). Shakeel's perfunctory, casual tone and his address of 'Bhaiya' (brother) indicate levels of comfort in opening up his self to the filmmaker. On the other hand, a further question arises about why the filmmaker would select a narrator whose truth claims are dubious and who elsewhere is revealed to be emotionally and physically abusive and therefore, as Bhaskar Sarkar states, very 'unlikeable'.[7] It is this question that goes to the heart of how this film relies not on the conventional rhetoric of authoritative persuasion or identification, but on a provocative subjective reckoning which is the work of the spectator. The decision not to pursue this line of inquiry to arrive at a causal or conclusive truth means that this fact remains another fragment of information rather than a defining epistemic frame. In fragmenting the expected response of empathy or the expectation of a traditional 'victim' subjectivity, the film forces the spectator to engage with a reality that requires multiple modes to re-evaluate what is considered real. For the spectator, Shakeel represents a character whose Self cannot be fully grasped, contained, or categorised through documentary discourse or narrative and, therefore, is more than an illustration or source of information. A feeling of perplexity overcomes our relation to the screen, an emotion stirred not so much by what we know but by the contradiction of what we thought we knew. In now making sense of Shakeel's behaviour, we are forced to place the knowledge within a larger context, requiring a relational understanding of historical and representational factors existing beyond the frame and the limits of our own rational knowledge.

Conclusion

In this chapter, I have argued that a visual focus on the embodied relations between bodies, space and subjectivity mobilises different forms of spectatorial engagement with people predominantly viewed as category or an undifferentiated socio-economic group. Framed as stereotypes and categories, poor and homeless human bodies become objects to be evicted so as to preserve the beauty and livability of urban public space.

To the extent that documentary accesses the experiential aspects of socio-political order, it allows a 'complex form of seeing'; in other words, by focusing on its inhabitants, documentary contains the possibility of a 're-imagining of the city' by using the body as the basis to interpret cities (Beattie 2006). By tracing the corporeal expression of homelessness, COS entrenches documentary's discursive function in 'making sense' of being in contemporary cities. Therefore, when we see Shakeel collapsed in a doorway, relating his bodily distress and fear of death: 'I saw a man being taken in an ambulance, maybe I will also die this way …' The words convey an oppressive urban reality perceived by us affectively rather than as abstraction or description of an urban experience of homelessness. At the same time, Shakeel's deceptive nature and violent behaviour dismantle a simple one-dimensional 'victim' subjectivity. The viewer's sympathetic gaze is discomfited and must re-evaluate benign but ultimately ineffective constructions of 'us' and 'them'.

And while it is true that the full sensual properties of Shakeel's state of being are perhaps diffused, nevertheless, an empathetic engagement with social reality accessed by subjective modes of inquiry acknowledges the complexity of reconciling lived experience and discourse. In her discussion, Laura Rascaroli (2009, 4) relates subjective inquiry to a mode of sense-making, or 'a reflection and a consequence of the increased fragmentation of the human experience in the postmodern, globalised world, and of our need and desire to find ways to represent such fragmentation, and to cope with it'. In depicting the performative and experienced dimensions of exclusionary and oppressive forms of urban habitation, *Cities of Sleep* calls on a personal relation with the subjects and the societies we inhabit as real, corporeal beings, a counter-discourse to its flattening as an effect, or simply landscape. The collapse of the symbolic remove between spectator and screen subject is crucial to this process.

Notes

1 Relatedly, the symbolic representation of Indian cities and urbanisms in popular and state media production is scrutinised in the scholarly literature (see, for example, Dutta et al. 2013) and documentary and non-fiction works; see, for instance, *Nostalgia for the Future* (2017, dir. Mukul Kishore and Rohan Shivkumar) and *Bombay Tilts Down* (2022, CAMP).
2 Among its successes, COS has toured US and UK college circuits, screened at several international festivals (such as the Taiwan International Documentary Festival and Dok Leipzig) and featured in urban studies labs in policy discussions on homelessness and outreach services. It was screened at the UCL Urban Laboratory on 25 May 2017, followed by a panel discussion with representatives from Camden NHS Homeless Outreach Services and Camden Safer Streets. The film is available for viewing by writing to Shaunak Sen at airborne2628@protonmail.com.
3 Figures according to GEOIQ, https://geoiq.io/places/Old-Delhi/9hFVEGB8yk.
4 These are the 2011 estimates, based on the figures collected through government agencies by the Housing and Land Rights Network, New Delhi, available at https://www.hlrn.org.in/homelessness [accessed 12 June 2021].
5 The Loha Pul or Old Yamuna Bridge is a dual-level rail-road bridge near the Red Fort, built in 1866 by the East Indian Railway Company of England. Approximately 100 to 200 people sleep here each night according to unofficial figures.
6 Featuring in the film's promotional materials. 'Sleep cinema' is the descriptive term used by the filmmaker to refer to the space in which the residents of Loha Pul watch video tapes of popular Hindi films.
7 Bhaskar Sarkar interviewed Shaunak Sen at the University of Southern California. The interview is available on University of California Television (UCTV), at https://www.youtube.com/watch?v=Xyij-Sykc28 [accessed 12 June 2021].

Works cited

Álvarez, Ivan V. (2015). *Documenting cityscapes: Urban change in contemporary non-fiction film*. New York: Wallflower Press.
Batra, L., and Mehra, D. (2008). The demolition of slums and the production of neoliberal space in Delhi. In D. Mahadevia (ed.), *Inside transforming urban Asia: Processes, policies, and public actions*. New Delhi: Concept Publishing Company.

Baviskar, A. (2011). What the eye does not see: The Yamuna in the imagination of Delhi. *Economic and Political Weekly, 46*(50), 45–53.

Beattie, K. (2006). From city symphony to global city film: Documentary display and the corporeal. *Screening the Past* 20. https://dro.deakin.edu.au/view/DU:30016120 [accessed 12 April 2021].

Bhan, G. (2009). 'This is no longer the city I once knew': Evictions, the urban poor and the right to the city in millennial Delhi. *Environment and Urbanization, 21*(1), 127–42.

Birdsall, C. (2014). Resounding city films: Vertov, Ruttman and early experiments with documentary sound aesthetics. In H. Rogers (ed.), *Music and sound in documentary film*, 20–40. New York: Routledge.

Booth, Wayne C. ([1961] 1983). *The rhetoric of fiction*. Chicago: University of Chicago Press.

Brosius, C. and Schilbach, T. (2016). Introduction: 'Mind the gap': Thinking about in-between Spaces in Delhi and Shanghai. *Mind the Gap: Thinking about in-between Spaces in Delhi and Shanghai, 7*(4), 221–26.

Bruzzi, S. (2006). *New documentary*. London: Routledge.

Buck-Morss, S. (1992). Aesthetics and anaesthetics: Walter Benjamin's artwork essay reconsidered. *October, 62*, 3–41.

Dore, B. (2018). Eyes wide shut. *The Hindu Business Line*. https://www.thehindubusinessline.com/blink/watch/eyes-wide-shut/article7872519.ece [accessed 18 July 2021].

Dupont, V. (2000). Mobility patterns and economic strategies of houseless people in Old Delhi. In V. Dupont, E. Tarlo and D. Vidal (eds), *Delhi: Urban space and human destinies*, 99–124. New Delhi: Manohar Publishers.

Dutta, M., Bhaumik, K., and Shivkumar, R. (2013). *Project Cinema City*. New Delhi: Tulika Books.

Fitzmaurice, T., and Shiel, M. (eds) (2011). *Cinema and the city: Film and urban societies in a global context*. Oxford: Blackwell.

Harvey, D. (2008). The right to the city. *New Left Review, 2*(53), 23–40.

Kawash, S. (1998). The homeless body. *Public Culture, 10*(2), 319–39.

Klaus, C. (2016). '*Cities of Sleep*: DOK Leipzig'. *DOK Leipzig*. https://www.dok-leipzig.de/en/film/2015193/cities-sleep [accessed 8 November 2023].

Koeck, R., and Roberts, L. (2010). *The city and the moving image: Urban projections*. Basingstoke: Palgrave Macmillan.

Le Roy, F. (2017). Ragpickers and leftover performances. *Performance Research, 22*(8), 127–34.

Lefebvre, H. (1991). *The production of space*. Trans. Donaldson Nicholson Smith. Oxford: Blackwell.

MacDougall, D. (2015). Social aesthetics and embodied cinema. Conference paper presented at *The Challenge of Atmospheres*. Munich: Institut für Ethnologie. https://nbn-resolving.org/urn:nbn:de:101:1-201509221384 [accessed 12 January 2022].

MacDougall, D. (2005). *The corporeal image: Film, ethnography, and the senses*. Princeton: Princeton University Press.

Nichols, B. (1991). *Representing reality: Issues and concepts in documentary*. Bloomington: Indiana University Press.

Otway, F. (2015). The Unreliable Narrator in Documentary. *Journal of Film and Video, 67*(3–4), 3–23.

Parsons, D. L. (2000). Introduction: Gendered Cartographies of Viewing. In *Streetwalking the metropolis: Women, the city and modernity*, 1–16. Oxford: Oxford University Press.

Rajagopal, A., and Vohra, P. (2012). On the aesthetics and ideology of the Indian documentary film: A conversation. *BioScope: South Asian Screen Studies*, 3(1), 7–20.

Ramnath, N. (2015). How and where do the homeless of Delhi sleep? A documentary uncovers an economy of the night. *Scroll.in*. https://scroll.in/article/755115/how-and-where-do-the-homeless-of-delhi-sleep-a-documentary-uncovers-an-economy-of-the-night [accessed 20 June 2021].

Rascaroli, L. (2009). *The personal camera: Subjective cinema and the essay film*. London and New York: Wallflower Press.

Renov, M. (2016). The facial closeup in audio-visual testimony: The power of embodied memory. In N. Apostolopoulos, M. Barricelli and G. Koch (eds), *Preserving survivors' memories: Digital testimony collections about Nazi persecution: History, education and media*, 238–48. Berlin: Stiftung Erinnerung, Verantwortung und Zukunft.

Sahdev, M. S. (2016). I think of cinemas, panoramic sleights. *Outlook India*. https://www.Outlookindia.Com/ [accessed 20 June 2021].

Sarkar, B. (2017). *Cities of Sleep, with Shaunak Sen*. Carsey Wolf Center, University of California Santa Barbara. https://www.uctv.tv/shows/Cities-of-Sleep-with-Shaunak-Sen-32227 [accessed 21 September 2021].

Sen, A., and Silverman, L. (2014). *Making place: Space and embodiment in the city*. Bloomington: Indiana University Press.

Sharma, A. (2015). *Documentary films in India: Critical aesthetics at work*. London: Palgrave Macmillan.

Films Cited

7 Islands and a Metro. Dir. Madhusree Dutta. Majlis Productions. 2006.
Bombay Our City. Dir. Anand Patwardhan. 1985.
Cities of Sleep. Dir. S. Sen. Films Division. 2015.
Jari Mari. Dir. Surabhi Sharma. 2001.
My Own City. Dir. Sameera Jain. Public Service Broadcasting Trust. 2011.
Quarter no 4/11. Dir. Ranu Ghosh. Streamline Stories. 2011.
Saacha. Dir. Anjali Monteiro and K. P. Jayasankar. Magic Lantern Movies. 2001.
The City Beautiful. Dir. Rahul Roy. Magic Lantern Movies. 2003.
Vertical City. Dir. Avijit Mukul Kishore. Public Service Broadcasting Trust. 2011.
When Four Friends Meet. Dir. Rahul Roy. Magic Lantern Movies. 2001.

2

'Canine spaces': Kolkata's slum dogs

Veena Hariharan

> *Indeed, that is the beauty of dogs. They are not a projection, nor the realization of an intention, nor the telos of anything. They are dogs; i.e., a species in obligatory, constitutive, historical, protean relationship with human beings. The relationship is not especially nice; it is full of waste, cruelty, indifference, ignorance, and loss, as well as of joy, invention, labor, intelligence, and play*
> (Haraway 2007, 11–12).

Indian documentary films have, until recently, largely remained indifferent to the representation of animals who are featured mostly by chance or as accidental backgrounds. Documentaries that did feature animals tended to be expository or pedagogical, concerning themselves with issues ranging from wildlife extinction, poaching and captivity, to animal suffering caused by inhuman corporations, food and packaging industries, human cruelty and greed. Usually made by wildlife enthusiasts, animal activists, or conservationists, these films travelled in environmental film festivals or as part of television programming as 'conservation films' and have played an important role in drawing public attention to these issues.[1] In recent years, however, we have seen a few animal films that strayed from this predominant impulse – the realist documentary *Pariah Dog* (dir. Jesse Alk, 2019) on Kolkata's slum dogs and their human care-givers; Prateek Vats' hybrid film *Eeb Allay Ooo* (2019), a moving satire on the plight of migrant workers employed by the City Corporation to catch monkeys in Delhi's elite neighbourhoods; Shaunak Sen's award-winning 'poetic documentary' *All That Breathes* (2022) on Delhi's black kites, their saviours and the city's multi-species life; and the Netflix documentary *The Elephant Whisperers* (2022) on the bond between an indigenous couple and an orphaned baby elephant set against the spectacular backdrop of the Mudumalai forests. I am interested in this particular trajectory of animal non-fiction films for the ways in which human/non-human entanglements are put into focus. The subject of this paper is Jesse Alk's *Pariah Dog* and its representation of canine-human entanglements in the crowded metropolis of Kolkata.[2]

Indeed, the history of the moving image has been snared with animals. Jonathan Burt (2002) claims that the desire to understand the minutiae of the animal body in motion precipitated the early cinema experiments of Eadweard Muybridge, Jules Etienne Marey and others. Yet, the 'animal turn' in critical discourse is of more recent vintage, even as it includes a substantial body of scholarship that has produced diverse ways of looking at the animal in narrative and non-fictional representations (Baker 2001; Berger 1980; Burt 2002; Cahill 2019; Haraway 1991; Hediger 2020; Lippit 2000; Pick 2011). Scholarship on animal documentaries tends to be largely focused on wildlife films (Bousé 2000; Chris 2006; Mitman 2012; Vivanco 2012; and so on), more recent works such as Belinda Smaill (2016) moves closer home to the domesticated and livestock animals that live in our midst, drawing attention to both their materiality and agentiality, while regarding the importance of the documentary form in producing 'knowledge about the non-human world' (7). By studying a corpus of films that offers a 'rethinking of human and animal agency, one that both generates the destabilisation of familiar codes of humanist vision and accentuates the corporeality of animal life' (Smaill 2016, 19–20), she delineates a new figuration of the animal in modern life. Aesthetically, the challenge then is to elevate the animal from the objectivity of thing life and imbue it with embodied-ness and materiality. At the same time, this agentic animal cannot be 'fully appropriated to human knowledge or representation' (Smaill 2016, 83).

As a representational form, realist documentary cinema is anchored in a spectatorial contract that binds the filmmaker and viewer in a shared partaking of the truth of the indexical-real, what Vivian Sobchack (2004) calls the 'charge of the real'. Animals are always-already documentary subjects, whether they are featured in fiction or non-fiction, in that their lives as much as their deaths carry the charge of the real, which according to Sobchack is an ethical charge. In her example, the real rabbit's real death in Jean Renoir's *Rules of the Game* (1939) punctuates the narrative universe of the film to plunge the viewer into a documentary space, 'one that calls forth not only response but also responsibility – not only aesthetic valuation but also ethical judgment. It reminds us reflexively to ourselves as embodied, culturally knowledgeable, and socially invested viewers' (Sobchack 2004, 284). This documentary space becomes particularly contestatory in the case of animal representations that come into conflict with the storied worlds of humans. The most famous instance of this can perhaps be found in Michael Moore's documentary *Roger & Me* (1989), about the brutal plight of workers in economically depressed Flint, Michigan, following General Motors' decision to close several auto plants. The film was widely rebuked by animal activists and the American Humane Association, as it shows the wife of one of the laid-off workers clubbing, gutting and skinning rabbits on screen, while she engages Moore in conversation, saying that she raises the rabbits 'for pets or meat'. Jennifer Ladino (2013) suggests that our cinema has long borne the perspectival lens of a 'speciesed gaze' that privileges an anthropocentric way of seeing (Disney animations and popular wildlife films are exemplary here) that tends to 'simulate, objectify and marginalize non-human animals' and fails to offer a political comment on the ecosystem or its inhabitants (130–31). In an effort to remedy this, Anat Pick (2011) asks that we renounce our anthropomorphic gaze on animals, in which human life is central to meaning-making and representation, and to turn instead to a 'zoomorphic' one where the non-human other and the human are seen through an equal lens. By focusing on the animal in the human-animal dyad, both in film (Pick calls this a 'creaturely cinema') and film scholarship, the spectatorial covenant can include attitudinal change and attention to an ethical cohabitation with animals.

Jesse Alk's documentary *Pariah Dog* (2019) looks at the life worlds of the eponymous street dogs in the city of Kolkata and at the humans whose lives are inextricably tied to them. Set amid the detritus of urban decay in Kolkata's slum neighbourhoods, where free-roaming dogs have reclaimed the nocturnal city streets as their own canine spaces, the film imbued with poetry and humanity produces a discourse about love and loving care through its representation of stray dogs, as well as intimate and humane portraits of the people whose lives are intertwined with them, as feeders or care-givers. In this article, I propose that *Pariah Dog* responds to the aesthetic and ethical challenges of documentary representation of animals by offering a zoomorphic lens through which to look at the perceptual life worlds of the city's stray dogs. In the background of human-animal contestations in the congested urban spaces of Kolkata, I argue that the film responds aesthetically by carving out 'canine spaces' – cinematic configurations of canine inhabitation with indexical moorings in the real – and ethically through an interventionist documentary gaze, where the filmmaker-witness intervenes discursively via the film's afterlife and in the course of the film's production. Thus, the film creates an imaginative geography of human animal entanglements against human-centric representations of the urban.

Pariah Dog

Charles Baudelaire, inspired by Joseph Stevens' paintings of dogs, wrote about them in *Paris Spleen*, in his realist prose-poems on 1850s Paris – a curious hybrid space of high living and low life, of poetry and poverty, of cafes, salons and slums. Not for him the 'dandified dog', the 'fatuous quadruped' in their 'silken padded kennels' but the 'poor dogs, stinking dogs, the ones that everyone shoos away as if pestilent and flea-bitten, except for the poor whose companions they are, and the poet who regards them with a brotherly eye' (Baudelaire 1869 [2008], 101–2). Separated across spatio-temporal epochs, Jesse Alk's 2019 film *Pariah Dog*, set in present-day Kolkata, captures the same sentiment. Alk explores Kolkata's slum neighbourhoods as the canine space of the film. I borrow the notion of canine space from Luke McKernan's commentary (2008) on the noticeable phenomenon of stray dogs in silent cinema. In his presentation of a compilation of a predominantly realist corpus of films from the silent era to a modern-day audience, he noticed:

> …the audience's attention was being frequently drawn away from the supposed subject and centre of the film's attention, and instead they were detecting action to the edge of the frame, or crossing the frame, interrupting the action or courageously ignoring it, creating a vital counter-narrative. In short, their attention was irresistibly drawn to stray dogs (McKernan 2008).

As he researched further into the 'distracting and engrossing' qualities of stray dogs in films, McKernan compiled a vast number of silent films in which the stray dog appeared by accident or design, mostly by accident.

> Anyone familiar with early films will know of the puzzled glances from passers-by that characterise street scenes, of the distracting matter which suggests that the camera operator was not in full command of the subject… What adds to the fascination, reinforcing one's belief in the essentially liberated nature of early films, is that stray dogs can be found in studio films of the period. The drama is enacted, the comedy routine performed, and in the background a dog watches, or wanders past, or joins in if it so desires, and this is accepted as part of the total action. 'Canine space' is therefore that other space, that world into which the camera has intruded (McKernan 2008).

Alk's film is a rediscovery and representation of this canine space, where the stray dog is the subject and centre of the film and Alk and his camera merely interlopers. The documentary spaces of Alk's film have indexical moorings in the real canine spaces of Kolkata's many neighbourhoods, forcing us to encounter such spaces, not just as cinematic formations, but as spaces with equivalences in the real world. In this way, the film subverts a familiar anthropocentric urban geography habituated to marginalising animals, in ways that instead centre the animal. Rather than representing dogs as background or accidental elements of the landscape, in Alk's film the focus is on the streetscapes of the dogs – their canine spaces and, in the course of the film, of animal-human entanglements.

Responding to Edward Said's call for an 'imaginative geography' (Said 1978, 54–55, 71–72), Chris Philo and Chris Wilbert (2004) emphasise the need to move beyond a singular focus on the human to one that looks instead at the 'complex entanglings of human-animal relations with space, place, location, environment and landscape' (4). In the received schema of anthropocentric geography, there is a neat classification of lived spaces into the city, countryside and wilderness. Philo and Wilbert draw our attention to the unclassifiable in-between or marginal spaces of the city's poor, homeless, outsiders and petty criminals – spaces that human eyes typically avoid. These are the abandoned land stretches typically next to sewers, railways and bus stations – spaces populated by rodents, feral cats and dogs. They describe these animals as 'curiously transgressive beings, neither purely wild nor purely tame, existing as "in-between" animals finding themselves, appropriately enough, utilising in-between spaces' (Philo and Wilbert 2004, 20). In turn, the presence of such animals renders these spaces marginal.

Offering a classic definition of the city as 'emblematic manifestations of the human will to live free of the vagaries of nonhuman nature', Krithika Srinivasan (2018) observes that, as 'free-living animals living in the midst of human habitations', stray dogs pose a challenge to such well-worn definitions of cities (236). They occupy a liminal position and are seen as 'outcasts' whom 'residents should avoid, control, regulate, and perhaps even kill, because they are seen as disorderly, dirty, dangerous' and are treated with 'indifference, scorn, and sometimes brutality [...] they blend into the urban landscape as one more feature of disorder and decay' (Arluke and Atema 2017, 126). The space portrayed in *Pariah Dog* is set among the detritus of urban decay, but it is also a space of poetry, love, humanity and, above all, of free-roaming dogs who have claimed the city spaces of the night as their own canine space.

In the opening scene of the film, the camera gently hovers over the nocturnal street while the crowded metropolis finally sleeps. A shepherd returns with his herd of goats, rats scavenge the city's dumpsters, and the desolate howl of a solitary stray dog pierces the night. As we follow his lone gaze down the alleyway lined with yellow taxis, overhead electric wires and cables, and ruined facades of buildings, we see that he is looking at a pack of dogs a block away. They have claimed the street, and they bark and growl at each other as they play, fight and engage in sexual intercourse. As our lone canine approaches, the barks of the group grow violent as they defend their territory, and he is forced to beat a hasty retreat. As Simon Foster (2019) captures perceptively in his review of the film, …

> The opening scene of the documentary *Pariah Dog* is one of heartbreaking poignancy; a beautiful young adult male pariah (or desi) dog, the native canine breed of South (and) East Asia, sits alone in an empty street in Kolkata, the tips of his golden coat covered in the city's dirt, his yearning howl a cry in the night for other members of his long-dissolved pack. The life he cries for – the wilderness existence with which every one of his instincts is primed to interact – has long been consumed by man's industrial expansion. He is native to a land that he no longer recognises, and one whose society has wilfully neglected to recognise him (Foster 2019).

At the end of this scene, as the camera closes in on the film's first dog protagonist, we see its flea infested abrasions, its dirty coat, as with the rest of the bedraggled canine pack. These are the 'ugly' dogs 'beset with skin conditions including mange and ringworm, malnourished and often coated in a layer of solid filth, are semi-furred, semi-naked, dusty and dirty with skin like cracked cement', while others are maimed from road injuries or suffer from hip fractures or joint dislocations (Arluke and Atema 2017, 137). They are not the adorable cinematic canines,[3] that 'most photogenic of all animals', according to Louis Delluc, that populate the screen (Lawrence and McMahon 2105, 40). Stray dogs in films are just that – strays who wandered into the film or the set and are part of the final film by accident.[4] In *Pariah Dog*, the presence of stray dogs is not accidental but intentional, as they are the focus of the film. Alk and his crew even nicknamed the street dogs – James Dean, Marlon Brando and so on – in order to identify them by their unique, star-like personalities. Although Alk decided to leave out of the final cut (all the more difficult because of the large amount of footage and hundreds of dog vignettes) the more gruesome-looking dogs with tic-infested ears or severely injured or bloodied dogs, the diegesis of the film is indeed a deliberately produced canine space populated by strays: 'To me they are beautiful, awesome, especially when they are well fed … incredible ears, tightly wound tails, the way they look at you … regal, soulful, muscular'.[5]

Since dogs do not come under the ambit of the ban on performing animals (registration rules only require the Fitness Certificate of the dogs, along with the dog vaccination record), they are liberally used in films, fiction and non-fiction alike. Alk says that the moment the 'dog steps into the frame, it is real. The dogs in Tarkovsky's fictional film are real, as are the horses' (personal interview). Hence, for Alk, the choice to make a realist documentary film rather than a fictional one was suggested by the always-already documentary real of animals on film. Alk claims that the films that made the greatest impact on him in terms of inspiring *Pariah Dog* and the particular documentary mode employed in the film were Robert Gardner's *Forest of Bliss* (1986), featuring scavenger dogs on the funeral ghats of India's holy city of Benares, and Swedish director Mikael Kristersen's *Kestrel's Eye* (1998), which captures the world from the point of view of European falcons. Other influences that he mentions in his interview were the gritty beauty of the Austrian filmmaker Michael Glawogger's documentaries; Charles Burnett's *Killer of Sheep* (1978), that classic of the LA Black Film Collective; Harvard Sensory Ethnography's *Sweetgrass* (2009); and the observational documentaries of Frederick Wiseman. Early in the making of the film, Alk knew that he did not want an interview-based film; rather, he wanted to deploy what he calls a 'multi-sensory filmmaking style' (Alk, in Bhavani 2019) that captured the entangled worlds of dogs and humans. There are no hand-held shots in the film, as Alk was going for a stable Steadicam cinematic aesthetic. The Glawogger-inspired soundscapes are an authentic representation of Kolkata's canine spaces invoked in the sonic realm with stereo sounds and multiple microphones that were deployed to capture the barks, growls and howls of canine packs (no monopods were used during filming to prevent the dogs from becoming aggressive). While these animal sounds recreate their brutal life on the streets, the background scores are populated by western tracks, including songs by Bruce Springsteen, an Ella Fitzgerald cover of 'No Strings Attached' and Dire Straits – which Alk calls Kolkata's favourite band. Except for a diegetic track that plays during the Pujo festivities, Alk's anti-orientalist motto was 'no slums, no sadhus, no sitars' (personal interview).

City of Dog

The city of Kolkata, host to infinite and contiguous canine spaces, became the perfect setting for Alk's film:

> I first visited Kolkata in 2010, and I was hypnotised by the city from the moment I landed. The street dogs were an immediate focus for me. Something about their intense suffering, their (in my experience) friendliness, and the way they were a part of the city, but also completely separate from it drew me to them.[6]

Although Alk hoped to present a 'timeless' film about the city, he also believes he 'captured a moment in which Kolkata in particular is undergoing rapid change':

> Old heritage buildings are being torn down every day and replaced with soulless glass and concrete storefronts. In twenty years, the city may be unrecognizable. The city itself is a main character in the film, and I'm happy we were able to preserve a bit of it in its current incarnation (director's interview).

While iconic signifiers such as the yellow taxis, narrow alleyways, festive pooja pandals, slums, waterfronts and large decrepit buildings suggest the old city of Kolkata, the Big Ben replica towering over the city, the bustling commercial life of Park Street with its selfie-couples suggest the more modern innovations in the city's colonial pastiche. Alk claims that he took great pains to avoid the pitfalls of an orientalist gaze, both at the city and its dogs, taking inputs from his local collaborators. 'We were very conscious during the shooting to avoid what westerners think of as 'exotic' images, when possible, to avoid unnecessary images of poverty, and to be as focused and specific as possible' (personal interview).

> Many people in the West have an idea of what Kolkata is like (or Calcutta, to use its former name). But there's so much more to that incredible, frustrating, beautiful city that we see in western documentaries. More than anything, I wanted to capture the feeling of being there, which I felt was so different from anything I saw in the many documentaries shot in Kolkata focusing on slums or social problems (director's interview).

The film is mostly shot in night lights when the canine packs are out in their element, under sodium vapor streetlamps, kitschy decorations that illuminate the festive Pujo season, or the haphazard 'neon cacophony' of Kolkata's billboard landscape (Savada 2020). However, Alk's flaneur-camera also captures the daytime streets of Kolkata – its stalls, hawkers and bystanders, as well as its dogs and dog lovers which are aplenty in the city. Indeed, as Alk filmed all over the city, especially South Kolkata from Dhakuria to Chetla, he notes that stray dogs were everywhere, notably in the poorer areas. According to figures consolidated by NGOs, it is estimated that there are about 80,000 stray dogs in this city of more than fourteen million.[7]

In Kolkata, as elsewhere in the world, it is the street that emerges as the canine space of strays. Animal legislation also classifies canines as either pet dogs or street dogs, thereby rendering the street as the stray's lawful habitat and indeed its primary home. At the same time, the distinction between pets and strays is not merely a semantic one but also marks the difference between the primitive and the modern city – the former where animals and humans are chaotically entangled, and the modern where a notional, even violent separation of the two is based in their value estimated by the extractive logic of capital. Pets 'are born, live, and die mainly within human affective and recreational economies', while street dogs are seen as 'ordinary', possessing no intrinsic 'economic value'; rather, they are seen to have a 'nuisance value'[8] as aesthetic blights, vectors of disease, sometimes even causes of injury and death to humans (Srinivasan 2018, 236). By focusing his attention on strays rather than pet dogs, the primary canine space in Alk's film remains the street with all its documentary possibilities. Siegfried Kracauer (1960) famously described the street as 'not only the arena of fleeting impressions and chance encounters but a place where the flow of life is bound to assert itself' and hence the 'medium's affinity for the flow of life would be enough to explain the attraction which the street has ever since exerted on the screen' (72–73).

As strays thrived on streets and amid trash, with the active participation of humans, it is not humans but the machinic that has been opposed to the animal. While strays occupied the night streets, where the odd car may whiz past, automobiles became positively menacing to the stray dog during the day. Indeed, automobiles have historically been the animal's enemy, displacing and eventually substituting them as transport and labour in urban modernity. As cars proliferated at the beginning of the twentieth century, efficiently churned out on Fordist assembly lines, they became a regular feature of not only cityscapes but also extended to the edge of forests and wildlife parks. Automobiles became a regular part of safaris aiding tourism, photography and the hunt itself. Rather than fix negative or positive connotations to the automobile, Heini Hediger (1985, 161) argues for its neutrality based on necessity and an inevitable passage into modernity. In Alk's film, the automobile has negative connotations, even though two out of the four human protagonists in the film drive auto-rickshaws for a living: 'A lot of the dogs in Kolkata have disabled legs from car accidents, and I came to look at the automobile as the natural enemy of the Indian street dog' (personal interview). As Subrata, one of the main protagonists, says in the film, '[t]hese days people have submitted to the *ajantrik* – there is no place for love, only the pretence of love'. Loosely translated from the Bengali, 'ajantrik' is the machine, the automobile that Ritwik Ghatak famously, if tragically, celebrates in his eponymous film; it is also a way of life.

Animal-human entanglements

> I sing the dirtied dog, the poor dog, the homeless dog, the loafing dog... I sing the unlucky dogs, whether those who wander, solitary, in the winding ditches of immense cities, or those who with their blinking, spiritual eyes have said to abandoned men: 'Take me with you, and perhaps out of our two miseries we can create a kind of happiness!'
>
> (Baudelaire, 1869 [2008], 104)

As Alk became progressively involved with the human care-givers of the strays, the film eventually became one about animal-human entanglements – intimate and humane portraits of the people whose lives are so intertwined with the animals. A review describes *Pariah Dog* as an 'ode to the ethical continuity between humans and other species' (IFFLA 2020). Emphasising this, Alk announced at the premiere of his film at the Melbourne Festival: '*Pariah Dog* centres around universal themes – loneliness, compassion (or lack thereof), personal fulfilment and the search for meaning' (director's interview). The analogous relationship between the pariah status of the 'urbanised native dog' and social outsiders is not lost upon the viewer.

> The film was originally intended to focus much more on the street dogs themselves. When I first moved to Kolkata, I thought it would be a film with very little dialogue, 70% footage of street dogs living their lives in the city, 30% observational footage of some of the people who feed them (director's interview).

Thus, even though at first glance we may expect a film after Turkish filmmaker Ceyda Torun's 2016 documentary about stray cats in Istanbul (many reviews make this reference), *Pariah Dog* is more a film about stray dogs and humans who care for strays. *Kedi*'s high-definition images of an inviting city by the Bosphorus is in stark contrast to the repulsive realist imagery of rodent-infested dumpsters on Kolkata's night streets in Alk's film. While *Kedi* anthropomorphises the cats, categorising them in 'man-types' that could have come straight out of a dating manual – 'player', 'gentleman', 'lover' and so on – in Alk's film, we have portraits of humans who care for the dogs, while the dogs themselves are not individualised. After many conversations, Alk finally settled on the four protagonists of the film – Pinku, Kajal, Milly and Subrata – who live in separate everyday worlds but are united in the universe of the film by their shared love for strays. As the film cuts between their stories, Alk describes the editing process: 'Because there were four people, all of whom required a lot of screen time, a lot of really incredible dog footage ended up being cut in the final pass. I think in the end we found the perfect balance, but that change in focus to the human characters was a profound shift that happened early in the process' (director's interview).

Pinaki 'Pinku' Dasgupta is a sculptor and artist, without a place in the modern city, with no patrons and no buyers for his delicate wood carvings. He finances his art, pays his bills and feeds his dogs all on his meagre earnings as a nightly 'toto' driver.[9] Dedicated as much to his art as to his strays, his penury is never an obstacle to his labours of love: 'If I have a little food, they [the dogs] get the same'. Some day he hopes to sell his artwork and be appreciated for his art, but in the meanwhile, he is happy to exist on the love and admiration of his dogs: 'They love me a lot', he says, referring to the dogs he takes care of, 'so I consider myself a rich guy'. At the end of the film, the wooden sculpture that he has been carving through the duration of the film is finally revealed to be that of a beautiful dog.

Although the four protagonists share a roughly equal amount of screen time, it is Subrata Das, the auto-rickshaw driver who feeds nearly seventy dogs across the city every day, who is the film's star. Alk says in an interview that it was his encounter with Subrata that his own 'thinking about the project changed'.

> Before I met Subrata, I just had a sense of the dog carers as lonely people, missing something vital in their lives. In fact, I thought the film would be filled up with close-ups of dogs and canine points-of-view of humans as they themselves would be framed from the waist down, faceless and glance-less. Then I met Subrata, and I knew he had to be a star of the film (personal interview).

Subrata is an auto-rickshaw driver, an entertainer and musician who had his fifteen minutes of fame back in the day when he appeared on *Dadagiri* – a Bengali-language quiz show hosted by the celebrated ex-captain of the Indian cricket team, Sourav Ganguly, or Dada, as he is popularly called. He is now a small-time local celebrity in his own right and is invited to judge local dog shows that promote fighting human cruelty against animals. Over the course of the film, a newly inspired Subrata (after his television appearance) decides to pick up his forgotten dreams, buys an electronic synthesiser with his last bit of savings and records a song that celebrates his love for humans, animals and plants. With some encouragement from Alk, he even embarks on a tour to the outskirts of the city as a traveling musician.

Even here, Subrata's dreams of hitting a jackpot of instant celebrity are not so much for himself as for his wish to have enough to care for ailing dogs. Even as he just about manages to survive, he tends to the masses of the strays he sees *en route* his auto-rickshaw rides, picking up leftovers from the city's many restaurants to feed dogs. Subrata remains a committed advocate of dog welfare and finds himself at the head of a protest march of animal activists at the end of the film.

Mallika 'Milly' Sarkar is a striking presence in the film – of Japanese-Russian-Indian descent, her looks, accent and relative affluence set her apart from the rest of the film's protagonists. But we soon realise that she is a mixture of delusion and defiance, and her glory, if it ever existed, is in the distant past. She complains bitterly about a country gone to the dogs, as squatters and politicians have taken over what once used to be the large mansion that she inherited. Alk had to take great care and attention in editing Milly's story and sculpting her character in the film as people tended to dislike her superior airs and defiant independence: 'She was a single woman with a giant house that she was trying to protect, dogs and all; in itself, it was a physically dangerous place to be'. She is committed to her life's mission to save dogs and of someday converting her ruined mansion into a dog ashram – a shelter for stray dogs. On more than one occasion she is seen taking cudgels on behalf of the neighbourhood dogs – fighting for their rights at protest marches that she initiates, or castigating those who attack care-givers at her dog clinic, hectoring them on humane ways to care for animals. Milly contemplates her single life on camera, focusing her attention instead on her relationships with the dogs. 'These animals are so trusting... they don't realise how human beings can destroy them', she says in one of the film's strongest lines.

Of the four protagonists, Kajal seems most intimate with the dogs as she nurses them through sickness and often carries them to their death. Over the course of the film, we see Kajal at several dog funerals, as she ceremoniously buries them while the camera lingers on her tearful reveries after each burial. She herself lives in a home no bigger than a kennel, next to the graves of the dogs she helps bury. But unlike her employer, she does not complain about her meagre resources: 'I don't have a problem with it. In fact, I like it'. In a particularly poignant moment in the film, she confesses to the camera that she lives in the present as she has no future; her life's happiness is looking after the strays, she says, as she rocks a pup between her breasts.

Alk gives us insights into the complex love-hate, master-slave relationship between the dogged Kajal and the high-handed Milly as they occupy two ends of the class-caste spectrum. Milly is pedigreed and always twice removed from dog-care, while the nitty-gritty of looking after dogs falls on Kajal. But this is only so in appearance, as there are more similarities between them than there are differences. Even though Kajal lives in a hovel no bigger than a kennel and Milly lives in a large inherited mansion, we soon see that the house is falling apart and can hardly keep out the elements or trespassers, and both have little else in their lives than the retinue of dogs they care for, as they constantly bicker and complain about each other. In the film's concluding section, a lyrical boat ride on Chilka Lake, away from the hustle and bustle of the city and its dogs, brings the two of them together as they realise that, in spite of their insurmountable differences, they are bound by their shared love and dedication to the ill, malnourished and maimed strays that they have adopted. The section ends with both of them joining in a protest march initiated by Milly under her Stray Animals Crusade, in the nearby city of Puri.

The discourse of love and 'loving care' looms large in the film, as in movements aimed at the rehabilitation of street dogs. As the loyal companion of man and the 'first domesticated animal on earth', Haraway (2008, 17) considers the dog to be a 'companion species', or a species with whom we share things ('companion' is derived from the Latin 'cum', meaning with, and 'panis', meaning bread, with the term thus having a sense of 'sharing bread'). For her, animal-human entanglements are emphatically underlined in 'co-constitutive' relationships with their dogs – 'we are constitutively, companion species. We make each other up, in the flesh. Significantly other to each other, in specific difference, we signify in the flesh a nasty developmental infection called love. This love is a historical aberration and a natural cultural legacy' (Haraway 2007, 39). Although Haraway is primarily referring to domestic and pet dogs specially curated for human companionship, this can be extended to stray dogs who exist in the liminal category. They may go up in the world as pets or be abandoned on the street when, for example, a household moves, leaving them behind. Arluke and Atema develop the concept of 'passive' and 'commensal ownership' of street dogs:

> More caring relationships with roaming dogs can occur in communities in which people form loose affiliations with dogs at the neighborhood level, rather than their being strongly connected to one family. This practice, which is widespread, is referred to as community dog-keeping. With weaker human-canine affiliations, there is tolerance or benign co-existence between residents and dogs on the streets, or even affection,

as people may feed the dogs and perhaps name or play with them but do not assume further responsibility for their care (Arluke and Atema 2017, 129).

An interventionist gaze?

The film made the minor festival circuit, winning Best Documentary Feature at the Big Sky Documentary Festival. Peter Keough (2020) of the *Boston Globe* called it 'heart-breaking and luminous', while Foster (2019), reviewing the film when it played at the Melbourne Documentary Festival 2019, saw it as a 'deeply humanistic film full of existential irony'. Rachel West (2020) calls the film 'experiential' and 'immersive': 'Eschewing a traditional voice over or explanatory talking head interviews, Jesse Alk immerses audiences directly into the world of these lowly dogs and the people who love and care for them'. However, Alk did not make it to the big festival league, since juries around the world were as confused by Alk's outsider/insider status as an Alaskan man filming in Kolkata as they were about the city's free-ranging street dogs and, as noted above, India's 'open waste reality'. In some countries where dogs are imbued with religious significance, juries reacted to the film's depiction of their wretched street life. A major festival such as Karlovy-Vary rejected the film's 'sweet and light tone' (personal interview). A particularly harsh review however says: 'With just one brief reference to population control ("Who should do this?"), Alk misses the chance to save more unfortunate lives (human and animal), who need to find meaning beyond a wagging tail and unrequited love' (Wegg 2020).

Why is it important to study canine representations, especially of the stray dog, in literature, media, cinema and other pop-cultural representations? Peter Kellett (2016, 74) uses the term 'rhetorical hotspots' to describe the 'rhetorical struggle over how pariah dogs are defined and consequently how they are treated by humans'. Drives to eradicate strays are often 'at their core about image and aesthetics'. As Kellett (2016) observes, strays mar 'the aesthetic of upwardly mobile neighbourhoods and are often borne on the bodies of dogs themselves' (164). Advocacy involves legislating, influencing public attitudes by 'reconstructing the image and symbolic representation and even naming of pariah dogs' and rescuing them from 'fear-based narratives' around street dogs as vectors of contagion, rabies, aggression and dog bites (Kellett 2016, 161). As fear of rabies and dog bites is exacerbated in public discourse, they can lead to brutal put-downs of dogs with cruelty and impunity. However, as Alk pointed out in various public screening fora, this cruelty is relative. In fact, strays are treated with relative humanity in Kolkata, he says, compared to the 'two million odd dogs that are put down in the US every year, simply because we cannot bear to look at them'. Alk himself makes no claim to being an activist filmmaker. His films are not aimed at advocacy for street dogs, although he does hope that the film would alter micro-perceptions about strays. By representing models of dog-carers, eminently worthy of emulation if not identification, Alk proposes that dogs eventually will be 'part of the community's moral responsibility' (personal interview).

Documentary scholars have long dwelled on the 'indexical bond' between the image and the object/subject captured as image. Nichols (1991) extends this further to include the bond between the 'image and the ethics that produced it. The image provides evidence not only on behalf of an argument but also gives evidence of the politics and ethics of its maker' (77). This is most evident in the event of the documentary's encounter with death. In Sobchack's phenomenology of documentary representation, she develops a classificatory system of ethical documentary 'gazes' possible in the filming of death on camera: the 'accidental', 'helpless', 'endangered', 'interventional' and 'humane gaze' (2004, 249). 'In other words, the filmmaker may accidentally record the death, may be helpless to prevent the death, may herself be endangered in the situation, may attempt to intervene to prevent the death, or may record an image of death out of compassion for the dying, all of which seem to justify the filming of indexical, documentary death' (Baron 2015, 156–70). As Sobchack (1984) explains in the ninth of her ten propositions on death, representation and documentary, '[d]ocumentary space is constituted and inscribed as ethical space; it is the objectively visible totalization of subjective visual responsiveness and responsibility toward a world shared with other human subjects' (294). If we expand this to include non-human subjects, then the documentary image also could be seen to contain within it the subjective ethical responsiveness to the witnessing of non-human deaths. In one of the film's memorable scenes, a maimed pup repeatedly attempts to cross a particularly busy traffic intersection as Alk's camera captures it from low-angle shots filmed through the menacing spokes of bicycle wheels, as bikes and cars whizz past. In a deux-ex-machina moment, a young boy appears, seemingly out of nowhere, but probably hanging around on the street corner, as many tend to do on Kolkata streets. He gathers the pup in his arms and sets it by the side of the road.

> This was one of the first scenes I filmed for *Pariah Dog*, in February of 2014. And it remains the hardest thing I've ever filmed. One of my favourite parts of this scene is that the kid, who I did not ask to do what he did, gives me a bit of an understandably dirty look as he walks away… It looks staged, but it definitely wasn't; the relief I felt was huge (personal interview).

The accident averted provokes all manners of questions regarding the ethical gaze of the documentary filmmaker, as he is poised between the happenstance of being at the scene – the accidental, even helpless gaze and the interventional gaze of the documentary filmmaker-witness. As Alk captures all kinds of dog tragedies, death and sickness, larger questions about the documentary filmmaker's interventions in mitigating the challenges that stray dogs in the city face are raised. As a 'present-tense film', *Pariah Dog* precludes historical explanations (personal interview):

> I try to get microscopic if possible … In relation to the street dogs, there is a lot of disagreement right now about their place in the future of India. Can a modern India exist alongside street dogs? Do the dogs have their own rights as a native breed that has remained in a semi-domesticated state for thousands of years? (Alk, cited in Bhavani, 2019)

Indeed, the film poses a larger question about the coevalness of strays in modernity. As urban planners envisage smart cities and argue for a large-scale eradication of strays from our midst, animal activists and animal lovers seek ways of accommodating them. Even as the film fails to depict human-dog conflicts or offer a vision of trans-species cities and justice for non-humans in our midst, its invocation of off-screen canine spaces provokes larger questions about street dogs and animal-human entanglements that remain unanswered by the film itself.

Notes

1 These include the films of Mike Pandey, Krishnendu Bose, Rita Banerji, Shekar Dattatri and Sunanda Bhat, to name a few.
2 The so-called pariah dog is a 'pure, indigenous and ancient race of dogs' – the 'long-term pariah morphotype' – whose characteristics include 'erect ears, a wedge-shaped head and a curved tail'. They can be found dispersed across the world, and particularly aplenty on the streets of India. See https://indog.co.in/ [accessed 23 November 2023].
3 From Flick in *Umberto D* (dir. Vittoria De Sica, 1952) to Uggie in *The Artist* (dir. Michel Hazanavicius, 2011), from Lassie the Collie and Rin Tin Tin the German Shepherd who starred in many movies to the digitally manipulated *101 Dalmatians* (dir. Walt

Disney, 1961; 1996), cinematic canines have shared the spotlight with human stars. Indian cinema also has had its share of adorable canine protagonists, such as the black labrador Moti in *Teri Meharbaaniyan* (dir. K. C. Bokadia, 1985), Tuffy the Pomeranian in *Hum Aapke Hai Kaun* (dir. Sooraj Bharjatiya, 1994) and the mutt Bhidu in *Chillar Party* (dir. Nitesh Tiwari and Vikas Bahl, 2011). From being flung from a high-rise in *Sacred Games* (2006) to being the moral centre of *Pataal Lok* (2020), recent Netflix shows have equally highlighted the canines in our midst.

4 Writing about an early photographic reproduction of a 'stately procession "photo-bombed" by a lone canine pariah', Vanja Hamzic notes, 'early photographs of Indian pariah dogs are notoriously rare. Unlike tigers, elephants, monkeys, snakes and other animals typically associated with India, pariah dogs are captured by the colonial-time photographer's camera almost exclusively by chance' (Hamzic 2014, 193).

5 Personal Interview with the director, 12 April 2020 [hereafter personal interview].

6 Director's Interview at the Melbourne Documentary Film Festival, 2019 [hereafter director's interview].

7 Figures provided by ORF (Observers Research Foundation).

8 Nuisance may include a spectrum of harmless activities, including persistent barking, ranging on private property, scavenging for food in trash and dumpsters, defacing public spaces with feces, marring street aesthetics by spilling trash, or indulging in 'unaesthetic sexual activity', whereby neighbourhoods may be perceived as 'messy or decaying'; obstructions to walkability, bikability and tourism, and causing road accidents or physical injuries to humans. 'Dog bites can make residents feel unsafe or insecure because they fear attacks, mauling, disease transmission, even death, despite the fact that vast majority of roaming dogs are friendly or submissive to humans and pose no threat' (Arluke and Atema 2017, 130–31).

9 This is a cross between an auto- and cycle-rickshaw used to ferry tourists and seen as a green alternative to auto-rickshaws.

Works Cited

Arluke, A., and Atema, K. (2017). Roaming dogs. In L. Kalof (ed.), *Oxford handbook of animal studies*, 113–34. Oxford: Oxford University Press.

Baker, S. (2001). *Picturing the beast: Animals, identity, and representation*. Champaign: University of Illinois Press.

Baron, J. (2015). The ethics of appropriation: 'Misusing' the found document in *Suitcase of Love and Shame* and *A Film Unfinished*. In D. Marcus and S. Kara (eds), *Contemporary documentary*, 156–70. London and New York: Routledge.

Baudelaire, C. (1869 [2008]). *Paris Spleen: Little poems in prose*. Indianapolis: Hackett Publishing Company.

Berger, J. (1980). *Why look at animals?* London: Penguin.

Bhavani, D. K. (2019, 21 March). [interview with Jesse Alk]. *The Hindu*.

Bousé, D. (2000). *Wildlife films*. Philadelphia: University of Pennsylvania Press.

Burt, J. (2002). *Animals in film*. London: Reaktion Books.

Cahill, J. (2019). *Zoological surrealism: The nonhuman cinema of Jean Painlevé*. Minneapolis: University of Minnesota Press.

Chris, C. (2006). *Watching wildlife*. Minneapolis: University of Minnesota Press.

Foster, S. (2019). Pariah Dog. *Screen-Space*. http://screen-space.squarespace.com/reviews/2019/5/14/pariah-dog.html [accessed 23 November 2023].

Hamzic, V. (2014). The unconscious pariah: Canine and gender outcasts of the British Raj. *Australian Feminist Law Journal*, 20(2), 185–98.

Haraway, D. (2007). *The companion species manifesto: Dogs, people, and significant others*. Chicago: Prickly Paradigm Press.

Haraway, D. (2008). *When species meet*. Minneapolis: University of Minnesota Press.

Haraway, D. (1991). *Simians, cyborgs, and women: The reinvention of nature*. New York: Routledge.

Hediger, H. (2020). Not the animal is blind, but the human being, blinded by consciousness and incapable of seeing the world: A Note on Roxy Miéville, Star of Jean-Luc Godard's First Animal Picture, Adieu au Language. *Senses of Cinema*, 100. https://www.sensesofcinema.com/2022/forms-that-think-jean-luc-godard/not-the-animal-is-blind-but-the-human-being-blinded-by-consciousness-and-incapable-of-seeing-the-world-a-note-on-roxy-mieville-star-of-jean-luc-godards-first-animal-picture-adieu-au-lang/ [accessed 1 July 2022].

Hediger, H. (1985). *Studying animal behaviour: Autobiographies of the founders*. Chicago: University of Chicago Press.

IFFLA Catalogue (Indian Film Festival of Los Angeles), 2020.

Kellett, P. (2016). *Communication and conflict: Transformation through local, regional and global engagement*. Lanham: Lexington Books.

Keough, P. (2020, 19 August). 'Far beyond truthiness, tending strays, traveling light'. *Boston Globe*.

Kracauer, S. (1960). *Theory of film: The redemption of physical reality*. Princeton: Princeton University Press.

Ladino, J. (2013). Working with animals: Regarding companion species in documentary film. In S. Rust, S. Momami and S. Cubitt (eds), *Ecocinema: Theory and practice*, 129–48. London and New York: Routledge.

Lawrence, M., and McMahon, L. (2015). *Animal life and the moving image*. London: BFI.

Lippit, A. (2000). *Electric animal: Toward a rhetoric of wildlife*. Minneaplis and London: University of Minnesota Press.

McKernan, L. (2008). First film dogs. *The Bioscope*. bioscopic.wordpress.com/2008/11/14/ [accessed 9 November 2023].

McLean, A. L. (2014). *Cinematic canines: Dogs and their work in the fiction film*. New Brunswick: Rutgers University Press.

Mitman, G. (2012). *Reel nature: America's romance with wildlife on film*. Seattle: University of Washington Press.

Nichols, B. (1991). *Representing reality: Issues and concepts in documentary*. Bloomington: Indiana University Press.

Philo, C., and Wilbert, C. (eds). (2000). *Animal spaces, beastly places: New geographies of human-animal relations*. London and New York: Routledge.

Pick, A. (2011). *Creaturely poetics: Animality and vulnerability in literature and film*. New York: Columbia University Press.

Said, E. (1978) *Orientalism*. New York: Routledge and Kegan Paul.

Savada, E. (2020, 17 August). Saving man's and woman's best friends: Jesse Alk's *Pariah Dog*. Filmint.
Smaills, B. (2016). *Regarding life: Animals and the documentary moving image*. Albany: SUNY Press.
Sobchack, V. (2004). *Carnal thoughts: Embodiment and moving image culture*. Berkely, Los Angeles and London: University of California Press.
Sobchack, V. (1984). Inscribing ethical space: Ten propositions on death, representation, and documentary. *Quarterly Review of Film Studies*, 9(4), 283–300.
Srinivasan, K. (2018). Posthumanist animal studies and zoopolitical law. In A. Matsuoka and J. Sorenson (eds), *Critical animal studies: Towards trans-species social justice*, 234–53. Rowan and Littlefield.
Vivanco, L. (2012). Pengions are good to think with: Wildlife films, the imaginary shaping of nature, and environmental politics. In S. Rust, S. Monani and S. Cubitt (eds), *Econcinema: Theory and practice*, 109–27. New York: Routledge.
Wegg, J. (2020). *Pariah Dog* [review]. jamesweggreview.org [accessed 21 June 2021].
West, R. (2020). *Pariah Dog* review: More than just a dog version of *Kedi*. *That Shelf*. https://thatshelf.com/pariah-dog-review-more-than-just-a-dog-version-of-kedi/ [accessed 21 June 2021].

Films Cited

ll That Breathes. Dir. Shaunak Sen. HBO Documentary Films. 2022
Eeb Allay Ooo. Dir. Prateek Vats. Nama Productions. 2019.
Elephant Whisperers. Dir. Kartiki Gonsalves. Sikhya Entertainment. 2022
Pariah Dog. Dir. Jesse Alk. Collective Eye Films. 2019.

3

'Threadbearing': Journeys with our subjects and our documentary narratives

Anjali Monteiro and K. P. Jayasankar

The filmmaker as a 'threadbearer'

As documentary filmmakers, we have always imagined ourselves as *Sutradhar*, tentative bearers of the multiple, complex threads of narratives that are not quite under our control, neither in their performance nor in their reception and interpretation. There are always many possibilities for both our subjects and our audiences to put their foot into the door of our stories that take them into unchartered realms – realms in which we could lose ourselves, but also potentially find ourselves anew. And sometimes we may not like what we find; it may tell us something about ourselves and our relationships with our subjects and our texts that might make us feel less than worthy. These moments of crisis are sometimes, although not always, moments of epiphany that shape our practice.

Sutradhar, literally meaning 'threadbearer' (*Sutra* in Pali and Sanksrit denotes thread, and *Dhar* is the bearer) is a non-diegetic, reflexive narrator, found in many Indian performative traditions. In the *Natya Shastra* (200 BCE–200 CE), a treatise on theatre and aesthetics attributed to Bharat Muni, the term was originally used to denote both a 'puller of strings' and a 'curator-director'. The original reference in the *Natya Shastra* was to the marionette manipulator who literally pulls the strings or *sutra*. Scholars surmise that the term made its way from puppetry to classical Sanskrit plays, where the *sutradhar* is the stage manager and performance coordinator (Ghosh and Banerjee 2005). This theatrical device is also found in numerous folk theatres across the Indian subcontinent and has equally been deployed by playwrights and directors, such as Girish Karnad (for example, *Hayavadana* and *Jokumaraswamy*) and Vijay Tendulkar (for instance, *Ghashiram Kotwal*), who adapted folk forms to look reflexively at contemporary themes. As Dharwadker (2005, 328) points out, ...

> The structure of (largely anonymous) folk drama usually consists of the interplay between an outer rhetorical frame, containing the *sutradhar* (literally, 'puppet master') and one or two ancillary characters, and a dramatized inner narrative [...] The frames also enable the playwrights to locate the performance (as distinct from the narrative of the inner play) in the historical and political present, and hence to create an ironic disjunction between the premodern narrative of the inner play and the postcolonial positioning of the outer. In its totality, the play then acquires an ineluctable contemporaneity.

We find this interactive heuristic narrative device to be productive in understanding our own practice and, perhaps, the documentary project itself.

In the beginning of our career as filmmakers in India in the 1980s, a 'voice-over' was an essential part of the narrative thread of a documentary. It helped ground and curate interviews and other materials that formed the narrative spine. These articulations certainly steered clear of the benchmark established by the Films Division of India (FD) documentaries with their pedantic, redundantly descriptive, male 'voice-of-god' narrator, often off-screen, bringing in more 'political' overtones, affective energy and more informal inflections.[1] Nevertheless, the voice-over remained disembodied, often choosing to stay self-consciously affect-free. This was to become passé soon. Our documentaries, too, in keeping with changing stylistics and peer practice, abandoned these voice-overs for a more 'thesis'-like format, impelled by arguments and interviews and other visual materials, as well as their collision with each other. Thus, the need for an expository narration was obviated by the tension between these diverse narratives, often contradictory, amplified by the syntactic juxtapositions. An argument by a government official or a figure of authority could be contested by another citizen-subject making a counter-claim, or more economically, by just using a 'cut-away' visual that contradicted or subverted its claim to truth. As filmmakers, we became *sutradhar*, albeit invisibilised, of the narrative, exploiting the ability of the documentary genre to absorb within its form, audience expectations and diverse aesthetic artefacts from animation to graphics. This invisibility afforded us a location of neutrality and 'immunity'. It offered us a safe space from which to speak, without contesting the 'normality' of that position, leading to the possibility of a rupture and of critiquing ways of seeing and being that underpin the project of essentialising the 'other' (Minh-Ha 1993). Nevertheless, discomfiture with this space was part of the process that led us to explore more reflexive ways of storytelling. It is not an accomplished journey, particularly for us as 'self-learning' filmmakers; it is a work in progress.

In this essay, we would like to share some of these experiences that gave new direction to our work. As *sutradhar*, we also weave ourselves into the delicate fabric of our narratives, the warp and the weft of the thread simultaneously constricting ourselves and our practice and giving it tangible shape. We have written before about the making of some of this documentary work (Jayasankar and Monteiro 2016). Other scholars, too, have written about our documentary texts and our cinematic praxis (Rutherford 2011; Kishore 2015, 2018). This essay focuses on a specific theme of our experience as *sutradhar* when engaging with subjects and with audiences. We use the word 'experience' rather than 'journey', for the latter tends to imply a purposive movement from one point to another, a notion of progress and completion. This is far from the often-muddled ways in which insights present themselves in the course of our work, not always adding up and often raising far more questions than providing answers.

Weaving multiple threads: *Kahankar: Ahankar (Storymaker: Storytaker)*

It was a dark night in the month of February 1995. We were somewhere in Dahanu, at the home of an *Adivasi*[2] activist of Kashtakari Sanghatana, conducting pre-production research for a film on some of the Warli stories that the organisation had been documenting for their youth-focused workshops in the area.[3] The residents of the pada were all there, and as the night wore on, they began to dance and sing – one song after another. And they would keep asking us: 'Is this good enough for your film?' We froze, unable to record the spectacle in shame and despair.

We recalled the story of the rat, a popular Warli story. A rat appeared one day, with a thorn in his tail, looking for some help. He saw a woman going to gather wood with her sickle and requested her to remove the thorn. As she tried, the sickle slipped, and the tip of his tail was sliced off. The rat demanded: 'Give me my tail back, or give me your sickle'. The rat took the sickle and moved on. The rat with a thorn in his tail became a rat with a sickle. And so the rat moves on, on a relentless spree of expropriation: a sickle, a few baskets, some pots, many vegetables, a big bullock and finally the Adivasi's wife. This is a Warli retelling of a history of exploitation that probably began in the mid-nineteenth century, when John Wilson, a British missionary, first entered the indigenous tracts of the Bombay Presidency. Subsequently, British administrators tried to 'tame' these heavily forested hills and valleys, through deforestation, land settlement legislation, excise duties on toddy and many other measures that opened the province to processes of expropriation – the rats who dispossessed the Warlis and other Adivasis of their forests and their lands.

As 'outsiders' trying to make a documentary with their stories and their paintings, we felt somewhat like rats with cameras. Was there any way in which we could deal creatively with this burden of history? Could we embed this self-doubt, and our subject-position, into the narrative? We drew inspiration from the titular story of the film-in-process. It speaks about the relationship between the story-teller (*Kahankar*) and the one who actively listens and affirms the story (*Ahankar*, literally meaning, the one who says '*han*' or yes). These two leave their homes, on a story-telling trip. They talk and listen, so absorbed in their stories that they die of hunger. The villagers of a nearby hamlet find their bodies and bury them together. This becomes a conundrum for their wives who have set out in search of them and want to take their bones home. They immerse all the bones in a pond. And such is the power of story-telling that the bones of the Kahankar, who gave his stories, are light and float in the water, while those of the Ahankar, who absorbed the stories, sinks to the bottom of the pond.

To us, *sutradhar* in search of a film, this was such a potent trope that it gave us the courage to insert ourselves in the interstices of the stories. For the Warli stories speak from the space of the oppressed; they who have been othered look with humour and irony at those who have othered them: the rat on a spree of dispossession who finally makes off with the Adivasi's wife; *Jum*, the god of death who comes down in the form of a liquor vendor and takes the Adivasi's life. A woman who has been beaten demonstrates with the first of her *chattis nakhre* (thirty-six ploys) how she can give her husband his come-uppance if she wants to. Men are far less efficient than women, a story tells us. Men brand women as witches because they cannot put up with the realisation that women are far cleverer than they themselves. These subaltern stories speak truth to power in subtle yet fecund ways. They pass on the seeds of resistance from one generation to the next.

We needed to place ourselves in relation to these profound stories. How have people like us looked at the Adivasis? And thus we went to the archives to trace the writings of the colonial others, missionaries and administrators, who have written about the Warlis. We found a rich body of research and administrative records, most of which adopted a coloniser's gaze. This gaze continued in the post-colonial period, with a few exceptions. Juxtaposing this writing with the stories, we felt, was our response as *ahankars* to the power of the stories. The film (*Kahankar: Ahankar*, 1995) shuttles between the Warli stories and our writings about them, an invitation to the viewers to become *ahankars* bringing their own experiences and prejudices to bear in their re-reading of the film. The two sets of narratives and their collision helped amplify the uneasy precarity of these communities and also create more critical readings, premised on their interstices. When we now reflect critically on this film, which was perhaps one of our first attempts to break out of the mould of linear story-telling about the other, we are painfully aware of its limitations:

> While the film is innovative in its formal narrative strategies, it fails to integrate the everyday lives and experiences of the Warlis into its structure. This tends to create a distance between the spectator and the subjects of the film. The film works more at the level of intellect than at the level of affect. It is a film about narrativity that in some ways does not engage adequately with the subjects/authors of the narratives. Its lack of indigenous voices makes the narrative speak on behalf of the subaltern. While the narrative attempts to emulate the non-linearity and precariousness of the stories, the neat structure, packaged for audience consumption, as a film, tends to overlook the dynamic nature of the very marginal traditions it seeks to represent, thereby reinforcing the division between 'us' and 'them', a relationship it proposes to problematise. The film also records and documents their stories, thereby running the risk of fossilising and fixing these precarious, porous, and open-ended narratives. These are some of the dilemmas that continue to haunt any process of archiving of marginal traditions (Jayasankar and Monteiro 2016, 182).

These limitations were in some measure due to our inability to forge close relationships with the subjects of our films, even as we were aware of this distance and tried to question the position from which we were coming. In subsequent films (*YCP 1997*, 1997; *Saacha: The Loom*, 2001), we continued to question the dividing practices (Foucault 1982) that mark the relationships of power between filmmakers and their marginalised subjects. Secondly, we began to work more deeply with the affective dimensions of image and sound, which became easier for us with a film such as *Saacha*. In *Saacha*, we were working in the space of the city where we lived and which was suffused with memory, past experiences and associations – a city that was changing fast and slipping away even as we gazed at it, as it were. For our next film, *Naata* (2003), we worked with subjects who were our friends, in a space where we had spent many months in discussion about the kind of film we should make. This level of collaborative endeavour and themes of community relationships that resonated with our life experiences provided the opportunity to explore our identity as *sutradhar* in a new way.

Threading our stories: *Naata (The Bond)*

Naata (The Bond) was perhaps the first film where we directly included our personal stories.[4] Set in Dharavi, *Naata* chronicles the production of a film by two protagonists, together with the larger resident communities as part of communal amity-building efforts of the mohalla committee movement (peace-building neighbourhood committee). The mohalla committees came into existence through the voluntary efforts of citizens after the disastrous violence of 1992–93 in the aftermath of the demolition of the Babri Mosque in Ayodhya.[5] Our two protagonists are Bhau Korde, an elderly retired school head clerk, and Waqar Khan, manufacturer and retailer of garments. Khan participated in relief work following the violence in 1992–93 and over the years has led efforts to bridge the rift between Hindus and Muslims living in Dharavi.

As filmmakers attempting to make a film on Dharavi with the involvement of the local residents, we felt that the story of Bhau and Waqar's video productions for fostering peace formed an interesting peg for the story of Dharavi. Dharavi was a bustling hub of informal industry that housed over 800,000 people from various parts of India. In our attempt to subvert the stereotypical representations of a 'slum' in the popular imagination, we also wanted to share Dharavi's long and complex history. However, we also did not want to make a 'feel-good' film about 'them', the residents of Dharavi, for consumption by people like 'us'. We wondered how we could implicate ourselves in this narrative. How could we share the commonality of struggles around identity, specifically along religious lines, that have become increasingly crucial to the definition of nation as well as individual and community spaces within it? We thought that we could perhaps include our own stories as people of different religions and ethnicities who came together and had a daughter who faces her own questions over her hybrid identity. These stories were the little events of everyday life, not dramatic or life-threatening moments, but events that called upon us as a family to articulate who we were or were not.

Although these were *our* stories, we wanted them to function as an alienation device within the film, moments when we pull back from the brimming, sometimes chaotic space of Dharavi, into a quiet, somewhat sanitised space. In the film, this appears as a clean white rectangle populated by personal objects of identity: toothbrushes, watches, credit cards and the like. We saw these trivial markers as an ironic reflection on the lives of people like us, people who guard the sanitised space of our apartments against incursions from the informal settlements out there and thus deny them the dignity of personhood. The preoccupation with things was a sad commentary on materialistic obsession that often took on pathological dimensions, as witnessed during the 2002 Gujarat pogroms where rich and middle-class people ventured on the streets, looting Muslim-owned shops. We were horrified by this phenomenon. Indifference to social strife, the normal response in a city like Bombay, was transformed into active greed, looting and humiliation of the Muslim 'other' by Hindus from all social strata in Ahmedabad.[6] These moments of pause within the film were also open-ended spaces inviting audience reflection where the film could move beyond a story about 'them' and become 'our' story, too.

> Their narrative of their families' lives is told through material culture – toothbrushes, toys, vegetables, and other objects. They describe this documentary as a sort of 'self-reflexive ethnography, low budget'. It negotiates the middle-class origins of their film and its relationship to the subaltern classes that make another film through gentle self-humor, so that while the subaltern speaks, the viewers/directors are not voyeurs nor patronizing 'others' but allied media (Srinivas 2007, 313).

As mentioned elsewhere, our relationship with our protagonists and with the space of Dharavi was perhaps different from that in other films. Bhau Korde had been a close friend for many years. We got to know Waqar through Bhau, when he came to us with the script of Waqar's proposed public service commercial that was interestingly set in Gujarat, which had experienced a powerful earthquake in 2001. The film juxtaposed the story of a Hindu and a Muslim boy who participate in a Republic Day parade to celebrate amity between the communities.[7] The earthquake disrupts the parade, and amidst the death and destruction both fathers set out in search of their sons. The Hindu man comes across the Muslim boy, and the Muslim man finds the Hindu boy. At the hospital, the doctor pronounces the need for urgent blood transfusion for both children. The Muslim man offers his blood to the Hindu boy, and the Hindu father to the Muslim boy. In the style of popular Bollywood cinema, the blood is transfused directly from the fathers to the children. This powerful albeit non-realistic trope affirms the oneness of all human beings, regardless of markers of caste or religion. In the popular imagination, blood is what unites families, blood is what determines one's 'nature' and trajectory in life. As the children recover, in a tearful reunion between parents and children of all religions, a jingle affirms the integrity of the nation, and a poster tagline of 'We all are one' appears.

When we first saw the script, we were somewhat incredulous at the leaps of rationality that it made (although we politely hid our feelings). Nevertheless, we decided to follow the process of shooting and making the film. We were amazed at how various communities came together to provide food, transportation, actors, properties and professional skills in order to make the film happen. There were over a hundred actors – children, parents, doctors and nurses – in addition to camera persons, directors, assistants, make-up artists, costume suppliers, set designers, caterers, the works. The good-humoured way in which this large team of people worked together for a common purpose was deeply inspiring. When the film was completed, Waqar and Bhau were able to leverage their contacts in the mohalla committee movement to get it broadcast on prime-time national television, no mean feat for first-time filmmakers. It was also screened and distributed widely through VCDs across the country. Our initial scepticism gave way to admiration as we realised that the process was as important as the product in bringing people together; moreover, the tropes of popular cinema had more affective charge and influence on viewers than our documentary on the same theme. We were reminded of the focus of Cultural Studies not only on the text but also on contexts of production and reception:

> One could spin off several text-based critiques of his film (and the earlier poster, from which the film derives its protagonists): 'Why four boys and not four girls?' (Bharucha 1998) or 'Why are figures of priests, particularly a Brahmin, deployed to represent various religions?' and so forth. However, we have noticed during many public screenings in Dharavi, how the spectators seized the opportunities offered by his film, perhaps transforming and opening themselves to the affective energy of his narrative practices, rooted in the idiom of the popular culture, obviating and making redundant the issues that such text-based critiques throw up. We have concluded our film *Naata* with Waqar's spot and have seen, on many occasions of the film's screening, how the patronising laughter of the audiences watching the making of the spot turns into a joyful applause at the end (Jayasankar and Monteiro 2016, 173).

Subsequently, Waqar decided to make a longer film with his commentary on Indian history illustrated by a pastiche of Hindi film clips and interspersed with interviews with eminent personalities on the theme of communal harmony. Our collaboration became two-way as Jayasankar filmed some of the interviews in Waqar's film. Waqar drew copiously on Hindi cinema, stitching together his own narrative through this act of semiotic poaching and appropriation of powerful, popular scenes from Bollywood, with scant regard for intellectual property regimes. This wise and judicious repurposing of media material, to a very different end, mirrors the recycling of the city's waste that Dharavi and other informal settlements in the city undertake even as this contribution goes unrecognized:

> Dharavi's ecological footprint is minuscule and its carbon credits worth a thousand green Oscars. It takes too little and gives back a lot. If places like Dharavi were destroyed, almost all the plumbers of the city would disappear, so would many policemen, taxi drivers, domestic helps, vendors, garbage recyclers... The invisible political economy of the slum is a compassionate bulwark that shores up Mumbai. Without these vital spaces, Mumbai would collapse and rot in its waste (Jayasankar and Monteiro 2009, 15).

Our encounter with a very different logic of media production and reception in the context of *Naata* and our ongoing relationship with Dharavi has helped us to critically examine our own efforts. It has increased our respect for and engagement with popular media. And so, when during our conversations Bhau took a dig at secular filmmakers like us who make films that are seen by miniscule secular audiences, we decided to embed this critique into our film. We may never be able to emulate the inclusive energy of Waqar's work, but an awareness of and respect for the resistance embodied by subaltern media helps to keep us grounded.

> [...] documentary films that showed 'real' material of demolitions and riots, in the context of a rational argument against religious intolerance, were regarded by the local community [in Dharavi] as too close to everyday experience and hence likely to arouse strong antagonistic and polarising sentiments. The use of the more melodramatic language of Bollywood, removed from 'real' events, yet in many ways connecting with raw emotions of grief, anger, love and compassion, were seen as having greater transformative potential, more able to engender conversation and dialogue between communities that had been torn apart by events beyond their control. This use of melodrama and more metaphorical imagery (e. g., blood transfusion between religious communities) tends to be looked down upon by media makers such as us, as non-rational, unreal exaggerated and implausible. Perhaps it is time to rethink our prejudices (Monteiro and Jayasankar 2020, 45–46).

Naata has been screened with various audiences around the world. The multiplicity of interpretations based on audience concerns bears witness to the many layers of the film, some of which are beyond our intentionality. In most cases, audiences are able to relate to our personal stories; often, younger audiences observe that they resonate with their struggles to understand their own identities in an increasingly polarised society. There are two responses that we would particularly like to note. The first was during the early screenings of the film, one for a group of activists and the other for a mixed audience of students and faculty, both in Ahmedabad. Both groups felt that the stories were 'too abstract' in their visualisation and that 'people' would not understand them. This sharply brought home to us how middle-class audiences, particularly those who see themselves as involved in education and social change, tend to make patronising assumptions about people. They feel the need to tie down meaning to unidirectional messages that they believe to be persuasive, as if watching the film not on their own behalf, but on behalf of millions of less powerful others in need of positive messages.

When we screened *Naata* at a large public gathering in Dharavi and for smaller groups of peace activists from Dharavi, the response was less predictable. People were quite intrigued by our narrative passages, and some appreciated our stories, which they said also gave them an insight into our world. Waqarbhai was very taken with the object animation and thought that it was something which he could probably try out in one of his future films.

To sum up, our work with Waqar, Bhau and the citizens of Dharavi in the making and screening of Waqar's films and of *Naata* helped us to critically examine our own position as *sutradhar* and to explore methods to include our subject positions into the cinematic text. It also helped us understand the many ways in which audience reception can surprise and give new insights into our own work.

The performing 'threadbearers': *Our Family*

In a few films, we have worked collaboratively with groups regarded as 'deviant'. Our work with artistes in Yerawada Central Prison, Pune, in *YCP 1997* (1997) and with the transgender family of Aasha, Seetha and Dhana from Tamil Nadu in *Our Family* (2007) are among them. The video documentation for *Our Family* was conducted in 2004. We mulled over the material for a long time, given the potentially voyeuristic gaze that the topic might evoke.

Ultimately, we decided to work with the solo performance of Pritham Chakravarthy titled *Nirvanam*, which narrates the difficult journey of a transgender subject tortured to conform by their families and subjected to rape and abuse when they venture into the world of popular performance.[8] Finally, they find their own space as they decide to go through with the procedure that liberates them from their male biological identity. As an actor from outside the transgender community, Pritham spent a long time researching the play in collaboration with the Thamilnadu Aravanigal Association (THAA).[9] The powerful and compelling narrative that forms the sutra (thread) through the film features three transgender subjects – Aasha, Seetha and Dhana – who perform their own normality and reflect on their individual life journeys.

The lifeworld of the family of Seetha, her male partner Selvam and her adopted daughter Dhana is narrativised through their everyday interactions: a neighbouring child helps Seetha clean rice as they chat about getting their TV repaired; Dhana and Seetha chop vegetables in the kitchen and prepare for Aasha's birthday (the film starts with the cutting of Aasha's birthday cake); with the women who lives next door, they play a common board game, and together they discuss the film that is being made. They speculate reflexively on its potential 'purpose' and 'mission'. These scenes of daily routine work to establish them as a family, a transgender family that lives in a non-transgender community.

> Their family, with the same daily rituals that mark any 'normal' family, destabilises the dominant idea that the heterosexual family is the only valid form of conjugality. The title of the film, *Our Family*, is an attempt at contesting both the construction of 'family' and of 'us'. Interestingly, the family of Seetha and Selvam reproduces, in many ways, the patriarchal mores of the larger heteronormative society into which it is inserted (Jayasankar and Monteiro 2016, 164).

At the same time, we see the fault lines when Dhana visits her natal home: her mother's resigned acceptance, her kindness towards her son-turned-daughter is not reflected in the attitudes of the other (absent) male members of the family, who shun her presence. The complexities of gender change are brought out when Dhana speaks of how, as a female subject, she no longer enjoys the freedom to occupy public space in the way in which she could as a man. The joy of belonging to the gender to which one aspires comes at a price.

The larger transgender community enters when we participate in the fortieth-day celebration of an Aravani who has undergone gender reassignment surgery. There is much merriment and good cheer shared by the members of the transgender community who have travelled from as far as Mumbai to celebrate this momentous occasion. The film cuts to Pritham's powerful recounting of the moment of Nirvanam, alternating between a stylised stage performance and a more everyday performance for an audience comprising the four protagonists of the film. In Pritham's telling of

Nirvanam, the procedure is undertaken in a somewhat old-fashioned way where the *Daima*, a traditional medicine-woman, severs the male organs by using a sharp instrument. The exhilaration of that moment of freedom, which might be difficult to understand, given its life-threatening nature, is left for the audience to reflect on as the screen fades to black. The film then cuts back to a discussion between Pritham and the four protagonists about Pritham's performance. They discuss the process of crafting Nirvanam, how it moves them and the issues that it raises about the acceptance of transgender people as members of society, with equal rights and access to resources. This is the note on which the film ends.

> The transgender communities, spread across the country are shunned (and at times violently persecuted) by their families, and socially ostracised. They also have limited opportunities for gainful employment. The film uses 'their' stories to raise questions about 'us' and our sexualities, thus contributing to the numerous struggles by the LGBTQ communities in the country to decriminalise same-sex relationships and question gender binaries. It attempts to problematise the dominant discourse on sexuality by familiarising the unfamiliar: the agency and the normality in the lives of Aasha, Seetha, Selvam and Dhana, perhaps brings one to question the futility of trying to straitjacket sexual identities and preferences (Jayasankar and Monteiro 2016, 164).

After completing the film, we took it to Chennai and showed it to Aasha. She was very moved and thought that it was a very poetic and lyrical film. She was only sad that Selvam could not watch the film since he tragically had passed away of a sudden heart attack earlier that year. We were not able to visit Coimbatore but sent a copy of the film to Seetha. We did not hear back from her. Dhana was no longer living with Seetha and was untraceable. For us, *Our Family* was a film that stretched and challenged our story-telling sensibilities. We feel that juxtaposing the lives of Aasha, Seetha, Selvam and Dhana with Pritham's powerful and often disturbing narrative helped us to navigate and deflect a prurient gaze and to invoke the pain and trauma experienced by Aravanis, without invading the privacy of our subjects. We jointly discussed events from everyday life which they wanted to include in the film and agreed with their choice and judgment about how they would like to represent themselves. For us as *sutradhar*, it was yet another opportunity to curate colliding discourses, a narrative strategy that we had first explored in *Kahankar: Ahankar* and later in *Naata*.

As documentary filmmakers, particularly in the Indian context, we bear the burden of the past, where the will to know has been the *raison d'être* of documentary practice, by and large. As filmmakers we have invariably had to address, in post-screening discussions the question: 'What did you want to say through your film, and what is its impact?' The documentary genre, popularised by the Films Division in India, with its prophylactic role against the excesses of the melodrama of Bombay cinema, has often bench-marked these epistephilic aspirations and audience expectations (Vasudevan 2001). Globally, too, there has been little place for the affective in the documentary text, affirming its evidentiary role (Rutherford 2011; Nichols 1991).

The filmmaker as *sutradhar* potentially offers possibilities for subverting these found expectations. The *sutradhar* helps foreground the notion of reflexivity and amplifies the plural diegetic possibilities of the documentary text, inviting the viewer to participate in a fluid, open-ended way, in the pleasures of the many narratives that could unfold. The audience is offered the possibility to occupy an agentic subject-position, with a window to that narrative's constructed nature. Thus, the *sutradhar* is not a single omniscient 'puller of threads', but an assemblage of textual pathways, where curators, subjects and audience find possibilities for critical engagement with their signifying practices and ideological frames. More than a device or a method, the *sutradhar* is a subject-position, a philosophical attitude that is at once visible and invisible, at once pre-modern and contemporary. In the context of a discussion of the work of Indian playwrights, such as P. L. Deshpande, Habib Tanvir and Girish Karnad, Dharwadker demonstrates how the *sutradhar* becomes a 'pivotal character who manages these multiple ironic discourses' allowing for a critical reception of the text:

> [T]he critique of ideology has entailed more than anything else a politics of form […] Since ideology is rooted in the structures of culture and in artistic forms, the pressing and priority task is to expose structure and form, to open cultural artefacts up to investigation and challenge (Graham Holderness, cited in Dharwadker 2005, 381).

'Both of us have changed – the speaker and the listener. Nobody remains fixed. No! It's a process going on all the time. It never stops abruptly. We die, we die, okay. But something remains. It's always there; it'll be always there. And we are all connected. Deep down we are all one!' concludes Matwala in *YCP 1997*, a film that brings together the poetry and music of prisoners of the largest and oldest prison in India, the Yerawada Central Prison in Pune. Matwala is reflecting on his experience in the prison and also on his relationship with us as fellow artists and *sutradhar*. The encounter with the collaborative subjects of our films has revealed the futility of essentialising and othering. These processes, which tend to mark our social fabric, help people make sense of the world through given categories: male and female, law-abiding and prisoner, normal and deviant. Most of our work attempts to actively resist the will to essentialise, thus encouraging us to explore a 'critical ontology of ourselves' (Foucault 1984, 49).

Notes

1. This not to suggest that all Films Division documentaries followed this mode. There were many remarkable exceptions to the run-of-the-mill Films Division documentaries.
2. 'Adivasi', literally the earliest inhabitants, is a term widely used to denote the various indigenous groups that live in India.
3. The Kashtakari Sanghatana is a movement-based organisation that has been working with the Adivasis in the Dahanu area since 1980, mobilising them around issues of land rights, access to forests, minimum wages and the need to affirm their cultural identity. They have been using these stories (which have also been painted by one of their activists, the late Bhimsen, who was an artist) in workshops with Adivasi youth. We collaborated with them in the making of this film, which they felt could help bring these stories to larger audiences.
4. This section draws from Jayasankar and Monteiro 2016.
5. On 6 December 1992, Hindu fundamentalists demolished the Mughal-era Babri Mosque (built by the emperor Babur in 1528), claiming it to be the birthplace of the Hindu god Ram. Following this demolition, violent clashes broke out across the country. In Mumbai, there were clashes between Muslims and Hindus, as well as systematic targeting of Muslim neighbourhoods by Hindu fundamentalist political parties and groups, sometimes aided by the police, resulting in over 900 deaths between December 1992 and January 1993. Many people also lost their homes and livelihood in this violence.
6. These were probably the foot-soldiers of influential and rich politicians who played with people's sentiments for political mileage.
7. A take-off on his earlier poster which showed four boys, visibly belonging to four different religions (Hindu, Muslim, Sikh and Christian) with the tagline 'We are all one'. This became an iconic image that was shared as a poster in Mumbai and elsewhere. Waqarbhai spent his own money to print and disseminate the poster through the Mohalla Committee Movement Trust network. He talks about this experience in *Naata*.
8. Also known as Aravanis in Tamil Nadu.
9. The Thamilnadu Aravanigal Association (THAA), based in Chennai, Tamilnadu, India, is a non-profit for the support of transgender communities.

Works Cited

Bharucha, R. (1998). *In the name of the secular: Contemporary cultural activism in India*. New Delhi: Oxford University Press.

Dharwadker, A. B. (2005). *Theatres of independence: Drama, theory, and urban performance in India since 1947*. Iowa City: University of Iowa Press.

Foucault, M. (1982). Afterword: The subject and power. In H. L. Dreyfus and P. Rabinow, *Michel Foucault: Beyond structuralism and hermeneutics*, 208–26. Chicago: University of Chicago Press.

Foucault, M. (1984). What is enlightenment? In P. R. (ed.), *The Foucault reader*, 32–50. New York: Pantheon Books.

Ghosh, S., and Banerjee, U. K. (2005). *Indian puppets*. New Delhi: Abhinav Publications.

Jayasankar, K. P., and Monteiro, A. (2016). *A fly in the curry: Independent documentary film in India*. New Delhi: Sage.

Jayasankar, K. P., and Monteiro, A. (2009). Jai Ho Shanghai: The invisible poor in *Slumdog Millionaire*. In K. Ashwani et al (eds), *Global Civil Society Yearbook*. London: Sage.

Kishore, S. (2015). On whose behalf? Ethics in Indian social documentary film and practice. *Senses of Cinema*. https://www.sensesofcinema.com/2015/documentary-in-asia/indian-social-documentary-ethics/ [accessed 20 November 2022].

Kishore, S. (2018). *Indian documentary film and filmmakers: Independence in practice*. Edinburgh: University of Edinburgh Press.

Minh-Ha, T. T. (1993). The totalizing quest of meaning. In M. Renov (ed.), *Theorizing documentary*, 90–107. New York: Routledge.

Monteiro, A., and Jayasankar, K. P. (2020). Mumbai sub-versions: The place of affect in digital video activism. In A. Monteiro, K. P. Jayasankar and A. Rai, *DigiNaka: Subaltern politics and digital media in post-capitalist India*, 38–55. Hyderabad: Orient Blackswan.

Nichols, B. (1991). *Representing reality: Issues and concepts in documentary*. Bloomington: Indiana University Press.

Rutherford, A. (2011). *What makes a film tick? Cinematic affect, materiality and mimetic innervation*. Bern: Peter Lang.

Srinivas, S. (2007). The Bond. *Visual Anthroplogy*, 20(4), 313–14.

Vasudevan, R. (2001). An imperfect public: Cinema and citizenship in the 'Third World'. In *Sarai reader: The public domain*, 57–68. Delhi: Sarai.

Films Cited

Kahankar: Ahankar. Dir. Anjali Monteiro and K. P. Jayasankar. SMCS, TISS, 1995.
Naata (The Bond). Dir. Anjali Monteiro and K. P. Jayasankar. SMCS, TISS, 2003.
Our Family. Dir. Anjali Monteiro and K. P. Jayasankar. SMCS, TISS, 2007.
Saacha. Dir. Anjali Monteiro and K. P. Jayasankar. SMCS, TISS, 2001.
YCP 1997. Dir. Anjali Monteiro and K. P. Jayasankar. SMCS, TISS, 1997.

Part II:
Representation of lived experience

4

Personal is political: Documentary and intimacy

Shabnam Sukhdev

> *His films that I never saw before*
> *Tell a story of pathos, compassion & void*
> *I discover the depths of a Man, who was a person first then all else –*
> *however, As a child I judged his love or lack of it*
> (Excerpt, *Knowing Papa*, 2005)

In this essay, I will deliberate on the first-person documentary form adopted in my film *The Last Adieu* (2014), which gives an understanding of the life and works of my father, the acclaimed filmmaker S. Sukhdev. Alisa Lebow (2012) describes first-person films as being poetic, political, prophetic, or absurd:

> They can be autobiographical in full, or only implicitly and in part. They may take the form of self-portrait, or indeed, a portrait of another. They are, very often, not a cinema of 'me', but about someone close, dear, beloved, or intriguing, who nonetheless informs the filmmaker's sense of him or herself. […] these films 'speak' from the articulated point of view of the filmmaker who readily acknowledges her subjective position (7).

For most of my filmmaking career, I worked with fictional narrative story-telling, mainly for Indian television. Thus, when I began my enquiry, I wanted to use my research to make a fictional piece. Although I had made a couple of short non-fiction films prior to venturing into feature-length documentary, I seriously entered the foray of documentary filmmaking only when I began investigating my relationship with my father. At the very outset I knew that this would be a deeply personal journey for me.

It was not until I migrated to Canada in 2002 that I started thinking about Sukhdev and his documentaries. I had presented a poem at a poetry festival organised by the CBC (Canadian Broadcasting

Corporation) that reveals the complicated relationship I shared with my father (later, it was this poem that informed the structure of *The Last Adieu*).[1] During my initial years in Edmonton, I made a few documentaries to keep my artistic identity alive and slowly began to comprehend the power of an independent personal voice. Apart from the impractical logistics of mounting a fiction feature and the desire to experiment with form, I was driven by an urgent need to make peace with my father. In 2009, I made a trip to India with a miniDV camera (Sony PD150) and documented a few interviews with people who had known my father. My mother, who is prominently featured in *The Last Adieu*, helped me to re-connect with some of his old friends and colleagues. Most of his close friends, who were his drinking buddies, were deeply involved in his work as well. Their fond remembrance of Sukhdev's friendship made me feel even more alienated from my father, since I was unable to form that kind of a connection with him. I met with Partap Sharma, Jatin Das, Shaukat Kaifi, Baba Azmi, Sohrab Boga, Bijon Das Gupta, Shashi Kapoor, Salim Sheikh, Uma Da Cunha, Zul Velani and Irshad Panjatan, to name a few. Through their stories, I discovered Sukhdev's contribution to the Indian documentary film movement of the 1960s and 1970s. While teaching a chapter on Indian documentary to post-graduate students, I knew I could not escape Sukhdev's role in it. This was the first time I started to watch his works critically. I could not find my father anywhere on the internet, except for one mention of the feature film *My Love* (1970) that he had directed. The project thus evolved into an urgent inquiry to revive Sukhdev's contribution to Indian documentary. I was conducting sporadic research while teaching, and I needed to commit full-time if I wanted to do justice to my project.

I knew that, if I were to make a truthful film, I would have to confront the uncomfortable spaces of our troubled relationship. I was concerned that my subjectivity may interfere with an objective representation of Sukhdev, but it soon became clear that my pursuit of objectivity would not only be impossible, but also unwarranted. Lebow (2012) writes that, 'when a filmmaker makes a film with herself as a subject, she is already divided as both the subject-matter of the film and the subject making the film. In the first-person film, the filmmaker's subjectivity is not only brought back into frame, but it also permanently ruptures the illusion of objectivity so long maintained in documentary practice' (5). Therefore, my portrayal of Sukhdev would be an authentic representation of my 'truth' and would remain a subjective interpretation of reality.

The 'state' of documentary

Making my film with the Films Division, a state-owned machinery driven by the Information and Broadcasting Ministry, was not my first choice. I wanted to make the film with full creative control, different from the kind of films they were known to commission. Films Division has had a monopoly on the documentary film scene in India since the early years of Indian independence. At the time, they were invested in newsreels, largely government propaganda, mandated to play in theatres before the main feature film screened. In the late 1950s, Jean Bhownagary was invited to re-vitalise Films Division. He believed that, in order to achieve transformation, the organisation needed to give voice to individual artists, '[f]or there can be as many approaches to documentary filmmaking as there are filmmakers' (Sutoris 2016, 168). Bhownagary was responsible for recognizing talented filmmakers of a new, creative kind, such as S. N. S. Sastri, Pramod Pati and Sukhdev, among others. He provided them with opportunities to make films under the tutelage of the Films Division. Jean Bhownagary had recognized Sukhdev's talent for making films that were deeply personal with a distinctive point of view, marked with passion and commitment. For instance, his film *India 67* (1968), commissioned by Films Division, has a uniquely poetic language without an overarching voice-over commentary, unlike any other documentary made at the time. Through compelling images and montage and a well-crafted sound design, it reflects Sukhdev's response to a *new* India after twenty years of independence (from British rule). He was in love with India, and this is why he accepted to collaborate with the state, but at the same time he was also anti-establishment. Sukhdev had created quite a stir in government circles. He was beginning to gain recognition as a fearless filmmaker who knew how to navigate his way around the Censor Board. Documentary film historian and critic Jag Mohan aptly called him the *enfant terrible* of documentary film: a 'rebel with a cause'. On the Indian documentary scene, creativity peaked during this period. Censorship, however, remained an impediment, forcing filmmakers like Sukhdev to creatively overcome limitations or engage in conflict with the Censor Board. For instance, Sukhdev fought to retain certain shots in his *India 67* (1968): 'Sukhdev, being Sukhdev, worked around the system and got it approved from the highest office', relates filmmaker and scholar Ashish Avikunthak in *The Last Adieu*. This struggle persists even today: apart from economic reasons, censorship remains a key deterrent to documentary film production, independent or otherwise.

When Mr V. S. Kundu, an IAS (Indian Administrative Service) officer, was appointed as head of Films Division in 2011, his mandate was to streamline the administration of Films Division. But being the person he was, he took it upon himself to become involved in the creative side to stimulate the documentary filmmaking sector which had lost its vibrancy. He invited several independent filmmakers, offering them creative freedom to tell their stories, which was attractive to me. He was open-minded and ready to take risks, welcoming newer genres of documentary filmmakers into the fold of Films Division. This reminded me of the creative period in the history of the Films Division when Jean Bhownagary was commissioning films. I decided to make *The Last Adieu* with the support of Mr V. S. Kundu, who approved the proposed structure that I had in mind, different from anything done before in the Films Division.

Finding my lens

Once I began formal work on my film, I was initially confronted with a lot of self-doubt. I suddenly realised the magnitude of the subject-matter and felt that I was not experienced enough as a documentary filmmaker to be entrusted with such a project. There were other filmmakers, more knowledgeable, qualified and entitled to make a film about this iconic figure. There was Vijaya Mulay, whom my father used to call '*akka*' (big sister) out of respect. She had been toying with the idea of making a film on Sukhdev as well.[2] A tribute had already been paid to Sukhdev in a short film by Gulzar, titled *Ek Akar* (1985). So what made me the right person to claim Sukhdev's legacy? I felt that an objective critical analysis of Sukhdev's films would not be enough to understand the entirety of his socio-political milieu that informed his worldview. Approaching his life's work from a personal lens gave me an additional edge. As his daughter, I was near him but never close to him because of his continued absence from family life. Through the journey of making this film I was confident that I could offer a more nuanced perspective, given that I could delve into the depths of Sukhdev's character, beyond his persona as a filmmaker. As an interviewer, I felt empowered that my interviewees would be talking to Sukhdev's daughter, not just recounting facts about Sukhdev and his work to another filmmaker. The stories I captured were told in an informal tone and style usually uncommon in interviews. Above all, I had access to my mother, Kanta Sukhdev, who had known him since his early days of struggle in the Mumbai film industry. I had in my possession a vast archive of photographs, access to his close friends and family, and a personal story to tell. I thus felt committed to offer my unique perspective.

Documentary filmmaker Pankaj Rishi Kumar was my mentor for this project. He kept raising the question: Why are you making this film? All my answers were unsatisfactory to him, until I became frustrated and said: 'I need to speak to him again, dammit!' His questions eventually stopped, and I understood how I needed to approach my subject-matter: my film was to be a series of conversations in which I confront Sukhdev. I lay down the premise of my film in the first ten minutes: 'I never had the courage before. Now that you are gone, there is so much I need to tell you about me, how I feel...' Giving my film a personal voice gave me the creative freedom to adopt performance as a key motif. Conversations with my father added a critical layer of discourse as we go behind Sukhdev the person and begin to understand how 'Sukhdev the person' was no different from 'Sukhdev the filmmaker'. Partap Sharma candidly confirms that 'Sukhdev couldn't distinguish between work and play; they were both the same to him, and it would eventually eat into his family life' (*The Last Adieu*). The several interviews with friends and colleagues took me through Sukhdev's filmmaking journey from his early days right until the day he died. Archival photographs helped construct a vivid picture of his life.

From denial to acceptance

Although I began my research in 2005, my formal approach to making the film had substantially evolved by 2013. As I delved deeper into the project, it became clear that the film was also developing into an intimate narrative about myself. I started to acknowledge my methodology and attitude towards filmmaking as an artform. I was beginning to recognize the power of personal cinema as my film slowly began to take shape on the editing table. I worked closely with my editor, Jabeen Merchant, who brought in a poignant objectivity in constructing the film's structure. The framework was informed by five pivotal 'conversations' between Sukhdev and me. The relationship journey was clearly from denial to acceptance, as I expose viewers to Sukhdev's work through my 'lens' along the way. I was conflicted about revealing Sukhdev's domestic life. Revealing deeply personal facts would make me and my family extremely vulnerable, and I was not sure if I was ready for it. Merchant convinced me that, in order to construct a truthful persona of Sukhdev, we must address those uncomfortable spaces. For instance, she felt that it was important to underline the violence in his personality. Sukhdev had slapped little Shabnam to get a shot depicting a young girl who had lost her family to violence. In the film, I confront Sukhdev, questioning the dichotomy of 'truth' and 'ethics' in documentary filmmaking. He has no definitive answer. This sequence also serves as a question for my own enquiry while approaching documentary filmmaking. Working with transcriptions of all the interviews helped Merchant construct Sukhdev's trajectory of work spanning two decades. We worked consistently on the editing, and within eight weeks we had a cut in place. This cut was thirty minutes longer than what was commissioned by the Films Division, but it was accepted since it presented a well-rounded biography of Sukhdev.

Authentic in its telling, *The Last Adieu* adopts different layers of audio-visual commentaries. The first is a direct address to Sukhdev in my voice, relating how I feel and what I know of him. This layer additionally gives information about the circumstances under which he made his films. The second layer comprises a performed dialogue between 'father' and 'daughter'. These allude to the underlying tensions in our relationship. Albeit fictionalised, they are drawn from facts of Sukhdev's life and present an authentic understanding of Sukhdev's persona, unpacking the impact of his work on himself and those around him. Archival footage provides a third layer of discourse through which I could objectively convey historical information about Sukhdev's films. A rich archive of photographs from Sukhdev's past helps construct his complex relationship with family and work.

Defining and growing as an artist

In January 1977, two years before he passed away, Sukhdev wrote an essay in which he makes a distinction between 'personal cinema' and 'social relevance' (Mohan 1984). He writes:

> Social relevance in art means that the artist, through his creation, tries to present, analyze, and expose the social reality and thus tries to create, among the spectators, an awareness which ultimately becomes a motivating force to change or improve upon the existing social norms, institutions and human behavior (96).

He claims:

> 'Personal Cinema' (per se) is not obliged to say anything or communicate anything; it becomes a mere exercise in form. But form, when practiced without content, is reduced to gimmicks. Form in itself cannot be art.

> Form is a vehicle to be used to communicate a given truth. Since each truth has its own peculiarities, every time an artist wants to state a truth through his art, he does invent, consciously or otherwise, a new form or radically changes the existing form (99).

My films are propelled by a personal quest to understand phenomena that directly impact or influence my life, compelling me to dive deep into its enquiry through a personal lens. My purpose is to arrive at a truth, adopting and challenging cinematic grammar to achieve my objective. The self-reflexivity of my praxis gives me an opportunity to expand and experiment with the language of documentary story-telling. By narrativising my film, I am able to achieve my purpose of forming an affective connection with my intended audience. With *The Last Adieu*, I wanted to reach a more generic audience. With my latest film, *Unfinished* (2021), on the subject of mental illness, my focus shifts to targeting a more specific audience (for example, mental health professionals, families and persons with lived experience).

In Jag Mohan's book (1984), Sukhdev lashes out at the popular genre of films made in India. He says:

> [T]here is no difference between commercial feature films and the *arty* 'personal cinema': they both avoid reality. They both hate social involvement and they both are acceptable to the exploiting classes because they both send the spectator into a coma – the commercial film through the opium of glamour, melodrama, and fantasy, and the 'personal cinema' through the gloss of mere form and intellectual masturbation (102).

I would argue that some experimental films urge audiences to actively engage with the content through their form; audiences must actively engage to interpret the film from the perspective of their individual sensibilities and life experiences. For example, the films of Philip Hoffman, Canada's pre-eminent diary filmmaker, uses the material of his life to deconstruct the Griersonian legacy of documentary practice. They have a marked affective resonance, the impact of which encompasses social intent and reflection. His films can safely be labelled as 'personal cinema' or 'experimental cinema'. Rather than lacking integrity, they are infused with a relentless personal commitment to connect with the spectator. Sukhdev's experiment with style and the intensity of his social commitment makes his cinema deeply personal, too. His commitment to excavating and show-casing the truth was complete. To that end, both Sukhdev and those filmmakers whose oeuvre of films fall under 'personal' have similar objectives. I find myself garnering this sort of a commitment in *The Last Adieu*, as well as in my overall practice of filmmaking. For example, my film *Earth Crusader* (2016), a character-driven film underlying Didi Contractor's persona, highlights her ideology for sustainability against the impacts of global warming. Through her crusade, the personal becomes political.

In March 2014, I had the premier screening of *The Last Adieu*. I was wary of critiques comparing my work to Sukhdev's. In the film, I question Sukhdev: 'How can "I" be "you"?' When I decided to pursue filmmaking as a career, I made a conscious effort not to identify with Sukhdev and his style. I resisted following in his footsteps:

> I was in denial of his existence
> In denial of the legacy he had left behind
> The legacy of a filmmaker
> As seen through his third eye (*Knowing Papa*, 2005).

Today, when questioned about whether I could ever have been like my father, I remind myself: we were two quite different people, the result of quite different circumstances. Our styles, ideologies and the times which influenced us were vastly diverse, and this is reflected in our films: his work is socially oriented, while I have discovered my style to be more introspective, arising from personal conflict. He rose from nothing to attain success in his field, while I had his example and legacy behind me through all my endeavours, whether I acknowledged it or not. He was completely self-taught, while I obtained a formal education in film at the Film and Television Institute of India, Pune. His struggles were thus different from mine.

I continue to be awestruck by the ways in which he managed to make such bold political films and adopted dynamic techniques using analog technology, exposing thousands of feet of film raw stock during times when there was no video or digital recording or non-linear editing. Sukhdev died on 1 March 1979. In the words of Jag Mohan (1984), …

> On that day ended the 25-year career of Sukhdev as the most intrepid, ubiquitous, vocal, talented documentary filmmaker […] Sukhdev revolutionized the Indian documentary film, both in content and technique, bagged innumerable awards, here and abroad, created controversies and established bridges of understanding through his film with people here and elsewhere. If Satyajit Ray brought renown to this country with his feature films, then Sukhdev did likewise with his documentaries (1–2).

The questions I have yet to find answers to may be considered by the reader: if Sukhdev were alive today, how would his films inspire the practice of a new generation of filmmakers in the digital age? What would his concerns be regarding the practice of filmmaking itself? What would inspire him today to continue his practice?

The question I ask myself is: Would I be making films if my father were alive today?

Notes

1 Shabnam Sukhdev, 'Knowing Papa', poetry recital (2005) https://www.youtube.com/watch?v=bUF47X-kPaQ
2 I regret not including her experiences of knowing my father in *The Last Adieu*.

Works Cited

Lebow, A. S. (2012). *The cinema of me: Self and subjectivity in first person documentary*. New York: Wallflower Press.
Mohan, J. (1984). *S. Sukhdev, filmmaker: A documentary montage*. National Film Archive of India, Ministry of Information and Broadcasting, Government of India.
Sutoris, P. (2016). *Visions of development: Films Division of India and the imagination of progress, 1948–75*. New York: Oxford University Press.

Films Cited

Earth Crusader. Dir: Shabnam Sukhdev, Films Division, 2016.
The Last Adieu. Dir. Shabnam Sukhdev. Films Division, 2014.
Unfinished. Dir: Shabnam Sukhdev, York University, 2021.

5

Making films from and about the margins

Lipika Singh Darai

The beginning

I applied to film school out of a sense of restlessness and an eagerness to make sense of my surroundings – my childhood, adolescence, prevailing inequalities, my body, my Adivasi identity, dreams, illnesses, love and greed – anything and everything around me. My training in Hindustani Classical Vocal Music was one of the reasons why I studied Sound Recording as a specialisation. In the first year of film school, while learning to translate stories audio-visually, many things in life which were not given enough introspection were addressed, many gaps noticed and bridged with newly acquired knowledge. A new way was found to look at image and sound and their capacity to create a language, even in silence.

In the initial months, I also realised that not many women studied Audiography or Sound Design in film. Neither were many making films, and an even more insignificant number from tribal communities like mine were making films. After all, filmmaking is an expensive medium, and spending that amount of time, money and effort in a film school is a privilege very few can afford. I was the only woman in the Audiography class in a batch of ten students that year. Apparently, I was the second woman who was admitted in the Audiography course from Odisha after more than a decade.

After film school, I looked for work in Mumbai where I worked on a few assorted projects before shifting base to my home state, Odisha. At that time, I had just finished editing my first film in Odia (the native language of my state). I was born and brought up in small villages and towns of Odisha, and my entire school education had been in the Odia language. After relocating to Odisha, I decided to set up a base in the capital city, Bhubaneswar. There were a few reasons for this choice: Bhubaneswar is well connected to other cities; it is the seat of the Odia Film and TV industry; and some of my film-school-seniors whose films were considered milestones of Odia Cinema lived there.

After moving to Bhubaneswar, around 2013, I realised that there was no active community of filmmakers in the city or the state in terms of documentary and non-mainstream films. There was no practicing woman filmmaker in fiction or non-fiction filmmaking at that time. There were barely a couple of journalists and activists making documentary films, and the production frequency of non-mainstream films was hardly two to three films in a decade. For several months, I tried to figure out ways to generate work and failed. I had received a National Film Award for Sound Recording for my student project film called *Gaarud* (2008) by then, but this was not helpful for getting any work in Odisha.

Around this time, I received a fellowship from SARAI CSDS, Delhi, for the 'City as Studio' art project. My project was called 'Listening to the city'. I chose Mumbai for this project. As a sound-recordist, I decided to record the soundscape of the city. The fellowship also included a residency period with other selected artists from across the country. The residency initiated a period of unlearning for me. In my case, the entire process was deconstructive of the self, which was somewhat burdened by the many pioneering films that I had seen and studied closely in film school.

Engaging with my surroundings through films

While recording Mumbai's soundscape, through the noise of dissonance, I became reconnected to the opposite: my maternal village's peaceful landscapes of childhood memory and the abundance of love I had received there. I started an imaginary conversation with my great-aunt in the process. I thought of making an essay film. At that time, my previous work sent to the National Film Awards was awarded the Best Debut Film. I was interviewed by both regional and national print media and TV channels. My film *Eka Gachha Eka Manisa Eka Samudra – A Tree a Man a Sea* (2013) was made in the Odia language, and I had started living in Odisha. Thus, an Odia girl making Odisha proud was an easy articulation for many media articles.

Along with that, it also became the achievement of a Ho-Adivasi young woman. My film was a 27-minute-long documentary on my childhood music teacher, made after his demise. The very next year, my 16-minute documentary *Kankee o Saapo – Dragonfly and Snake* (2014) received another National Film Award for Best Narration in a film. Prior to this,

Figure 5.1 Still from *Dragonfly and Snake* (2014). The film appears as a split screen with two different images running on each half of the screen, visualising a conversation between the filmmaker and her great-aunt. Picture courtesy of author.

in Odisha people had mostly received this award only for feature-length fiction films.

My work being adequately written about in regional media encouraged many film enthusiasts and students of film in Odisha to write to me, enquiring about the filmmaking process, how to apply for film school, how to obtain a certification for a film, how to apply for the awards and so on. One day at a local railway station in Balasore, I met a man with his daughter. The man told me: 'We have seen you talking about your film, which was dedicated to your childhood teacher. The small parts of the film which we saw on television were nice. My daughter is very good at the arts, and I would encourage her to do something like you'.

A few similar incidents made me realise that language is extremely powerful. It connects people. And in my films, Odia language was getting used in a unique way as my works were mostly personal narratives. I felt that, however small it was, my films were initiating a definite change. Through the films, I was engaging with my surroundings, and this is precisely what I had set out to do as a filmmaker – to position my people's voices in their own language. I was even more determined that I needed to continue working from Odisha.

My awards did not help to generate work in Odisha. There were no funding organisations for fiction films or documentaries in the state. And it was a conscious choice to not make corporate films for survival. As I could not find any local documentary film editors, I also started editing my own films. With the small budget for my films, it was even more difficult to hire someone from outside my state. And another hurdle was language.

Even if one managed to translate everything to the editor's spoken language, still it would take a lot more time than usual and hence would increase the expenses. There is so much to learn, understand and adapt, especially when someone is starting out as a filmmaker. Many choices needed to be established, which would eventually reflect one's politics but also narrow down the possibility of work. I was slowly processing the complexity of it all. My former partner Indraneel Lahiri, cinematography graduate from the Film and Television Institute of India, and I worked together from Odisha for nearly five years, until we parted ways. I believe that, had we not worked together as a team, juggling several roles such as cinematographer, director, editor and recordist, as people having a similar work ethic, we would not have produced the kind of work we did under a very tight budget, or I could not have sustained myself through these most important initial years of being an independent documentary filmmaker in Odisha.

How my films are born

For my documentary *Some Stories Around Witches* (2016), I travelled to a village next to a town called Rairangpur, in the Mayurbhanj district of Odisha, where a dreadful witch-hunt incident had taken place. A woman in her fifties, branded as a witch, had been stripped naked and tied to an electric pole in the middle of a moderately populated and developed village called Jodapokhari. I had seen a close-up photo of the woman on the front page of a local newspaper. The distinctly appalling thing about the case was the manner in which this news and the mobile-phone recorded-video of the event were circulated; within hours, thousands of people from nearby villages and towns had gathered to witness the event, jamming long stretches of road leading to the village.

Five months after the incident, I was going to travel along the same road under the supervision of the sub-divisional police officer. The officer, whom I had met in an anti-witch-hunt awareness meeting, when asked about the incident, insisted that I should come to the village and investigate the reality myself. Two police constables from the rescue team were supposed to take me to the place and provide an account of the entire incident. This incident had happened on 27 July 2014, after the Anti-Witch Hunting Bill had already been passed in Odisha in 2013.

One of the petitioners of the bill, Sashiprava Bindhani, had gotten in touch with me, and she later introduced me to a few cases under her personal supervision. Not knowing how to pitch a documentary for funding, I tried several options, including one or two international forums. But my pitch material was not sufficient. There was a lot of waiting time to receive even a research grant, and in-depth research was money-intensive. But somehow, over the next six to eight months, I was able to start the process of making the documentary, which was produced by the Public Service Broadcasting Trust (PSBT), India, to be screened on national television. The funding offered was very little, but I felt that, for the kind of films that PSBT was producing in India for Doordarshan, no one else was supporting such subjects at that point in time, especially for new filmmakers. I decided to investigate a few devastating yet important cases of witch-hunts in Odisha and make the film.

Upon reaching the village, the police constable began with a nutshell description of his encounter with that event. It had been a Sunday morning. Just as he had bought some chicken meat to prepare a good Sunday lunch, he received the news of the incident. He arrived at the spot with another constable. By that time, hundreds of people had already gathered, and more were coming. When he asked some people to untie the woman to let her sit down, some of them said: 'Do not untie her, or else she will fly away'. Soon a police force team also arrived, and it took them hours to rescue the woman from the situation. Some onlookers thought that the police were taking the woman away to punish her in private. The entire day passed. In fact, when the police constable finally came back to his pack of meat, it had turned rotten inside his motorbike's carrier case.

Listening to the constable, I was amazed by his description of the events and by the volatility of the situation. I learned that the woman was sheltered at an old-age home. I met her. Her presence remained with me. A new chapter began, and I knew that it was going to stay with me. One woman was victimised as a witch, and another woman with a camera was trying to make a film around that issue. In that context of irony, I had found an unknown strength to make the film happen anyhow. The woman's village resembled mine; the woman resembled my grandmother. Having been born in a village similar to this one, I had indeed come a long way. I could learn filmmaking, learn about the world, develop a point of view and make my own decisions. While filming and recording these stories, I constantly thought how rare it was for an Adivasi woman like me to pick up the camera and represent her own people. During that period, I understood why my presence as a filmmaker in my home state was so important.

Addressing my Adivasi identity

While working on *Some Stories Around Witches*, I became very aware of my Adivasi identity. I realised that there exists the notion that witch-hunt cases are prevalent only among Adivasi people. We hardly realise that it prevails in all societies and that these instances manifest differently. Coming from a tribe called Ho in Odisha, I was not attempting to defend tribal communities or their customs in my film. I was trying to say that witch-hunting cases are not an outcome of superstition or ignorance alone; it is a societal and systemic problem, and one should not ignore this. During my research, I had seen a few films produced by big sponsors on the same subject, and what I found in most of these films was that the portrayal of communities and people who were victimised lacked empathy. The fiction TV shows around these subjects had unusual interpretations. There was always a sense of othering and an attempt to sensationalise the plot. I worked on the cases that happened in Odisha. The language, culture, landscape, people were familiar to me, and there was a sense of camaraderie. Hence, the outcome of the film was a collaboration, indirectly made by the people through their participation. I was just weaving the various strands of narratives together. A sense of connection with people is crucial, as empathy can bridge divides, too.

When I was still a student at the Film and Television Institute of India (FTII), I had an opportunity to perform location-sound-recording and assist a director on a documentary project. The director did not speak or understand Odia, and the film was on the food-security of the K-B-K (Kalahandi-Balangir-Koraput) districts of Odisha, infamous for poverty, starvation deaths and famine. It was a fifteen-to-twenty-day schedule across all three districts. I was the only woman in the four-member crew. During interviews, I had to ask the local people questions prepared by the director, add a few of my own and briefly make the director understand their responses. I had my reservations about several of his questions. Considering the circumstances under which the questions were being asked, I felt that they were inappropriate in tone. I conveyed my disappointment to the director who became extremely unhappy with me. He would still repeatedly tell me to ask certain questions around hunger and food but would allow no time for the respondents to warm up to those questions.

I used to feel embarrassed and stopped asking those questions. This annoyed the director, and he began to argue with me. He claimed that I had no knowledge and was trying to undermine his authority. Finally, I left the project. I had failed to make him understand that there needed to be some compassion and a language of kindness while conducting the interviews. I wonder why this was so difficult for him to understand. Why did the things that bothered me not bother him, too? It was probably because he was so far removed or alienated from the subject and setting of his film, the people and the place featured in the work. Hence, he could 'other' the people very easily. But I felt an immediate connection. I felt that they were my people, that this was my land and that I belonged there; not only did I speak the language, but I could also feel it, too, and I wanted to resist the humiliation through which the film was putting them. I felt protective of them. This incident and several thereafter made me realise the importance of identity and belonging, and how they transpire in the stories we tell and choose to represent on screen.

I am reminded of another incident that happened during the making of my film *The Waterfall* (2017), about a waterfall called Khandadhar in Odisha, which is under constant threat from mining companies that have taken over the region. Several local tribal communities are fighting to keep the waterfall alive. During the filming, Bilua Nayak, an elderly local Adivasi community leader who fought against the giant mining companies for the preservation of forests and rivers, told me that he noticed something very unusual in cities – everyone was busy consuming something or other, eating all the time, buying, or selling too many things, consuming something on the phone. He said: 'If you consume all the time, when will you think? When will you get the time to be kind?'

I have travelled across Odisha, which is full of forests and rivers and rich in folk art. In every corner, there are fine artists. But I have also seen utter poverty: schools without teachers for years, hospitals without doctors, villages without electricity, farmers committing suicide, witch hunts and so on. Most of the Adivasi communities (along with other communities) are displaced from their land in the name of development. They are struggling to protect their homes and natural habitats. Hills are wounded by heavy mining. There is large-scale migration to other Indian cities in search for work. A large section of the population is deprived of a decent education.

Over the past ten years, I have not come across any other woman documentary filmmaker in Odisha. I sometimes wonder who among us would ever want to be a filmmaker when there are more pressing challenges surrounding us every day? Children of farmers or displaced communities, or of families who are selling everything to give a better education to their children so that they can migrate and contribute to the financial well-being of the families? There is an extremely small segment of society who can afford to study filmmaking or become a filmmaker. And will their journey be only validated through an affirmation from a European Film festival or the creation of a consumable content, film, or series? Trying to make films from Odisha, in the language I speak, has become my practice for the past ten years. And eventually it has enabled me to address my Adivasi identity, which would not have been possible so profoundly if it were not for a morphosis of self through filmmaking.

Films Cited

Dragonfly and Snake. Dir. Lipika Singh Darai. 2014.
Some Stories Around Witches. Dir. Lipika Singh Darai. PSBT, 2016.

6

Against all odds: A filmmaker's quest to make films in Northeast India

Haobam Paban Kumar

Locating my documentary lens

In 2002, I enrolled in the Direction and Screenplay Writing Department at the Satyajit Ray Film and Television Institute (SRFTI) in Kolkata, India. It was the best thing that happened to me. In my second year, I shot the documentary film *AFSPA 1958*. I went home for the holidays, and on 11 July 2004 a woman named Manorama Devi died in custody. I was told that this was the first time that a woman had died in custody in Manipur. In the entire state, there were unprecedented protests against the custodial death of Manorama Devi. I immediately started covering the incident with a cameraman friend and kept recording the incidents each day. Normally, I do not shoot a film without a script, but here the situation was such that I was already shooting a film without a story or script. And I was continuously looking for the story or elements to make a story while I continued to shoot.

Slowly I started researching AFSPA 1958, the controversial Armed Forces Special Power Act 1958.[1] I studied the various clauses in the act. The reason why people call it draconian is because the Indian army can kill anyone on mere suspicion. This was quite shocking for me, because I had been hearing from people that this act was the root cause of all their worries; now, I had seen the proof with my own eyes. How could India, the world's biggest democracy, have an act such as this? For years, the rest of the country had been hearing about the problems in Northeast India. I wanted them to watch and decide for themselves about the wrongdoings in this part of the country. This reasoning determined the treatment of my film. I was quite aware that a purely observational film was not in fashion those days. But I took the risk, as I thought it was the best way to tell this story.

Figure 6.1 Still from *AFSPA 1958* (2005). Picture courtesy of author.

I kept on shooting for almost a month. Every evening, I would watch the uncut news on the local cable network and look for footage that might be useful for the film. Those days all the journalists in Manipur would exchange footage, as everyone believed that it was for a good cause. I was doing two things simultaneously: shooting a film, as well as shooting for news. My co-producer was an electronic journalist, and through his network I could easily collect all the important footage of the day. We also shared our footage with other journalists. Finally, after following the protest for around a month, I had to stop shooting, even though my camera person continued, as he was also a journalist. A student leader died during a protest, setting himself on fire. After this incident, the local government became extremely strict, and only journalists were allowed to cover the events. Incidentally, this is where my film ends.

This was a zero-budget film, and we had managed to shoot with my friend's camera and used my motorbike. Now the real problem was to edit the film. Luckily, my editor and close collaborator on all my films, Sankha, had recently bought a new editing system, and he was kind enough to join the project without bothering about money. He also was a fellow student at the SRFTI. We completed the film in no time, as I was clear about the structure of the film. Although we had more than 100 hours of footage, it was one of the easiest edits we ever accomplished. We immediately sent it to the Mumbai International Film Festival 2006, where it was selected for the International Competition section. Since Mumbai, the film has been screened at many festivals and events around the globe. Later, it became the first Manipuri film to win the Swarna Kamal for Best Non-Feature Film at the 56th National Film Awards 2008. Here I would like to mention that from the same footage I made another film called *A Cry in The Dark* (2006) for Finnish Television YLE to recover some of the money that I had invested in the project. This was a major decision that I made, because around that time I also came to know through Doc Edge that we could do a Director's Cut and another cut for another organisation. This film also travelled the world and had its premiere at the prestigious Toronto International Film Festival 2007.

How cinema?

While growing up, I was only exposed to Hindi love stories and Chinese martial arts films because of the boom in VHS cassettes. My schooling happened at the central-government-run Kendriya Vidyalaya, as my parents wanted me to learn Hindi which could later help in connecting with mainland India. Therefore, I was more comfortable with the Hindi language as well as Hindi cinema than with the cinema in my home state of Manipur. While discouraging cinema, my parents were quite open and encouraging when I participated in co-curricular activities. I participated in recitations, drama (English, Sanskrit) and debates. Also, I was fortunate to be born around dance and theatre. I grew up watching the rehearsals and plays of my maternal uncle, theatre legend Ratan Thiyam, and my grandfather is an important guru of Manipuri dance. When I was in the final year of my studies in Computer Science, I suffered a breakdown and felt incredibly low. I felt restless and thought that I might not be able to succeed at anything in life. There was a strange urge to do something beyond my studies. I had heard about film school from a friend and wanted to explore this avenue.

I attended a crash course in cinematography which helped to prepare for the entrance test at the film school and offered a brief introduction to cinema. I began to enjoy this new world of film, and there for the first time I saw the photograph of Pabung Aribam Syam Sharma, the doyen of Manipuri cinema. After completing the course, I joined Aribam Syam Sharma as an assistant; luckily, he was about to shoot a new feature film.

It was during the shoot of his film *Shingnaba* (*The Challenge*, 1998) that I learnt how to give a clap, write continuity, lensing, how to hold and carry a reflector. The seniors were very welcoming and helpful. Aribam Syam Sharma taught me many things. For example, as a director, one should always look at the shot from behind the camera. In this way you can be very clear about the look and position of the character and the camera level. I also learnt the basics of lensing while writing the continuity sheet, as I was allowed to peek at the viewfinder to write the shots. I continued to assist Aribam Syam Sharma for about four to five years, and I slowly realised that, if you are open to the process, there is so much more to learn.

Representing Manipur on and off screen

After finishing my film education at SRFTI, I returned to Manipur to start my career in filmmaking, while my batchmates migrated to cities with big film industries, such as Mumbai, Chennai, Hyderabad and Kochi. My intention was clear from the beginning – that is, to tell stories about Manipur to the world, which was possible only if I lived there.

Before going further, I should mention a small film which I made for the Programme Production Centre (PPC), Doordarshan, Guwahati. It is called *The First Leap* (2008), and it is a film about the making of the first film ever made in Manipur. When I started thinking about this film, I was yet to watch the first Manipuri film or meet anyone involved with the film, except for my teacher Aribam Syam Sharma and M. K. Binodini who scripted almost all the best-known films of Manipur. The idea was to make a documentary for the public. I started thinking about the treatment of the film. Slowly I started researching and found out that the entire film crew came from outside the state and that only the actors were from Manipur. Within the limited budget, it was impossible for me to go and meet the technicians who were based in Kolkata. But it was easy to find the actors, as most of them were from Imphal, the capital of Manipur. Soon I met all of them and found out that they had not watched the film in the thirty-six years since its premiere. Hence, this became the treatment of my film. I planned to arrange a meeting of the actors of the first Manipuri film in the context of a special screening. I decided to capture the moment of the meeting. The moment of watching the film and remembering the making of it is history in itself. It was easy to shoot this film, as I had to wrap up most of the shoot in a day. The interviews of the actors took another two days to shoot. The pre-production and the planning for the get-together of the actors took most of the time. This is one of my personal favourites.

I started looking for producers, but for documentaries or non-fiction films the only option was Doordarshan. Those days, Doordarshan was still commissioning films in Northeast India and Jammu and Kashmir. I was lucky to get projects to sustain and continue my passion. But the Programme Production Centre (PPC) Doordarshan had a very peculiar rule: Films could be made only in English and Hindi. Even subtitles were prohibited. One can imagine what kind of films were made: a Manipuri historical serial with a Manipuri cast speaking in English and Hindi; a Sahitya Akademi Naga short fiction film with a Naga cast speaking Hindi. But we all did it because there was no other option, and we had to think of our survival, too. I was disappointed with this work of mine. But I came up with the idea of making my kind of films with the little money I received by making the Doordarshan films. Thus, the film *Mr. India* came into being.

Mr. India (2009) is about the legendary bodybuilder Khundrakpam Pradip Kumar who became a bodybuilder after discovering his HIV status and went on to win the Mr India title. The idea for the film was given by my editor friend and long-time collaborator Sankhajit Biswas, who had read about Pradip Kumar in the newspaper. We decided to make the film with the available resources – with help from friends and the little money we earned by doing other projects. We then approached my cinematographer-friend Irom Maipak, who agreed to loan us the camera almost for free for the project and did not charge his remuneration. Another friend from SRFTI, Avijit Nandy, shot several parts of the film without bothering about money as he believed in the project. Thus, *Mr. India* was made by primarily using the resources of my friends and their generous participation. Fortunately, the film was screened at festivals around the world and went on to win the National Film Award.

Documentary OR fiction filmmaking?

While the films that I made for Doordarshan and other governmental departments helped to sustain myself and my family, deep down I always wanted to make feature films. In 2011, I received a call from the National Film Development Corporation (NFDC), informing me that I had been selected as one of the emerging talents of Indian cinema to represent India at the Cannes Film Festival. This was aimed to expose younger filmmakers in India to the biggest film festival and film market in the world.

After this experience, I started to concentrate on my feature film script. I had been so involved with documentaries that I was unable to write a proper feature film. Unlike with documentaries, one has to write more for a fiction project. Besides, I had to continue making documentaries for survival. Thus, both had to happen in parallel. One thing that I learnt from my trip to Cannes is that there are many support systems around the world to make your first film. In India, the NFDC organises many labs and workshops to support filmmakers. One can start by applying for grants to write scripts, then attend a script lab and apply for production funds and so on. Around the world, there exist opportunities that support filmmakers especially during their first and second feature film projects.

I felt encouraged to start working on my first feature film. I had a story in mind, about the gun culture in Manipur. This was a story about contemporary Manipur where guns matter, where owning a gun often is equated with being as powerful as a king. Both insurgents and the army personnel feel equally strongly about guns. I consciously went for an adaptation for my first film. I started looking for a story roughly similar to my idea. I found a short story written by the famous Manipuri author Sudhir Naoroibam. But then it was not easy to stretch a short story into a feature length film. It was almost like writing a new story; finally, the entire script changed, but the central idea remained intact.

In the meanwhile, I was granted the opportunity to present my project at the National Film Development Corporation (NFDC) co-production market in Goa in 2012, and I was selected to attend the co-production market at the Rotterdam Film Festival in 2013. After attending all these events, I was still struggling to find potential financiers for my film. However, I also realised that there is a market for all kinds of films, and one only needs to find someone to slot it in the right place. With this thought I decided to go ahead and self-finance my film, using the resources I had available around me.

From the very beginning, I had planned to make my first feature like a documentary. Even though it is said that documentaries and fiction feature film approaches are different, I was quite confident that I could approach it like a documentary. I was planning to use real people in real locations. I tried to find my character from real life. For example, how do we shoot a documentary? First, we create a friendship with the character and slowly start rolling the camera only when the character forgets the camera. I was quite sure that I could use this technique for fiction films as well.

I began the groundwork for my film. Manipur is famous for its beautiful locations and natural surroundings. It is famous for its lakes where people live in floating huts. I wanted to shoot on this lake. I went there with an environmentalist friend, Salam Rajesh. As soon as we reached the lake, he was astonished to see that the floating village was missing. It was not to be found. A local told us that the government had evicted the residents and burnt down all the huts. It was a perfect story for an investigative documentary. I immediately decided to shoot the documentary first, not only because it was a good subject, but also because making the documentary would help me understand the people and the place better. This was in the year 2011. I made the documentary primarily with my own means. During this period, I had the chance to present my project at the Films Division and find funding to shoot the film, which took me almost three years to complete. The film was titled *Phum Shang* or *Floating Life* (2014); it was widely shown around India and the globe and hugely appreciated.

Documentary AND fiction filmmaking

My feature film was delayed as a result, but the documentary that I made turned out to be very useful for my fiction film. During the shooting of the documentary, I was somehow able to mould my script to the real-life situation of the people who lived on the lake. Later, the first people whom I met on the lake while shooting the documentary – Tomba and his wife Tharoshang – became the main protagonists of my film *Loktak Lairembee* (*Lady of the Lake*, 2016). The protagonists were fishermen who lived on and earned their livelihood from the lake.[2] Their life was very uncertain, even though they have always lived on the lake, for many generations. All the characters in the film were selected from the lake's fishing community. I purposely decided to use a small camera, as we were going to shoot on small boats and mostly in floating huts. Land was an hour's drive from this village.

We usually shoot documentary films with a very small crew and with the available resources. I applied the same practice to my feature film. The crew of my feature film consisted of only six members, including friends from film school who worked for free and brought along their equipment, too. The location was a floating village in the middle of the lake. It was an hour's drive from the nearest shore. Motorboats are not allowed on the lake, and so we only had access by the wooden boats that the fishermen also used. These small boats can hardly carry two people, including the driver. Hence, we were completely dependent on the people of the lake. I had made many friends while shooting the documentary. Our stay was arranged in two floating huts, as these unique huts which are made by thickening the floating biomass can hardly accommodate more than three or four people. There is no electricity on the lake, except for solar panels. This also was taken care of by one of my fishermen friends who goes to the shore every day to sell fish. We arranged a charging point in one of the houses near the shore. We had to be careful about our equipment and rations, because once we entered the village in the middle of the lake, we could not leave easily, as we were surrounded by water and the tide was not always in our favour. The film would not have happened without the help of the fishing community, which, again, was possible only because of the time I had spent with the people while making the documentary – trying to understand them, sharing their pain and anger, living and eating with them and trying to become a part of them. Their performance in the film is testimony to my friendship with the community and our mutual trust.

My ideas or stories for fiction films emerge from my surroundings. This could be because of my long-time association with documentary cinema. My next venture is another feature film on the ethnic divide in Manipur, which is a major cause of conflict among thirty-five different tribes and sub-tribes, each demanding its own land, forest and separate state. Like all my work so far, I continue to return to tell the stories of my native land through my films. Cinema, to me, is an archive as well as a chronicle of my people and our stories.

Notes

1 The Armed Forces (Special Powers) Act of 1958 extends to the whole of the states of Arunachal Pradesh, Assam, Manipur, Meghalaya, Mizoram, Nagaland and Tripura. Under the provisions of the act, the governor or administrator of these states has the power to declare the states to be in a disturbed or dangerous condition, requiring the aid of the armed forces. Source: Ministry of Law and Justice, Government of India, New Delhi, India, available at https://www.indiacode.nic.in/show-data?actid=AC_CEN_28_38_00003_195828_1517807319490&sectionId=27972&sectionno=3&orderno=3 [accessed 7 April 2023].
2 *Loktak Lairembee* (*Lady of the Lake*) premiered at Asian New Currents: 21st Busan International Film Festival 2016 and the Forum: 67th Berlin Film Festival 2017. So far, the film has won fifteen awards, including the Rajat Kamal for the Best Environmental Film at the 64th National Film Awards 2016, Best Feature Film at the 18th Mumbai Film Festival 2016 and Special Mention – Cultural Diversity Award at the 11th Asia Pacific Screen Awards 2017, Brisbane.

Films Cited

A Cry in the Dark. Dir. Haobam Paban Kumar. 2006.
AFSPA, 1958. Dir. Haobam Paban Kumar. 2005.
Lady of the Lake. Dir. Haobam Paban Kumar. Oli Pictures. 2016.
Mr. India. Dir. Haobam Paban Kumar. 2009.
Phum Shang. Dir. Haobam Paban Kumar. Films Division. 2014.
The First Leap. Dir. Haobam Paban Kumar. Doordarshan. 2008.

Experiencing and representing conflict: Encounters of a Kashmiri filmmaker

Raja Shabir Khan

When I was seven years old, my father took me on his bicycle to the local TV station to participate in a children's show. I remember feeling excited and anxious. My eyes grew wide with wonder, marvelling at the cameras and the sets. I instantly fell in love with the world of images. After that initial encounter, I worked as a child artist in several radio plays, spending hours in studios re-enacting stories with other actors. Unfortunately, my rendezvous with this beautiful world of creativity and art lasted but a few years.

Kashmir started to witness political disturbance and bloodshed, and soon all theatres and video parlours were shut down. As I grew up, I learned to live without cinema, but never forgot about it either. Cinema halls were converted into military barracks to accommodate the vast number of government security forces sent to Kashmir. Our bedtime stories were replaced by the stories of horror and survival of the people of Kashmir. Ghosts and demons would not scare kids as much as the thought of security forces barging into our homes at night. The quietness of the night was regularly breached by the sound of gunfire and the blaring of freedom slogans through the loudspeakers of the local mosques. In such a situation, entertainment was the last thing on the minds of the people. Everyday survival became a challenge. Families would consider themselves lucky to have dinner together. Every evening, I would stand by the roadside, waiting for my father to return from his office. We lived amidst constant fear and uncertainty.

I have seen my eleven-year-old cousin being shot dead. I was barely thirteen then. We were accompanying my uncle to his wedding ceremony, and just before we could reach the bride's house, we were fired on. When I was seventeen, I was picked up by the security forces, because my cousin objected to one of the drunk soldiers hitting me with his gun. I spent the night in prison, never expecting to be free again. My father, a senior bureaucrat, was labelled a Pakistani National and arrested by the Uttar Pradesh police during a visit to Delhi. These tragic events were part of my experience while growing up in Kashmir.

I carried these memories and experiences with me to film school in Kolkata. I had seen very few films while growing up in militancy-ridden Kashmir and had not seen a film on the big screen until I was twenty-five. I did not know the difference between film and video, nor was I aware of the National Film Institutes of India. When I met the other applicants, I was intimidated by their knowledge of film. Luckily, the admissions panel at the SRFTI (Satyajit Ray Film and Television Institute of India) was able to recognize my creative potential and accepted me into the programme.

Why I make films

At film school, some of my classmates would often call me names. I was not sure if they did it for fun or if, in fact, they were serious when they called me an ISI agent. I decided to make a documentary, *Broken, Silence* (2006), about the arrest of my father by the Uttar Pradesh police while working in Delhi and what we went through after that. It also gave me an opportunity to talk about the incident with my family, as we had never discussed the event amongst ourselves before I made the film. We had kept our feelings to ourselves. Although we all knew how broken we had felt, we never spoke about it, thinking it might make the other person weak, worsening the already existing trauma. The film was also my way of telling my story to my classmates. I chose to resort to cinema to tell the stories that are important to me.

Upon obtaining a film degree, I relocated to Mumbai and worked there for a year but soon felt the urge to return to Kashmir and make films there. There are very few filmmakers from Kashmir, and most of them have left Kashmir to work in other parts of India. I decided to make films about Kashmir while living there, films that could reflect the true spirit of the place. Many films have been made in and about Kashmir, but they lack an insider's perspective. Those films generally focus on larger political issues but miss out on the smaller nuances of daily life. After all, only the wearer knows where the shoe pinches.

Unfortunately, there are some filmmakers who visit Kashmir for a few days or months and claim to know everything about us. Recently, I met such a filmmaker claiming to know everything about Kashmir, the conflict and its politics. His knowledge was derived from books and newspaper articles about Kashmir, but living here is a different ordeal which no book or research project can fully convey. It must be experienced to be understood. The lived reality is often quite different from academic research findings. Being a filmmaker in Kashmir is also not easy. Kashmir is a very conservative place, and one must be particularly careful not to hurt people's sentiments. Besides, one may also be under the surveillance of the security agencies when making a film or documentary about the political situation in Kashmir.

Unfortunately, there is a very small audience for documentary films in India. Not many people have seen my films in Kashmir, either. There have been a few attempts to organise film festivals in Kashmir, but those attempts have remained unsuccessful. My films have been received well when screened in other parts of the country and internationally, but I wish that more people could see them in Kashmir. Another challenge for documentary filmmakers in India is the permanent problem of funding or lack of funding agencies. There are only a couple of funding opportunities made available by the Government of India. My first two films were funded by The Asian Pitch. Now, with the help of the internet, it is possible to access and apply for international funding, to which I have availed myself for making documentaries.

While in film school, all the films I made had a permanent reference to death and violence. I simply could not think of anything else, because the bloodshed that I had encountered while growing up in Kashmir refused to leave my psyche. In a post-screening Question & Answer session, I was once asked if my films were political in nature. I said that you cannot separate the camera from politics. Based on my personal experience, no documentary film on Kashmir can be separated from politics. It may or may not be visible in the film *per se*, but politics is always lurking in the backdrop. It offers context to the film.

My film *Shepherds of Paradise* (2013) seems to be a simple film about shepherds who have nothing to do with politics. However, when watching it closely, one realises that these shepherds are also affected by the politics of the region. Is there anyone who remains unaffected really? The main character of the film narrates the story of his detention by the army because he had provided food to an armed fighter fighting against Indian rule in Kashmir. He says that he could not deny food to the armed fighter because of fear and explains how they as shepherds are perennially caught in this crossfire.

Filmmaking in a conflict zone

I have been watching nomadic shepherds since my childhood and always wondered where they came from and where they went. In *Shepherds of Paradise*, I followed the shepherds on foot all along their traditional hilly tracks of about 300 kilometres. It was a challenging task to film because of the tough terrain, rough weather, long journey and limited resources. On the way, the inhabitants of the militancy-infested areas, who had never seen a movie camera before, thought it was a machine gun and reported me to the police, assuming I was an armed militant. The police let me go only after thoroughly checking my baggage and equipment.

To make matters worse, the horse carrying the equipment skidded and broke the solar charger. This limited the shooting hours. I had to use the camera judiciously to save battery life. This had both positive and negative effects: we did not have to go through a lot of footage in the editing process, but it also reduced the choice of the selection of shots available to us. Besides, the last leg of the journey was extremely challenging. The weather on the mountains deteriorated abruptly; the wind turned strong and icy. My feet and hands went numb. Every single one of us, including the shepherds, had to struggle for survival. These experiences are not captured in the film, but filmmaking in Kashmir is beset with unending challenges. It was some satisfaction when *Shepherds of Paradise* received the National Award for Best Non-Feature Film and Best Cinematography.

Frequent clashes between the locals and the government forces are a common sight in Kashmir. It is difficult and risky to film these occurrences, especially in politically disturbed areas. On most occasions, the common people cannot distinguish between news reporters and documentary filmmakers. They are also angry with the national media which is biased in reporting news from Kashmir. The government forces, however, have little understanding of documentaries and prevent filmmakers from recording events because we do not have an identifying press card. Another difficulty involves the selection of a location from which to record the conflict. When filming from the protester's side, one is prone to get hit by bullets; when choosing to remain on the government forces' side, protestors will identify you as a spy working for the police. These are my personal observations, and I have been harassed on several occasions for similar reasons.

It also proves difficult for a Kashmiri filmmaker to procure the necessary permits from the authorities. I was stopped by the security forces from visiting a village near the Line of Control (LOC) when I was making a documentary about the divided families of Kashmir along this line. This was done despite securing all the necessary permits needed to film. I was also questioned by the investigative agencies while making this documentary, which required me to travel to Pakistan for research and filming purposes. The Pakistani authorities were not very friendly, either. One of the people associated with the ISI confiscated my mobile SIM card. Finally, I was denied permission by both India and Pakistan. Still, I managed to complete the film with the material that I had filmed during my research trips to the Indian side of the LOC, together with scenes shot in Pakistan on a mobile phone camera by some associates.

On another occasion, when I was filming my first independent documentary, *Angels of Troubled Paradise* (2011), I was detained by the police and taken to the police station along with 'the kid' (the main character of the film). They kept me there for hours. My film is about 'the kid' collecting smoke shells and selling these to a scrap dealer. It shows how the conflict is taking a toll on the lives of people in the valley, especially children. The police officers refused to understand my reasons for filming.

Sometimes, I feel that hailing from Kashmir is a major disadvantage while asking for permits or seeking any sort of cooperation from the government (both Indian and Pakistani). It seems that filmmakers and journalists visiting from outside Kashmir frequently receive help from the government. The same courtesy is not extended to us, making it further difficult for a local filmmaker to work in Kashmir. The challenges thus are numerous, but I am determined to tell stories and show the insider's perspective while living and making films in Kashmir.

Films Cited

Angels of Troubled Paradise. Dir. Raja Shabir Khan. The Asian Pitch. 2011.
Shepherds of Paradise. Dir. Raja Shabir Khan. The Asian Pitch. 2013.

8

Documentary and oppositional Bahujan agency

Jyoti Nisha

In 2009, when I was a screenwriting student at the Film and Television Institute of India (FTII) in Pune, my professor Anjum Rajabali, a very passionate teacher and celebrated screenwriter in the Hindi film industry, introduced us to author Robert Mckee's book *Story: Substance, Structure, Style and the Principles of Screenwriting* (1997). A remark by Mckee that stories are about archetypes and not stereotypes, consumed me in ways of which I had no comprehension of. My entire life, I had consumed (and still consume) popular cinema and stories in every possible format from India and the world over. It slowly dawned on me that 'story' indeed was the only common factor across everything – people, cultures, books, literature, religions, mass media, advertising, cinema, music, love, family. It was everywhere – raising scientific questions, questions of feminism and intellectual and cultural discourse. Most importantly, these stories were about people, and they were told by people. French philosopher Louis Althusser in his 'Ideology and Ideological State Apparatuses' said that 'people are ideological' (Althusser 1971, 41). This indeed held some truth for me. People dream, and they create! They want to tell stories, and they want to be themselves because stories are powerful. Those whose stories were told repeatedly have retained their power. Epics such as the *Mahabharata* and *Ramayana* are some of the finest examples of establishing a Brahmin ideological framework in India. We have grown up with stories of Mahatma Gandhi's satyagraha and Amitabh Bachchan's Angry Young Man image, but there was no woman's story to which I could relate.

Producing was not a choice!

All my life, I saw films and read books but, unfortunately, I did not find my story in popular culture – whether in mass media, literature, or sports. Where was my story then? I saw that the 'medium' of telling stories was of significant value. It became a personal quest. This writing is a sincere attempt to transgress the Brahmanical archive of image-making, via methodologies of Bahujan spectatorship and the oppositional Bahujan gaze and agency, to inspire people to 'witness' the question of caste and intersectionality and marginalised representation as a rational self-respecting thinking human being to arrive at truth.[1] I share a very personal story of making a political film, of finding articulation and epistemological arguments to make this knowledge palatable in the context of Brahmanical ideology and aesthetics, extending from reel to real life.

We all go through a unique life. I recall my adolescence and see a very different kind of struggle; of being a teenager, of being a woman, of being dark-skinned, of knowing what it meant to be a Scheduled Caste in India.[2] If you dressed well and spoke fluent English and told people your caste – it shocked them. I never understood that behaviour. All my life, whenever I had to answer a question about my caste identity, I was assertive. It was about self-respect. In retrospect, I see that I was just imitating my Ambedkarite family.[3] But back then, I could never figure out the surprise or disdain in the circles of which I was part. Perhaps I saw them as human beings, but they saw my caste. School, college, friends, life, love – caste was to be found everywhere. It was a certain kind of looking. A certain kind of othering. Conditioned and approved by the popular image and culture, it was a way of seeing, reserved for the marginalised. There were only stereotypes of people like us, until I found Rene in Pa Ranjith's Tamil film *Natchathiram Nagargiradhu* (2022).

The movie opens with a top-angle shot of Rene (played by Dushara Vijayan) and Iniyan (played by Kalidas Jayaram) lying exhausted in bed; Nina Simone's 'Feeling Good' is playing in the background, revealing that they have just made love. Rene pauses the music and asks Iniyan: 'Should we get married?' Sleepy and tired, Iniyan answers: 'Let's'. She wonders about the significance of marriage. 'But what's love if it sustains only because of an institution of marriage, not otherwise? That won't do with me. I won't'. Iniyan seconds Rene mindlessly and irritably: 'Let's not then!' Lying next to him, feeling his skin, Rene starts singing an Ilaiyaraaja song that irritates Iniyan further, and he asks her to stop singing.[4] He is sleepy, but Rene is not. He shuts her mouth, but she continues singing. He loses his cool and throws a fit. Rene takes offense: 'What ya? You can listen to Nina Simone, but you can't listen to Ilaiyaraaja?' Iniyan answers: 'I don't want to listen to any song. I want to sleep'. Rene provokes him further and continues singing. Iniyan yells: 'Tamil!!' An attack on Rene because her name is Tamizh! Rene corrects him by explaining the correct pronunciation of her name: 'It's not Tamil. It's Tamizh! Call me Rene. It is I who decides how I should be addressed'. She continues singing. Irritated, Iniyan takes another dig at Ilaiyaraaja: 'Birds of the same feather flock together'. This is the trait of a casteist person. Rene is aware that they are ideologically opposite, but she plays cool, somewhat funny, defiantly and calmly. She says: 'You know your problem is not Ilaiyaraaja. It's me' (*Natchathiram Nagargiradhu*, 2022).

Throughout watching this film, I wondered why Ranjith chose to give Rene a song and why she laughs in this first scene. During this scene, Rene's sarcasm and laughter are a defence mechanism to ward off the casteist gaze at her social identity and being. I do the same – dance, laugh, or indulge in both. As a person from the community, I can say for sure that we know the experience and have the awareness to identify how and when someone looks at us with a casteist gaze. It is irrational, blasphemous and small-minded. Thus, Rene's defiance and laughter hit home in a personal way.

Rene was the Ambedkarite heroine whom I needed to see in popular culture in my adolescence, but I found her now, when I am in my forties. I questioned where we learn those lessons. I found answers in the words of Ambedkar, bell hooks, Jyotiba Phule, John Berger, Louis Althusser, Noam Chomsky, Periyar and many dear friends and comrades' struggles and personal stories, which connected one thing to another: caste to gaze, ways of looking to spectatorship, spectatorship to ideological state apparatuses to cinema and mass media, and cinema came back to the TV sitting in our homes. Those were the lessons on which families were raised. It was a part of everyday humdrum. Children returned home from school and were glued to the TV. I was one of them, watching an image of one of us in a certain (victim) way and one of yours designed to rule. It was everywhere. It was Sujata in Bimal Roy's *Sujata* (1959), Kasturi in Frank Osten's *Acchut Kanya* (1936), Kachra in Ashutosh Gowariker's *Lagaan* (2001), Dukhi in Satyajit Ray's *Sadgati* (1981), Laxmi in Shyam Benegal's *Ankur* (1974), Dhaniya in Bikas Mishra's *Chauranga* (2016), Alice in Mira Nair's *Monsoon Wedding* (2001), Krishna in Mira Nair's *Salaam Bombay* (1988), Deepak Kumar in Prakash Jha's *Aarakshan* (2011), Tara in Subhash Kapoor's *Madam Chief Minister* (2021) and Jatav, Gaura, Nishad and the two Dalit girls in Anubhav

Sinha's *Article 15* (2019), to name a few. They just remained stories of the oppressed, all victims of an upper-caste victim gaze. They did not dare ask the scientific socio-political question – why does caste exist? They did not disturb the status quo. Nobody questioned, how did we become oppressed? The popular culture trained and conditioned a gaze to see each one of us with a different humanity. It so far served class as caste and legitimised inappropriate amounts of stereotyping and branding of marginalised communities as low people.

Claiming your (my) space was the only way

Ambedkar and Kanshiram both inspired the caravan of anti-caste movements. They did so by being the leaders that they were. I understood that claiming your (my) space was the only way. It became imperative to have a conversation with popular culture in India. It was essential to tell them our part of the story. To provide them with appropriate methodologies to see marginalised people. To address what has not been addressed in Indian/Hindi Cinema for what it is – the question of caste, its genesis, mechanism and development via an Ambedkarite methodology and informing its context with the question of patriarchy vis-à-vis a marginalised representation in Indian cinema. These questions are our deeper questions of life – gaze, feminism, equity and equality, love, land and fraternity in Indian democracy. For that very reason, the old pedagogies of the *Natyashastra*[5] need to be addressed, and new pedagogies of marginalised assertions must be created. I saw no harm in asking questions to understand the process and intention behind the representation of us marginalised people in cinema over the years. As a critic, I observed a lack of connection between image and knowledge when they represented marginalised subjects.

Filmmaker Karuna Kumar's *Palasa 1978* (2020) is a good example of making a connection between knowledge and representation. Set in Palasa, a town in the Srikakulam district of Andhra Pradesh, *Palasa 1978* is a story about two brothers: Ranga Rao (played by Thiruveer) and Mohan Rao (played by Rakshit Atluri), who belong to a backward community of Bahujans and are musicians and drum players by their caste occupation. The narrative follows their struggles and revolt for dignity, power and self-respect, against the oppressive casteist political machinery embodied in two high-caste brothers' fight for dominance in the political sphere.

What is different and unique about this film is the assertive gaze and resolution to Mohan Rao's rage presented in the narrative. In one scene, sharing his own lived experience of belonging to the community of manual scavengers, Sebastian, the honest police officer, not only gives a direction to Mohan Rao's anger but also a second chance by introducing him to Dr Ambedkar's leadership as a weapon to fight systematic caste violence and oppression. Instead of abandoning Mohan as a victim of systematic discrimination, the director provides a poignant solution to Mohan Rao's character, which demands deep reflection on the social and spiritual emancipation of Bahujans in India. Karuna's film's contextualisation of the struggle and values of the Ambedkarite ideology of equality, liberty, social justice and fraternity is distinct and unique in comparison to popular cinema's contemporary utopianism or tokenism.

Knowledge applied are methods devised

I have raised questions of gaze, agency and aesthetics in popular cinema because I see possibilities of radical change in the politics and language of the representation of the marginalised in Indian cinema. I see stories that will set us free and bring fraternity for real. I see opportunities for the appropriate and dignified representation of marginalised people in cinema and popular culture via Bahujan collaborators with agency. I see a space for marginalised integrity. I thought that I could help, and that is why I defined The Oppositional Bahujan Agency.

The Oppositional Bahujan Agency locates the social identity of a marginalised subject (Shudra and Ati Shudras and women), community culture, dance, dress, music, language, folklore, cuisine, traditional medicine, religious symbols, sacred objects and so on in Indian cinema, by using Ambedkar's historical methods – a non-Brahminical critique of positivist history – as a methodology/epistemology/language/aesthetic in contrast to popular culture's monolithic aesthetic of the Hindu *Natyashastra* in India. The Oppositional Bahujan Agency observes five forces working in alternative combinations in the making of a narrative where cinema functions as Ideological State Apparatus: (a) the Story and the fate of the protagonist, (b) gaze and ideology, (c) filmmaker, (d) funding, and (e) demanding greater accountability and responsibility for greater literacy, for a conscious cultural production in relation to the representation of Bahujans and women in Indian cinema.

Finding an identity became an intimate exercise

I observed that popular culture paid little attention to the idea of lived experience and shared histories of oppressed communities and their historical context in the making of India. Realism was not realistic enough. It was based on rasa-sutra.[6] That was not our culture. Thus, finding an identity became an intimate exercise. It took a political turn in 2017, when I went to the Tata Institute of Social Sciences (TISS) in Mumbai and studied Cultural Studies and understood caste for the first time. As a screenwriter, having a slight understanding of culture and lived experience of being a Bahujan from a family of Ambedkarites, I understood the scope and the responsibility to bring historical context to the representations of marginalised communities in popular images. The intention was to clearly inform, educate and draw out connections where the popular image was inaccurate or distorting or appropriating representation and doing more harm than good. I saw an opportunity to address our experience of consumption of marginalised representation via 'Bahujan Spectatorship'. It was important that they knew how we felt about their gaze. 'Bahujan spectatorship' relates to an oppositional gaze and a political strategy of Bahujans to reject the Brahmanical representation of caste and marginalised communities in Indian cinema. It is also an inverted methodology to document a different socio-political Bahujan experience of consuming popular cinema.

The popular gaze has been repulsive to us for nearly a century. The popular gaze conditioned and transmitted a casteist way of looking, and it still continues to do the same through mass media and cinema, even though a different kind of cinema has emerged in the last decade, through the works of filmmakers such as Pa Ranjith, Nagraj Manjule, Mari Selvaraj, Neeraj Ghaywan, Rajesh Rajamani, Jenny Dolly, Leela Santhosh and others.

Intersectionality required witnessing

Meditation made me aware of an ability to experience witnessing. I became deeply interested in the quality of the way in which popular culture has looked at us, the marginalised. It was a question of love and ethics. That became essential. Hence, I decided to look inwards. They say that *Vipassana* (a meditation technique) is witnessing, and I myself will not claim to be a witness, but I noticed a resonance in the way in which bell hooks defined a phenomenon of being an 'enlightened witness', a certain way of looking in her theory of *Cultural criticism and transformation*, in a YouTube series:

> Being an Enlightened Witness is really not about freeing ourselves of representation. It's really about becoming critically vigilant about both what is being told to us and how we respond to what is being told to us. Because the answer is not in the kind of censoring, an absolutism of right-wing political correctness but in fact a proactive sense of agency that requires all of us on a greater level of literacy (hooks 2006).

I hoped that someone would aspire to that kind of witnessing when they looked at the question of caste and its intersectionality with class, gender and sexuality. I had gotten tired of the stereotype of marginalised people – broken, poor people, prostitutes, criminals, bar dancers, drug peddlers, homeless people, people with no dignity, uncivilised, dirty people with no clothes. Our characters were stereotyped to the core. I wanted one positive story. It became essential to question: Who was telling our stories? Who was telling stories of women and children? Who defines and also distorts our identity? And who was funding these stories? That is why finding my own voice in the rich magical world of India and the even more magical world of Mumbai became an excruciating quest. It was also about authenticity. We barely had any representation!

Documentary was the befitting form to tell this story

Thus, the only possibility I saw was to have a conversation with people. bell hooks insists that talking is revolutionary, and I found that documentary was the most befitting form to tell this story. It is also an expository and reflexive piece of work from a Bahujan woman's feminist gaze, which is heavily informed by the struggles and philosophy of revolutionaries of the anti-caste movements, deriving its arguments from Dr Ambedkar and bell hooks.

Dr. Bhimrao Ambedkar: Now & Then is a feature-length documentary film that explores deep questions of liberty, equality, fraternity, social justice, exclusion and marginalised representation through me, Jyoti Nisha, a Bahujan woman filmmaker's gaze in an upper-caste Indian film industry. The film aspires to translate the praxis of Ambedkarite politics to image-making and the representation of marginalised subjects' culture, history and politics in popular cinema and media. Driven by Dr Ambedkar's philosophy epistemologically, the film symbolically and politically documents the representation and assertion of Bahujan people in the contemporary era. Questioning the institution of caste in India, this film is a commentary on religion, revolution, politics and the freedom of speech.

What kind of steps are involved in telling a non-fiction story?

To truly understand independent documentary film practice across development, production, post-production, distribution and exhibition in all its political and aesthetic diversity, one would have to go step by step. What kind of steps are involved in actually telling a non-fiction story? Serious questions arise. Why should I tell this story? What is the premise? Research. Scripting. Who is going to fund the story? Is it relevant? What is the socio-political context? And in terms of marketing strategies, who acquires documentaries in India? What films have been acquired in the past? And if you dared to dream the dream and tell your story, what should be the strategy for making a sociopolitical film? I began by using my savings as seed funding. I borrowed from friends and family to shoot and make a three-minute pitch video. After shooting for two and half years across eight states in India, I eventually crowd-funded 20 lakhs with Wishberry in a two-month crowd-funding campaign for the post-production of *Dr. Bhimrao Ambedkar: Now & Then*.

A brief background of film school education definitely helped. I had seen that conversations did happen if one had a story to tell but, truth be told, beyond production, nobody teaches you anything about how to sell anything, fiction or non-fiction. Most non-fiction filmmakers, despite having critical acclaim in the festival circuits, still sell their work to educational institutions via DVD copies or on their websites. Mass distribution was a far reach. What are the right festivals, right people, right curators? How do you connect with distribution agencies? Who are the right sales agents? How do you network with festival curators? Who are the distributors? What is impact-producing? These are questions that one has to figure out by oneself, based on the themes and budgets, and this requires real patience as documentary films take time to come together. I began in 2016 and went about my story based on instinct, knowledge and an audience study, as well as a real urge to tell this story.

Khushboo Ranka and Vinay Shukla's documentary film *An Insignificant Man* (2016), which follows the rise of the Aam Aadmi Party (AAP) and records its first election campaign in the state elections of Delhi in 2013, was the first film that received worldwide attention for its content in the popular domain. In an interview with *Film Companion*, the filmmakers revealed that, even though they received a great response from the film fraternity, nobody really wanted to touch the film because it was a political film (T. M. et al. 2022). *An Insignificant Man* later had a limited theatrical release, through an app that allowed them to screen the film in different cities. Vice Media acquired it later for international distribution.

Documentaries have struggled to find producers, distributors, platforms and audiences in India, but when seeing the increasing number over the past few years, one can be hopeful, even though it remains woefully meagre compared to the fiction market.[7] Selling a documentary becomes even more difficult in India if the themes are in any way perceived to be anti-state and explore socio-political issues or deal with advocacy. Very spookily, this brings us back to seeing oneself (and especially a political film) and the business of cinema through the relation between the production of knowledge and practices of power, power relations, the relationship between ideology and ideological state apparatuses. Producing is not a choice. It is a decision between telling your story or ignoring that instinct for good.

Conclusion

Documentary films are very real stories, like any other story. They draw you in, they keep you engaged, give you an adrenaline rush and also float you. It is more personal for me, because here I get to explore deeper questions of life, intellect, culture, art and revolution, by identifying and connecting with people of similar thoughts, ideologies and advocacy. The form helps one capture their subjects and circumstances as they are. Sometimes we can craft our scenes and design our visuals, but only very serendipitously life unfolds in front of you, and you should be both present and lucky to be able to capture that. It is certainly more challenging than fiction any day, because the format is very dynamic, tense and vibrant. It demands utmost patience and presence to watch hours of footage to convey on screen in brief moments the germ and essence of the story. Personal stories make the best stories and find their own space in the market. I think that people have connected with my work from a personal and political point of view. This means that a place for such nuance and articulation existed in popular culture. Those methods are political; if applied, if witnessed like a rationale, one can bring radical literacy, nuance and transformation to the image-making of the marginalised. It can be instrumental in addressing questions of human rights of the marginalised communities in popular discourse and, lastly, to annihilate caste for real. Through Wishberry and a common friend I partnered with Pa. Ranjith's Neelam Productions. Now, Neelam Productions are my co-producers. I am optimistic. I have created methods from my knowledge, and the application of these methods depends on one's own choice, ethics and politics.

Notes

1 Found in Buddhist texts, 'bahujan' is a Pali term which literally translates to 'majority of people'. Articulated by Gautama Buddha, the word appears in the dictum '*Bahujana sukhaya bahujana hitaya cha* (For the happiness of the many, for the welfare of the many)'. In modern context, it refers to the combined population of the Scheduled Castes, Scheduled Tribes, Other Backward Classes, Muslims and minorities, who together constitute the demographic majority of India. Kanshi Ram, the messiah of Bahujan politics in India, propounded the concept of '85 vs 15', where the 15 per cent were the Savarnas ruling the 85 per cent of Bahujans in India. Kanshi Ram's significance lies in the fact that, while everyone was aware of the '85 vs 15' status quo, only he knew how to transform it into political power – a power that was never imagined by any of the predecessors of Kanshi Ram, except for Ambedkar. Kanshi Ram spearheaded organisations such as the All India Backward and Minority Employees Federation (BAMCEF) in 1970 and the quasi-political entity Dalit Shoshit Samaj Sangharsh Samiti (DS-4). BAMCEF was an alternative to the political aspirations of countless Bahujan government employees. Without this initiative, the evolution of the Bahujan Samaj Party (BSP) as a colossal Dalit organisation would not have been possible. On 6 December 1984, the death anniversary of Babasaheb Ambedkar, DS-4 metamorphosed into the BSP. Kanshiram rightly said: '*Jiski jitni sankhya bhari, uski utni bhagidari* (The greater the number, the more the share)'.
2 'Scheduled Caste' is a term derived from the government listing of certain castes which could be defined as Untouchable in a schedule in 1935. The castes qualified for reserved seats in legislatures, educational benefits and reservation in government jobs now accepted as part of government policy. The concept behind the word was that special attention to these castes in the social and political sphere was necessary to raise their level to that of the 'clean castes'. The Mahars under Ambedkar's leadership used the term 'Scheduled Caste' over 'Harijans', although it did not come into common use until a political party for the Scheduled Castes was founded by Ambedkar in 1942.
3 An Ambedkarite is one who follows the philosophy of Dr Bhimrao Ramji Ambedkar, Indian jurist, economist, social reformer, political leader and constitution-maker who committed his life to the annihilation of the caste system in the twentieth century. Dr Ambedkar emphasised individual freedom and self-representation and was critical of Hindu caste society, calling for renouncing all Hindu scriptures in 1936 in order to annihilate the caste system. His final masterstroke was when he adapted Buddhism as a way of life in 1956, along with lakhs of marginalised people of the country.
4 Ilaiyaraaja is a film composer, singer, songwriter, instrumentalist, orchestrator, conductor-arranger and lyricist. His extraordinary career has spanned more than four decades, encompassing over 7,000 songs and 1,000 films in at least seven languages. Over the decades, his music has become an intrinsic part of Tamil life. There are two often-repeated arguments used to dismiss the politics of Ilaiyaraaja's works. The first is that he refuses to claim his oppressed caste identity. The second is that he has become a

devout Hindu and in the process has Brahmanised himself. Both arguments have over the years become a legitimised part of the discourse around the maestro.
5   The *Natyashastra* by Bharata is the oldest surviving Indian work on the performing arts.
6   The theory of rasa is part of Bharata's *Natyashastra*. Rasa is an emotion evoked in the audience by the art.
7   Investigative documentary series and crime series – such as Leena Yadav's *House of Secrets, The Burari Deaths* and Umesh Vinayak Kulkarni's *Indian Predator*, as well as the Netflix Original documentary anthology series *Bad Boy Billionaires* – are some of the series available on Netflix. Sikhya Entertainment's *Period End of Sentence* and Kartiki Gonsalves' *The Elephant Whisperers*, an Academy Award winner for Best Documentary Short, are available on Netflix now. Payal Kapadia's *In a Night of Knowing Nothing*, which won the L'Œil d'or Award for Best Documentary at the 2021 Cannes film festival, is not yet available anywhere. Shaunak Sen's *All That Breathes* won the Best Documentary at Sundance and the L'Œil d'or Award this year and has been acquired by HBO. Rintu Thomas and Sushmit Ghosh's *Writing with Fire* was nominated for Best Documentary feature at the 2022 Oscars and is available on Apple and Amazon, but not available to stream in India, as reported in the *Film Companion*.

Works Cited

Althusser, L. (1971). Ideological and ideological state apparatuses. In *Lenin and philosophy and other essays*, 121–176. New York: Monthly Review Press.

hooks, b. (2006). Pt 3, Cultural criticism and transformation. *YouTube*. www.youtube.com/watch?v=I0whHz7PLGY [accessed 23 November 2023].

Mckee, R. (1997). *Story: Substance, structure, style and the principles of screenwriting*. New York: ReganBooks.

Rajamani, R. (2020). To appreciate Ilaiyaraaja's anti-caste politics, you have to listen to his music. *HuffPost*. https://www.huffpost.com/archive/in/entry/to-appreciate-ilaiyaraaja-s-anti-caste-politics-you-have-to-listen-to-his-music_in_5eda5614c5b6817661649db5 [accessed 12 November 2024].

Singh, R. (2022). Kanshi Ram gave Dalit politics 'new Bahujan genes'. Today, Mayawati is wedged in nepotism. *The Print*. https://theprint.in/opinion/kanshi-ram-gave-dalit-politics-new-bahujan-genes-today-mayawati-is-wedged-in-nepotism/874117/ [accessed 12 November 2024].

T. M. and T. M. (2022). The trouble with making a documentary film in India. *Filmcompanion*. https://www.filmcompanion.in/features/the-trouble-with-making-a-documentary-film-in-india-shut-up-sona-all-that-breathes-writing-with-fire [accessed 12 November 2024].

Zelliot, E. (2013). *Ambedkar's world: The making of Babasaheb and the Dalit movement*. New Delhi: Navayana.

Part III:
Resistance in practice

9

Curating documentary film and video art in a museum: Reflections from *Loss and Transience*

Rashmi Devi Sawhney and Lucía Imaz King

In 2020, we were invited by Zoe Yeh, Director of the Hong-gah Museum, Taipei, to curate an exhibition of Indian video art. The invitation was issued to us as co-founders of the international film and visual arts network VisionMix,[1] which we set up in 2014 as a UK-India transnational entity. Drawing on this particular project which involved an India-Taiwan-UK collaboration, we lay out certain key concerns around documentary films, spectatorial address and transnational curation. This essay is meant as invitation to a dialogue around documentary film curation in gallery and museum settings, and the interventions possible through newer modes of public engagement, as well as the possible implications that this holds for the documentary form itself. While a substantial debate has emerged within the visual and contemporary arts about the important role that curation plays, this discourse has not yet been extended to Cinema Studies or Documentary Studies in South Asia. We hope to make a small contribution towards this, drawing on our own experience of working variously (and differently) as writers, academics, artist-filmmakers and curators (see also Sawhney and King 2018).

Trans-locationality as a paradigm of collaborative cultural practice

The idea of the 'transnational' has gained much significance since the 1990s, in the wake of economic liberalisation and globalisation, spearheaded in the Indian context by the opening up of the media and television industries to foreign investment and privatisation. The sudden flurry of abundant media content that began to be broadcast via satellite television by the Hong-Kong-based Star TV (followed shortly thereafter by Zee and several others) opened the floodgates of 'globalised desires', expressed through youth cultures and a radically transforming social landscape. Not surprisingly, the political response was of cultural conservatism, expressing anxieties about the erasure of 'traditional Indian value systems', erupting as violent agitations against cultural markers seen as 'non-Indian', ranging from films such as *Fire* (dir. Deepa Mehta, 1996) depicting lesbian relationships, to protests against McDonald's entry into India (also in 1996) and the first Miss World pageant to be held in Bangalore in the same year. Popular commercial cinema exploited this milieu by creating a new genre of ideologically conservative films often located in North America and Europe, targeting diasporic nostalgia for 'Indian culture', while maximising box-office revenue.[2]

In the international context, transnationalism acquired currency through an urgent interest in issues of migration, cultural diversity, the call to resist rising sentiments of Islamophobia and the economic consolidation of the European Union. Inter-disciplinary work addressing the transforming landscape of Europe, Australia and North America, with debates around citizenship, cultural diversity and multi-culturalism formed the core anchors of these new enquiries.[3] In the study of cinema, visual arts, literature and other creative forms, a heightened sensitivity towards pluralities of cultural and personal histories emphasised ideas of hybridity, liminality and subjectivities that were shaped by more than one identity, location, nation, language, or religion.[4] These recalibrations of plural belonging led to significant theories of multiplicity, including the argument that unique aesthetic characteristics could be identified in creative work (cinema, literature, visual arts) produced by migrants and people of colour from formerly colonised nations (see, for example, Naficy 2001; Bal 2009; Bayraktar 2017). Documentary cinema saw a surge of films addressing many of these issues while challenging the conventional documentary form, and the visual arts responded by questioning the power-structures and art-historical narratives embedded within the power centres of the Western world.[5]

In the three decades that followed (after the 1990s), India witnessed a great tussle on ideological and political grounds, between conservative neo-liberalism and what has popularly come to be known as 'the idea of India',[6] deeply marking artistic and documentary practice and theory, especially through the emergent category of the 'contemporary'[7] pre-dominantly within the visual arts. We sketch out this generalised (and hugely simplified) overview in order to locate the show that we curated at the Hong-gah

Museum from March to May 2021 – titled *Loss and Transience* – within this broader trajectory of historical events and discourses addressing the transnational. When VisionMix was formed as a UK-India network in 2014, it needed to be attentive to this wider context, further complicated by Britain's colonial history. In order to elaborate on the conceptual issues that emerged from *Loss and Transience*, which we wish to address here, we need to take a brief detour via the conditions and concerns that marked the formation of VisionMix. Readers are warned that our writing in the following section may take on a non-singular voice, as we comment on our individual locations and contexts through the lens of our collective and collaborative curatorial practice, a mark of what we propose to be seen as 'trans-locational practice'.

The formation of a transnational network

VisionMix started in 2014 with a meeting convened by Lucía Imaz King, of a small group of ten South Asian-British and other London-based filmmakers and video artists who had previously lived in, conducted long-term research, or made films in India and Pakistan. These discussions led to the articulation of a desire for an international network that would enable critical conversations between artists, filmmakers, critics and curators from or connected to South Asia.[8] Forming an initial partnership with Rashmi Devi Sawhney for our first India-based symposium, this created the juncture for a new stage where Rashmi became co-director of the network, planning our first event in India, the VisionMix Artists' Filmmakers and Curators' Workshop (2015).[9] The symposium was held at the School of Arts and Aesthetics, Jawaharlal Nehru University, and the Max Muller Bhavan, New Delhi, and included thirty-five film screenings and artists' presentations, as well as performances and research presentations. Established artists such as Sheba Chhachhi, Gigi Scaria, Avijit Mukul Kishore, Asim Waqif, Atul Bhalla, Sunil Gupta, Marc Isaacs, Alia Syed and Anupama Srinivasan presented their work, along with emerging artists such as Priyanka Chhabra, Pallavi Paul, Adele Tulli, Moutushi Chakraborty and others.[10] The workshop also invited scholars and curators as participants and interlocutors; these included João Laia, Phoebe Wong, Nicole Wolf, Lata Mani, Rustom Bharucha, Charu Maithani, Parul Dave Mukherji, Shukla Sawant, Shaunak Sen and Brinda Bose.[11] Postcolonial theorist Leela Gandhi delivered a keynote that addressed the 'politics of friendship', establishing the tone of the discussions that unfolded.[12] The workshop had been convened to explore issues of common interest to artists in the UK and in India, since the extended transnational axis brought a new vantage point to VisionMix's plans. Amidst the excitement of witnessing a great many films and inspiring presentations, participants in a closing roundtable recognized the need to co-determine what the purpose of VisionMix would be as an international group of collaborators, exploring ideas towards sustaining the network, which included asking and answering some difficult questions.

Partnering now as co-directors, the raison d'être of VisionMix developed as one in which we were keen to create small, laboratory-like platforms to share practices, films and critical thinking between friends and fellow artists, broadening this out to public conversations; sites that allowed us to explore the immediate cultural and political conditions that influenced our respective enquiries and projects. Since each of us existed in very different socio-economic and political milieux, it was important to remain attentive to the different contexts of producing and exhibiting work across locations. The network continued to expand and walk a tightrope of complex transactions across India and the UK with minimal resources. The pattern of applying for funding, predominantly from British and European funding sources and consulates, also came with underlying biases in their template of 'disseminating expertise' from western cultural agents towards the Indian partners, even with ongoing attempts to counter such neo-colonial modes of patronage by these organisations. Currency rates meant that funds generated in pounds would go a much longer way in India, and the often informal and spontaneous work culture in the Indian cultural and creative industries made it easier to organise events in India, when compared to the United Kingdom. Our partnerships also began to extend to other regions – for example, the artists' video collective Videotage in Hong Kong – where past and present tensions around colonial politics have an entirely different set of political implications, and later the Honggah Museum in Taipei with its own colonial history. VisionMix, therefore, was constantly marked by and engaged with questions of the transnational through a heightened attention to the trans-locational, as this played out in our varied and specific contexts. We emphasise trans-locationality over transnationalism as a defining characteristic of cross-border collaborative work in the creative industries and propose this as a framework to forge a deeper understanding of nuanced and complex regional contexts. This theoretical framing, we believe, is crucial at a time when much creative work is bound and determined by set time frames and a necessary engagement with the 'local' in artistic and curatorial work, particularly in pedagogies such as the short-term 'residency'.

Genre-crossing and spectatorial address: A garden and a forest

Julian Stallabrass' article 'Contentious relations: Art and documentary' (2013, 2) points out that, over the past two decades, it has become increasingly difficult to define what a 'documentary film' is; he goes on to suggest that it is largely sustained exposure to 'recognizable' international conventions that help viewers determine what constitutes a documentary. He cites an impressive range of theoretical re-evaluation of documentary for its new roles and its new social and political work, by authors such as Azoulay, Butler, Sebastião Salgado and Levi-Strauss flagging many filmmakers (from Trinh T. Minh-Ha to Hito Steyerl) who have challenged documentary paradigms of eliciting standardised emotions (such as anxiety, anger, fear, or empathy) among their audiences and emphasising the aesthetic dimensions of documentary practice (Stallabrass 2013).

There is an established history of documentary filmmaking that defies the classical distinction between artistic and documentary approaches in the Indian context, including through unconventional distribution and exhibition methods (see Sawhney 2021, 2022). The role of the Films Division in supporting form-breaking documentary and animation films in the 1960s under the Directorship of Jehangir Bhownagary has now been canonised (see Mukul Kishore 2018). Documentary filmmakers and scholars themselves have been conducting an ongoing debate, pushing the boundaries of 'documentary practice' in many exciting directions. It is impossible to chronicle or even provide a cursory outline of these debates here; however, interested readers may find valuable material in the conference Visible Evidence XXI, held in New Delhi in 2014.[13] Within the visual arts space, platforms created by the Kochi-Muziris biennial, the Raqs Media Collective, Khōj (New Delhi), Experimenter (Kolkata), Desire Machine Collective (Guwahati), Studio CAMP (Mumbai) and Experimenta (Bangalore) have become important sites for interrogating new media developments and constitute significant reference for innovative curatorial practices. In addition, there is a long tradition of the convergence of theatre, visual arts, literature, documentary and folk music, and many exciting histories which are gradually emerging, locating multi-disciplinary histories of creative practice.[14] The important contribution made by Okwe Enwezor through Documenta XI, whose second platform 'Experiments with Truth: Transitional Justice and the Processes of Truth and Reconciliation' which was held in New Delhi from 7 to 21 May 2002, cannot be overlooked in this narrative. The exuberant and passionate debates that this platform enabled have made an indelible mark on contemporary art in India, especially through what Geeta Kapur refers to as the 'cultural conjuncture' between art and documentary practice (see Kapur 2008). Although these debates may have formally entered the art world only in the twenty-first century, their lineage can be traced back through the films of Mani Kaul and Kamal Swaroop in the late 1980s, the Vision Exchange programme in the late 1960s, the Films Division productions of the 1960s and to 1940s popular cinema through filmmakers, writers and poets associated with the Progressive Writers Group and the Indian People's Theatre Association. Our objective in providing a cursory overview of these histories and events is to suggest that strict delineations of the space and form of art and documentary have periodically been challenged and conventions dismantled to generate new forms of participation, dialogue and audience engagement.[15]

We return now to *Loss and Transience*: the brief given to us by the Honggah Museum was to exhibit film and new media works from India, raising the usual questions about categorising the 'national'.[16] Avoiding any attempt to anthologise contemporary film movements, we sought to approach the process of curating as a practice where instability and change – which was also foremost in the projects that we identified – became the focus of engagement between our audiences and the work on display. Projects responding to very specific local and environmental urgencies over the last decade were selected; these included (among others) responses to rising levels of pollution in the Yamuna River, as well as the forced migration since 2019 of thousands of undocumented Muslims as a result of the Citizenship Amendment Act.[17] The exhibition's title, *Loss and Transience*, also referred to a particular moment of loss due to the COVID-19 pandemic, which in its second wave hit India particularly severely during the exhibition period. The documentaries and essay films featured in the exhibition included Abhinava Bhattacharyya's *Jamnapaar* (2017), Ambarien Alqadar's *The Ghetto Girl* (2011), Avijit Mukul Kishore's *The Garden of Forgotten Snow* (2017), Ayisha Abraham's *En Route or Of a Thousand Moons* (2011), Devshree Nath's *Noor Islam* (2019) and Madhusree Dutta's *7 Islands and a Metro* (2006). The artists' videos included works by Ranbir Kaleka (*Man with Cockerel*, 2002; *Fables from the House of Ibaan*, 2007; *Forest*, 2009), Gigi Scaria (*Hour Glass*, 2013; *Political Realism*, 2009; *Expanded*, 2015; *The Ark*, 2015), Mochu (*Wake*, 2008) and Ranu Mukherjee (*Home and the World*, 2015; *Succession*, 2018). The locations in India across which these projects were filmed spanned from Kashmir, Assam, Rajasthan, Delhi, Karnataka and Calcutta to Mumbai.

The combining of documentary films with artists' video installations within a single exhibition, although not uncommon in the history of exhibition, was an unusual approach for the Hong-gah Museum, which is known for the Taiwan International Video Art Exhibition (TIVA), a canonical video-art festival. The expectation of visiting audiences tends to bear heavily upon the kind of work that might be deemed acceptable or unacceptable by a museum's marketing team. There were several questions raised around the verbosity of some of the documentary films, and showing the films in Taiwan meant an elaborate process of getting the English subtitles translated into Mandarin. The far-from-ideal viewing conditions offered by museums and galleries for watching longer duration content did not dampen our decision to install documentary films along with artists' videos, as we sought to show creative responses rooted in activism along with work that used the transformative power of poetry and visual *poiesis* to address trauma or explored environmental exigencies through allegory and fable. This curatorial intervention sought to prompt audiences to identify connections in the 'in between-ness' of the films or artworks displayed, while rejecting art-historical categories that may make unbreachable distinctions between studio-based art practice and the more collective forms of documentary filmmaking.

In order to elucidate the implications of this cross-genre curatorial strategy, we offer a brief commentary on two works featured in *Loss and Transience* – a documentary film by Avijit Mukul Kishore and a video artwork by Ranbir Kaleka – focusing particularly on questions of 'spectatorial address'.[18]

The Garden of Forgotten Snow (dir. Avijit Mukul Kishore, 2017)

Avijit Mukul Kishore is a cinematographer and documentary filmmaker who has carved out a unique niche in making films about visual and contemporary artists.[19] He describes his process as a director/cinematographer who frequently collaborates with artists as a 'practice of translation', developed over time. His engagement with the eminent visual artist Nilima Sheikh, who is portrayed in *The Garden of Forgotten Snow* (henceforth referred to as *The Garden*), began when making *Sundari, an Actor Prepares* (1998), with theatre director Anuradha Kapur, in a film directed by curator/activist/filmmaker Madhusree Dutta, which included paintings by Bhupen Khakhar and Nilima Sheikh.[20] He produced another film with Dutta and Sheikh: *Scribbles on Akka* (2000), a theatrical/cinematic exploration of the female devotional body – drawing on the saint-poetess Akka

Mahadevi – and its relationship with Sheikh's work. Among several other films, he has produced a two-part documentary on twenty-seven Indian artists, *To Let the World In* (2013), in collaboration with art critic and curator Chaitanya Sambrani.[21]

The Garden presents Nilima Sheikh's reflections on her practice as a painter with close studies of her paintings from the series *Each Night Put Kashmir in Your Dreams* (produced between 2003 and 2010). Poems by the fourteenth-century mystic female poet Lal Ded and the twentieth-century American Kashmiri poet Agha Shahid Ali are read out as we view scenes of everyday life in Kashmir. Expansive landscapes and lakes glide across the richly coloured surfaces of the paintings, shown in microscopic detail, including their references to miniature painting traditions and Kashmiri embroidery patterns. Sheikh speaks about her long-term engagement with the history, literature and art of Kashmir, as well as her rejection of the false hierarchy between visual arts and crafts. She mentions her struggle with overcoming a 'guilt about engaging with certain traditional [craft] practices'; although the 'decorative arts' were rejected by many of the modernist/leftist intellectuals of her generation, she is interested in creating an Indian modernism rooted in older cultural and artistic traditions, including the crafts, which are integral to everyday life and sustenance for many communities.[22]

Figure 9.1 Detail, painting from the series *Each Night Put Kashmir in Your Dreams* by Nilima Sheikh, featured in the documentary *The Garden of Forgotten Snow* (2017) by Avijit Mukul Kishore. Image courtesy of Nilima Sheikh.

The Garden presents an interesting perspective on the representation of cultures from a close distance, or from a distant closeness, which is at the heart of any trans-locational practice. Both Mukul Kishore and Sheikh are Indian nationals coming to Kashmir as relative 'outsiders' not subject to its citizens' everyday conditions.[23] This article cannot address the entire scope and complexity of Kashmir's political life here; however, one has witnessed with horror the manner in which Kashmiri people were unconstitutionally stripped of their liberties overnight on 5 August 2019 by revoking Article 370 which protected their cultural rights.[24] The question therefore arises in the film, also addressed by the artist herself, about her choice to make artworks of such beauty in the context of Kashmir, where violence is enmeshed in everyday life.

Kishore mentions the difficulty of framing Kashmir through the camera lens as a cinematographer, drawing attention to the popular binary through which Kashmir has been depicted in Indian media either as a paradise on earth or, since the 1990s, as a place of terrorism, strife and violence perpetuated by militant groups as well as the Indian state.[25] Mukul Kishore describes working on this project as being a challenge of composing film frames that unravel these paradigms and contradictions in their full complexities.

For Sheikh, the process of trans-locationality, in being able to make work about Kashmir, began when she witnessed the trauma aftermath of the state-supported pogrom against Muslims in 2002 in Gujarat. She relates how, at this juncture, it was the poetry of Agha Shahid Ali that offered a route to begin to position herself in relation to Kashmir's history and ongoing troubles. The poetry, in that moment of crisis, gave space for other emotions; ones beyond the limitation of relating only to events within one's own locale. In a verse from Shahid Ali recited in the film, we are reminded of how poetry enables us to defy time, but also to shield ourselves from inescapable trauma:

> Don't tell my father I have died, he says, and I follow him through blood on the road. And hundreds of shoes they left behind at the funeral, victims of the firing. [...] Army convoys all night, like desert caravans. [...] Your history gets in the way of my memory. [...] I am everything you lost. You can't forgive me. Your memory gets in the way of my memory (Shahid Ali 1997, 11).

Shahid Ali's re-visitation of the disturbed valley is accompanied by inclusions in the film of super-8 footage of Sheikh's holidays spent in Kashmir as a child, adding one more layer of loss and memorial. In another scene, as the camera moves slowly across Sheikh's paintings, enlarging the minute details for us, we hear the following lines from Salman Rushdie's novel *Shalimar the Clown*: 'There are things, that must be looked at indirectly, because they would blind you, if you look them in the eyes. Like the fire of the sun. The village of Pachigam existed on the maps of Kashmir. But that day, it ceased to exist anywhere; except in memory' (Rushdie 2005, 309). The image on screen is of two women in Sheikh's painting: one covers her eyes with her hands, while the other behind her looks out into the near distance. We wonder what has made the woman cover her eyes, which the second woman is now seeing (out of frame).

The question of whether art is powerful enough to heal the atrocities of war, or to offer learning for future generations to humanise inhuman acts, was posed a long time ago by the German philosopher Theodore Adorno. Having witnessed the ravages of the Holocaust, Adorno claimed that 'to write poetry after Auschwitz is barbaric',[26] referring to the concentration camp exterminations where over a million Jews were killed by Nazis in Poland during the Second World War. Many writers and artists responded to Adorno's provocation, leading to new idioms and forms of expression devised to render the tragedies of human civilisation visible, more sharply.

The film and the paintings offer their vision on the vexed problem of representing Kashmir. Sheikh's primary interest is in discovering the multiple aspects of the history, lineage and political and social constructions of Kashmir, thus giving it a visibility beyond stereotypical and polarised views and opening up new vantage points, echoing Mukhul Kishore's own approach in the film.[27] The documentary, paintings and poetry powerfully engage with the ways in which art reaches across cultures when faced with questions that are impossible to answer.

At the Hong-gah Museum show, Kishore's film was installed on a single screen inside a small black-box in the gallery, where four documentary films were shown, one after the other, throughout the day. These included Abhinava Bhattacharyya's *Jamnapaar* (2017), Ambarien Alquadar's *Ghetto Girl* (2014) and Devashree Nath's *Noor Islam* (2019). The sound from the documentaries flowed into the room, and the single bench available to viewers meant that not more than two persons could view the film simultaneously. The viewing conditions sought to create an intimacy between the vastly different cultural, aesthetic and political contexts of the films' narratives, for viewers in Taipei. However, the process of cultural translation is extremely complex and unpredictable, and much work remains to be done here. Key questions of spectatorship and exhibition practices are crucially linked to grounded inter-disciplinary research drawing on audience studies, psychoanalysis and aesthetic theories.[28]

Ranbir Kaleka's Forest *(2009)*

Along a long wall of the gallery adjacent to the black box, a single screen showed the work of Ranbir Kaleka, one of India's most eminent visual artists, whose projects centre around memory, loss and human/ethical questions. This is a very unusual way of installing or encountering Kaleka's work which is usually shown as spectacular multi-screen projections, commanding the entire gallery space, and we place on record our gratitude to the artist for permitting his work to be shown on such a reduced scale, a constraint partially imposed by the resources at hand. However, showing the work on a single screen also contributed to our attempts at bringing documentary and video art into a shared frame of reference.[29]

Kaleka states that his work is often experienced as 'an artifact for a product of the imagination', allowing greater interpretive freedom for audiences to connect with the work's themes through their own interior life.[30] He is known for his innovative use of film projection techniques, especially after 1998, projecting video images onto pre-painted canvas and superimposing moving images onto still image to create an entirely distinct form, idiom and a new materiality of the image:

> There is the painted image and the image made of light. Both have been my interest. The painted image has a physical presence: it has its weight, it has gravity, it is tactile… And then there is the image made of light which has an aura of a presence. […] I wanted to see what would happen if I brought [together] the physicality of one with the non-physicality of the other. […] Time *sits* in a painting in a particular way, and it's not still time, it's not time stilled. And then there is cinematic time. I was looking to view these two times simultaneously, where the two gel together.[31]

Forest, too, demonstrates this inter-medial positioning between filmmaking and painting. It was originally presented at the Arario Gallery, Cheonan, Korea (2012), and later at the Nam Seoul Museum, projected onto a large painted canvas (3.4 × 6 metres), from floor to ceiling.[32] While our display of this work at the Hong-gah Museum on a 42-inch video monitor (alongside two other works by Kaleka)[33] diminished the immersive impact of the work, its performative characteristics remained as alluring in this more intimate setting.

Kaleka addresses human, cultural and environmental dilemmas, making no attempt to translate his visual iconography for the viewer. His method is one in which the world he establishes is deliberately an artifice, featuring protagonists who are symbolic, not real. In this 11-minute (looped) installation, we are transported into Kaleka's interior world as a painter in scenes that take place in a staged forest, conjured into an imaginary world. Both Mukul Kishore's and Kaleka's projects, within their different styles, collapse the distinction between the forms of spectatorship that have been theorised as being specific to painting and cinema. Mukul Kishore's method is dialogic: it enters the mental landscape of Sheikh, the painter, using her paintings as its vehicle, whereas Kaleka's work follows an oneiric logic experienced from its interior.[34]

Forest begins with a large theatre curtain opening to reveal an exterior setting: a clearing in a mythical forest. The characters move in slow-motion, sporadically appearing and disappearing magically. A man climbs a ladder and disappears up a tree; clothes fall randomly from the branches; flowers grow magically from the ground; a man is flagellating himself, while another man runs through the foliage chased by arrows. A lion enters, becoming the guardian of knowledge stored in a metaphorical bookcase, the animal symbolising the world of the imaginary. There is a suggestion that hidden atrocities are taking place off-set. The lion is driven away as the library is set on fire. Finally, a lion cub returns to a city which emerges from the ashes of destruction, flowers blooming from the burnt ground.

While Kaleka would not describe himself as an activist, *Forest* goes

Figure 9.2 Ranbir Kaleka, still from *Forest* (2009). Image reproduction courtesy of artist.

further than being a surreal tale. It implies that environmental sustainability crucially depends on inter-generational listening and exchange. Much of contemporary environmental discourse promotes the notion that sustaining the environment is a future-facing act of resisting or averting an imminent catastrophe. *Forest*, in this context, offers the less obvious view, such as that put forward by art historian and activist Yates McKee, that sustainability is 'articulated with historical concerns as much as with future-oriented appeals to the rights of generations to come' (McKee 2009, 71).

Forest's vision of human destruction is a revelation about rebirth through the powers of the imaginary; a kind of 'wake-up call', but one that applies different tactics than the ones we expect to see in documentary filmmaking, which have conventionally appealed to both reason and emotion. Kaleka, working more in the mode of fiction, makes use of allegory and fantasy to engage viewers. The exhibition of *Forest*, alongside other more politically discursive documentaries and essay films in *Loss and Transience*, mobilises their audiences by means of strikingly different aesthetics, to generate a more complex narrative of India or Indian documentary and video art.

Curatorial practice and translation

If one accepts that the point of curatorial work – or indeed, any creative work as an artist, filmmaker, writer, performer – is to enable different modes of seeing and experiencing the world in our immediate contexts, as well as in societies and cultures that are distant and removed, it generates a new challenge for classical interpretations of spectatorial address, which tend to treat the 'text' as a whole, as indeed we have done in the previous section. The fundamental difference in film studies between the 'spectator' and the 'audience' as quite distinct consumers of cinema throws an interesting light on the idea of 'collectivity' vis-à-vis the moving image. Two more terms need to be thrown into the mix here: 'mass' and 'publics'. At the outset, one might make it clear that gallery spaces within museums are mostly built to cater to small numbers of individual spectators, which may extend to an audience of multiple works held within a common space (and not of the same work, as would be the case in a movie theatre or a film festival). The notion of the mass is entirely alien to museum spaces; their audience and visitors usually have to undergo some kind of security check to gain entry to the site, hence surrendering the anonymity of the masses as a transactional act. The public is a very special category, which may intersect with fans in the case of popular cinema, and which carries with it an agency that could potentially be fatal for the powers-that-be.

The work of the curator, then, is to try to convert the lone spectator of the art gallery into an audience or public, in order to make possible a sense of collectivity. Admittedly, the joy of art is personal, while the pleasure of cinema is shared, in their systemic characteristics. The experience of an intimate viewing of a film or video, followed by a collective 'making sense of' or sharing of responses through discussions or special walk-throughs that deliver informational commentary on the exhibits is now a standard format followed in art museums. These were modes we leveraged in *Loss and Transience*, too, as this was the museum's preferred pedagogy, and in our concluding section below, we draw attention to one specific example to highlight the complexities of cross-cultural and trans-locational translation.

Through a special collaboration with Jamie Wyld, director of videoclub UK, a programme of online screenings, artists talks and panel discussions was organised as a collateral of the Hong-gah Museum's exhibition, particularly for students and audiences who would not be able to visit the exhibition in Taipei. Among these was a panel discussion with Mochu, Gigi Scaria, Nilima Sheikh and Avijit Mukul Kishore, with an intervention by the Taiwanese artist Li Kuei-Pi, proposed by the director of the Hong-gah Museum, Zoe Yeh. The event included complicated technical manoeuvres, with Zoe and Kuei-pi speaking to the audience in the Hong-gah Museum in-person, as well as to international audiences who had joined the discussion online, along with Mukul Kishore and Sheikh in the final talks session. The format planned was such that Rashmi would respond to Mukul's work as a filmmaker, through a free-flowing conversation, and Lucía would do likewise from her position as an artist, in response to Sheikh's work. Kuei-pi was to offer concluding observations from her position as a 'cultural translator' for the Taiwanese audience, since she had conducted a residency at Niv Art Centre, New Delhi, in 2017. Kuei-pi's website states that her work engages with 'transnational mobility and labor experience, in which she converts objects created from labor and intervenes in the labor process, transforming the meaning of the products to convey her critical viewpoints about the modern material world'.[35] The entire panel discussion involved a two-way process of live translation: everything that was spoken in English by the panelists was translated into Mandarin for the Taiwanese audience, and vice versa for the panelists and audiences joining online.

Many nuances may have been lost in translation; however, Kuei-pi's intervention primarily emerged from the experience of a 'tourist', seldom

Figure 9.3 Installation view of *Loss and Transience* at the Hong-gah Museum, Taipei, Taiwan, 2021. Image courtesy of Hong-gah Museum. Photo credit Hsiang-Ling Huang.

shifting beyond surficial 'impressions', reminding one of the many ill-informed colonial travelogues about India. As curators we had to respond nimbly to correct the simplistic narrative that was put forward by the Taiwanese artist, and larger geo-political and historical issues became apparent in the nature of the engagement that unfolded.

Experiences such as these continue to influence our own work as academics and curators, and we see trans-locationality as an important theoretical framework through which we can continue to develop a more nuanced and grounded understanding (and practice) of addressing normativity, power, privilege and difference. One of the important interventions in this context is proposed by the New York-based curator and writer Maura Reilly, through her idea of 'curatorial activism', a term she uses to designate the practice of organising art exhibitions with the principal aim of ensuring that certain constituencies of artists are no longer excluded from the master narratives of art. 'It is a practice', writes Reilly, 'that commits itself to counter-hegemonic initiatives that give voice to those who have been historically silenced or omitted altogether – and, as such, focuses almost exclusively on work produced by women, artists of colour, non-Euro-Americans, and/or queer artists' (2018, 17). Extending this important framework further through our work, we seek to interrogate the politics of trans-locationality through its many difficult dimensions, including the negotiation of perception, everyday experience, circumstance, history and the politics of solidarity.

Our discourse on trans-locationality is conditioned and generated by our positions as curators who have worked together for several years, and these are 'positions' to be continually questioned in a self-reflexive manner. Perhaps the work of curating cannot be other than an exposition of trans-locationality, extending (in social and spatial terms more than theoretically) into the sense by which we act and negotiate. Positionality alters dynamically among friends and interlocutors: exhibiting filmmakers, museum curators, partners, investors and audiences. We find the 'play' or oscillation between terms within the discourse to be of great significance here. The movement by which languages, artworks, films and their systems of reference become historically constituted is a continual interweaving of differences in flux.

Acknowledgement

The authors acknowledge the generosity of Nilima Sheikh, Ranbir Kaleka and Avijit Mukul Kishore who provided valuable information about their projects, as well as the images used in this article. We also thank all the exhibiting artists and Zoe Yeh as the Curator of the Hong-gah Museum, Taipei, for their contribution to the exhibition. *Loss and Transience* was financially supported by the University of Brighton, to whom we are also grateful.

Notes

1 Information on the network, its associates and past and current projects can be found at www.visionmix.info.
2 The film kicking off this trend was the hugely successful *Dilwale Dulhaniya Le Jayenge* (dir. Aditya Chopra, 1995, Hindi), soon followed by a number of films by Karan Johar, whose debut in this genre began with the 1998 Bollywood film *Kuch Kuch Hota Hai*.
3 Indicative titles include Kymlicka 1995; Parekh 2000; Modood 2010; and Brennan 2001.
4 A most influential text in this regard was Appadurai 1996.
5 For interventions in the visual and contemporary arts, see Reilly 2018.
6 'The idea of India' is a term that became popular through Sunil Khilnani's 1997 book by the same title, which alludes to the ideals of secularism, democracy, diversity and tenacity.
7 'The contemporary' is a term that marks a break from older art historical categories such as Modernism and the Avant-garde and that, over time, has become synonymous with 'conceptual art'. Influenced by critical theorists and philosophers ranging from

Giorgio Agamben to Walter Benjamin (and others), its interpretation has tended towards a 'sensation' or 'feeling' of co-existence across time and space, rather than generic or formal characteristics. See Benjamin 1968; Agamben 2009; Raqs Media Collective 2010; and Koepnick 2014.
8 Lucía. I. King's doctoral dissertation obtained from the SOAS, University of London, is on post-1990s Indian experimental documentary filmmaking practices. She spent several years living in India, explaining her abiding interest in South Asian film and media culture.
9 Rashmi was teaching at the School of Arts and Aesthetics (SAA), Jawaharlal Nehru University, New Delhi, at the time, and the collaboration started through a conference that Lucía had earlier proposed to host at SAA.
10 Sheba Chhachhi is a renowned artist and photographer; Gigi Scaria is a video artist and sculptor; Asim Waqif is an installation artist known for his public art work; Atul Bhalla is a conceptual artist working on environmental issues; Sunil Gupta is a photographer, writer and activist; Marc Isaacs, Anupama Srinivasan, Adele Tulli and Priyanka Chhabra are documentary filmmakers; Pallavi Paul is a video artist and writer; Moutushi Chakraborty is a painter and Alia Syed is an experimental filmmaker and artist. For more detail, see https://www.visionmix.info.
11 Many of the theorists/critics cited here were also faculty members of the School of Arts and Aesthetics, Jawaharlal Nehru University (JNU), at the time of the workshop: cultural theorist and dramaturge Rustom Bharuch, artist and art critic Shukla Sawant and art historian Parul Dave Mukherji were based at the School of Arts and Aesthetics, JNU; literary and cultural theorist Brinda Bose was in the English department at JNU. João Laia was curator of Videobrasil, Sao Paolo, at the time (now chief curator at Kiasma, Helsinki); Pheobe Wong was curator at Videotage, Hong Kong; Lata Mani, Charu Maithani and Shaunak Sen are independent scholars and filmmakers. Sen's film *All That Breathes* won the L'Œil d'or Award for best documentary at the 2022 Cannes Film Festival.
12 Leela Gandhi's 'politics of friendship' in this forum was a discussion around the ethics of 'solidarities' where these converge around concepts of nation, locality, community, race, gender and sex. Her position (albeit impossible to summarise in a footnote) prioritises the 'minor politics' of friendship, as understood from the vantage point of decentralisation, anarchy, horizontality and anti-coloniality; networks able to resist and re-set the more traditional forms of community mobilisation, such as labour unions or political parties that engage directly with state systems. For a more detailed elaboration of this concept, see Gandhi 2006.
13 Visible Evidence XXI was jointly organised by documentary filmmakers Shohini Ghosh and Sabeena Gadihoke from the Media Research and Communication Centre, Jamia Milia Islamia University, Delhi, and faculty at the School of Arts and Aesthetics, JNU, Delhi. Conference details are available at https://www.visibleevidence.org/conference/visible-evidence-xxi-2/.
14 Indicative titles include Chatterjee 2021; Deshpande 2020; and Misrahi-Barack et al. 2020.
15 The locus of spectatorship when moving away from black box (festival/theatrical) screening is also instrumental to questions of audience address and the mode of engagement with screened experience – for example, how corporeal immersion in the

work, being able to move around the screen, projections onto objects and public sites influence the interpretation of the work.
16 Attempting to distil what 'national' meant raised various questions for us. Were we expected to limit ourselves to artists and filmmakers who lived and worked in India, or could the remit include diasporic artists living in other parts of the world? Could the scope include Bangladeshi and Pakistani artists as residents of a former pre-nation subcontinent? These are delicate issues in the South Asian geo-political context, where acts of inclusion can also be mistaken as the negation of other sovereignties.
17 The Citizenship Amendment Act of 2019 was passed by the Parliament of India on 11 December 2019 as the BJP party's amendment of the 1955 Citizenship Act, which provided a pathway to Indian religious-minority citizenship from India's surrounding nations, who had arrived in India before the end of December 2014. The new law, however, excluded Muslim citizens from these neighbouring Muslim-majority countries. The act was therefore criticised for its overt use of anti-Muslim criteria for granting citizenship under Indian law, as well as for denying citizenship to many who already had settled in India at the time when the act was passed.
18 Until what came to be known as the 'cultural turn' in the 1990s, much of film theory focused on issues of spectatorship and 'spectatorial address' – such as the large and influential body of work in the 1970s (driven by the journal *Screen*) drawing on psychoanalysis and ideology to demystify the cinematic apparatus, the gaze, point-of-view and so on. Since reference to this influential material is beyond the scope of this essay, we presume that readers are familiar with these foundational aspects of film history and theory.
19 Mukul Kishore works in documentary films and inter-disciplinary moving-image practices, often collaborating with visual artists on video and film-based art works. His works have been shown at Documenta 14 at Athens, the Chicago Architecture Biennial and the Dhaka Art Summit, in addition to several film festivals, academic and cultural spaces. His films as director include *The Garden of Forgotten Snow, Squeeze Lime in Your Eye, Nostalgia for the Future* (co-directed with Rohan Shivkumar), *Vertical City, To Let the World In* and *Snapshots from a Family Album*. His films as cinematographer include *Lovely Villa, Kumar Talkies, Kali Salwaar (The Black Garment), John and Jane, 7 Islands and a Metro, Bidesia in Bambai, I am Micro* and *An Old Dog's Diary*.
20 Bhupen Khakhar (1934–2003), self-trained painter, artist and writer, became one of the most iconic figures of the Baroda School of Art in the second half of the twentieth century.
21 *To Let the world In* (2013) is a documentary in two volumes, featuring conversations with ten of India's leading artists of two generations born in the 1940s and 1950s, as well as the 1960s and 1970s. Artists featured include Arpita Singh, Gulam Mohammed Sheikh, Vivan Sundaram, Nilima Sheikh, Nalini Malani, Sudhir Patwardhan, Ranbir Kaleka, Pushpamala N., Anita Dube and Atul Dodiya, as well as art critic and curator Geeta Kapur. The artists talk about the evolution of their practices, fondly invoking the memory of Bhupen Khakhar, a key artist of the group, who had passed away in 2003. The second volume of the film looks at a period of monumental change in art-practice in India, following economic liberalisation and the resurgence of religious fundamentalism in politics.
22 Quoted from Nilima Sheikh, from the video documentation of a panel discussion held as part of *Loss and Transience*, 27 March 2021.

23 Sheikh qualifies that, although she is an 'outsider', she was already familiar with the valley through frequent childhood visits, which informed her work long before consciously engaging with Kashmir in her painting series (correspondence with the artist, 1 November 2021).
24 On this date, India's parliament passed a resolution to revoke the temporary special status, granted under Article 370 of the Constitution to Jammu and Kashmir, which consisted of the larger part of Kashmir and a disputed territory between India, Pakistan and China since 1947. Thousands of security forces were deployed to curb any uprising, and leading Kashmiri politicians were imprisoned, including the former chief minister. Government officials justified the revocation, claiming that it was enabling people to access government programmes such as reservation, rights to education and so on. The Kashmir Valley was effectively reduced to silence through the suspension of communication and imposition of Section 144 (curfew) in this Muslim-majority area.
25 Panel discussion held online as part of *Loss and Transience*, 27 March 2021.
26 This is a much-cited passage from 'Cultural criticism and society' by Theodor Adorno (1949 [1983]).
27 Because information about Kashmiri painting histories is scant, she explores Persian, Turkish and Central Asian sources as a 'stand-in' for that unknown history. Kashmir is extremely rich in crafts, but in her account most histories of painting traditions focus on the Shaivite iconic paintings or see other Kashmiri paintings as an offshoot of the Persianate tradition. Her practice thus becomes a 'fabricated history' drawn from a decades-long research process.
28 An interesting reference in this context is Raminder Kaur and Parul Dave Mukerjee's 2014 book *Art and aesthetics in a globalising world*, which frames its enquiry through anthropology and aesthetics in a globalising (rather than a national context). Situated thus, contributors to the book remain attentive to the power dynamics that establish norms, practices and expectations within the artistic domain.
29 Perhaps one of the reasons why museums and galleries prefer shorter, non-narrative works is precisely because of the complexities of interpretation by diverse audiences. More 'poetic' work that hinges on the power of images and sound alone (rather than speech or narrative) may evoke a more immediate and sensory response from audiences across cultural contexts. Narrative and the spoken word, on the other hand, are among the central ethical and emotive considerations for documentary films, and this has implications for their exhibition and audiences.
30 Personal correspondence with Lucía I. King, 4 November 2021.
31 Kaleka, quoted from *VisionMix Short Cuts* (dir. Lucía Imaz King, 2014).
32 Lalitha Gopalan comments that Kaleka's artworks centre on the question of the video's ontology, by staging what she calls a 'theory of adjacency'. Reading the intermedial links of Kaleka's video works are 'another way of reading the propinquity between mediums, despite the distinctiveness that is afforded by the distance between [painting and film]' (Gopalan, in Sareen 2018, 144).
33 The other works screened were *Man with Cockerel* (2002) and *Fables from the House of Ibaan* (2007).
34 For a detailed discussion of this oneiric/poetic logic in the work, see Sareen 2018.
35 http://www.likueipi.com.

Works Cited

Adorno, T. (1949 [1983]). Cultural criticism and society. In *Prisms*, 17–34. Cambridge, MA: The MIT Press.

Agamben, G. (2009). What is the contemporary? In *What is an apparatus? and other essays*, trans. D. Kishik and S. Pedatella, 39–53. Palo Alto: Stanford University Press.

Appadurai, A. (1996). *Modernity at large: Cultural dimensions of globalization*. Minneapolis: University of Minnesota Press.

Bal, M. (2009). Migratory aesthetics. *Irish Review*, 39, 93–100.

Bayraktar, N. (2017). Introduction: Cinematic/artistic takes on migration and mobility in contemporary Europe. In *Mobility and migration in film and moving image art: Cinema beyond Europe*, 1–22. New York and London: Routledge.

Benjamin, W. (1968). Theses on the philosophy of history. In H. Arendt (ed.), *Illuminations*, trans. H. Zohn, 253–63. New York: Schochen Books.

Brennan, T. (2001). Cosmopolitanism and internationalism. *New Left Review*, 7, 75–84. https://newleftreview.org/issues/ii7/articles/timothy-brennan-cosmopolitanism-and-internationalism.pdf [accessed 12 November 2023].

Chatterjee, M. (ed.) (2021). *Moving focus, India: New perspectives on modern and contemporary art*. Mumbai and Stockholm: Shoestring Publisher.

Deshpande, S. (2020). *Halla bol: The death and life of Safdar Hashmi*. New Delhi: Leftword.

Gandhi, L. (2006). *Affective communities: Anticolonial thought, fin-de-siècle radicalism, and the politics of friendship*. Durham: Duke University Press.

Gopalan, L. (2018). Intermedial circularities in Ranbir Kaleka's video works. In H. Sareen (ed.), *Ranbir Kaleka: Moving image works*, 138–61. Berlin: Kerber Verlag.

Kapur, G. (2008). A cultural conjuncture: Art into documentary. In T. Smith, O. Okwui Enwezor and N. Condee (eds), *Antimonies of art and culture: Modernity, postmodernity, contemporaneity*, 30–59. Durham: Duke University Press.

Kaur, R., and Mukerjee, P. D. (eds) (2014). *Arts and aesthetics in a globalizing world*. London: Bloomsbury.

Khilnani, S. (1997). *The idea of India*. New York: Farrar, Straus & Giroux.

King, L. I., and Sawhney, R. D. (eds) (2018) Special issue: South Asia moving image. *Moving Image Review and Arts Journal*, 7(2).

Koepnick, L. (2014). *On slowness: Toward an aesthetic of the contemporary*. New York: Columbia University Press.

Kymlicka, W. (1995). *Multi-cultural citizenship: A liberal theory of minority rights*. Oxford: Oxford University Press.

McKee, Y. (2009). Questionnaire on 'The Contemporary'. *October*, 130(3), 63–73.

Misrahi-Barack, J., Satyanarayana, K., and Thiara, N. (2020). *Dalit text: Aesthetics and politics reimagined*. New Delhi: Routledge.

Modood, T. (2010). *Still not easy being British: Struggles for a multi-cultural citizenship*. Stoke-on-Trent: Trentham Books.

Mukul Kishore, A. (2018) 'You've told me that three times now': Propaganda/anti-propaganda in the Films Division India documentary, 1965–75. *Moving Image Review and Art Journal*, 7(2), 222–35.

Naficy, H. (2001). *An accented cinema*. Princeton: Princeton University Press.

Parekh, B. (2000), *Rethinking multiculturalism: Cultural diversity and political theory*. Cambridge, MA: Harvard University Press.
Raqs Media Collective (2010). Now and Elsewhere. *e-flux, 12*. https://www.e-flux.com/journal/12/61337/now-and-elsewhere/ [accessed 12 November 2023].
Reilly, M. (2018). *Curatorial activism: Towards an ethics of curating*. London: Thames and Hudson.
Rushdie, S. (2005). *Shalimar the Clown*. London: Jonathan Cape.
Sareen, H. (2018). *Ranbir Kaleka: Moving image works*. Berlin: Kerber Verlag.
Sawhney, R. (ed.) (2022). *The vanishing point: Moving images after video*. New Delhi: Tulika.
Sawhney, R. (2021). Between screen and gallery. In P. Mitter, P. D. Mukherji and R. Balaram (eds), *20th century Indian art: Modern, post-independence, contemporary*, 480–81. London: Hudson and Thames.
Shahid Ali, A. (1997). I see Kashmir from New Delhi at Midnight. In *The country without a post office*, 11. New Delhi: Ravi Dayal Publisher.
Stallabrass, J. (2013). Contentious relations: Art and documentary. In *Documentary*, from the series 'Documents of contemporary art'. London: Whitechapel Gallery/The MIT Press.

Films Cited

7 Islands and a Metro. Dir. Madhusree Dutta. Majlis Productions. 2006.
En Route or Of a Thousand Moons. Dir. Ayisha Abraham. 2011. (8 mm, digitally transferred).
Jamnapaar. Dir. Abhinava Bhattacharyya. 2017.
Noor Islam. Dir. Devshree Nath. 2019.
The Garden of Forgotten Snow. Dir. Avijit Mukul Kishore. 2017.
The Ghetto Girl. Dir. Ambarien Alqadar. Public Service Broadcasting Trust. 2011.

10

Working with time: Editing the documentary

Sameera Jain

The process of non-fiction editing typically negotiates several potential emerging structures and keeps the director and editor in a state of alertness, with all possibilities open, making continuous choices, engaging with transformations that occur as the work evolves, seeing forms emerge that are yet unknown, latent somewhere. There are new discoveries of the documentary moment; sightings of unanticipated relationships between the mundane and the metaphorical; the sensing and enabling, of resonance.

Writing about this is difficult, as the editor's work is complex and multi-faceted and disappears right into the body of the work as the film grows. It is amorphous and overwhelming, and I have not figured it all out, at all. I approach it tentatively, sharing some thoughts as I go along. There is intensive labour, and many creative turns taken while engaging with the multiple content-form mysteries that constitute the film. But these need rambling time to share, hence I will keep them to a minimum. I write with reference to some of my own work as editor and director, and to student work that I have mentored. I will keep to circumstances where the edits have had some freedom from imposed templates or censorship.

I am trying to find a way to start with something small. The first glimmer comes like this … *A Season Outside* (1997).[1] The film carries a series of reflections and interrogations concerning conflict, and violence:

> The tree on the left is ours
> But the two trees in the centre are theirs.
> Do you know of a way to relate to wheat fields with gigantic transparent walls?
> On the outside, and in the inside
>   Deep inside you discover particles with different truths
> And in the flash of their haughty orbits probably lie the roots of violence

> You could have your position and you could be armed with your truth
> But what happens if instead you start arming your truth?

One may imagine that the edit would be made simpler by the overarching frame of the text within which it moves. Yet, the film posed a series of challenges, and I will write of just one of them here. It was to do with sound and silences. In a timeline that was being led by a voice that spoke almost relentlessly, the silences were critically important, and I do not mean just silences on the soundtrack, but silences in the edit itself, in the movement of time in the film. In case this suggests otherwise, let me clarify that this is not a long-duration film with lengthy shots. The film moves swiftly across conceptual, temporal and geographical terrains, within thirty minutes. It feels like watching an hour-long film, and most viewers are surprised by the actual duration.

Silence, sound and time

With *A Season Outside*, we had to deal with a fresh understanding of silence really, reckoning with how many kinds of silence can exist, exploring the nature of a pause in cinema, music, text. As we worked, the emerging timeline suggested music, the kind of music that could build with time precisely and minimally, yet with intensity and strength.[2]

Given that both arts move in time, a cinema timeline working well with music is no surprise. What is interesting here is that the movement was contrary to what is usually the process, wherein music is composed closer to the completion of the film and laid into the track. In this instance, the edit itself started to suggest the need for a structuring of silence, and of sound. The kind of decisions taken while editing – of cut point, pace, rhythm, transition – seemed to ask for an equally exact soundscape. This music, once composed and edited in, was doing the absolute opposite of what we may normally ask of music. It was not creating seamlessness, not *covering* the cuts. In fact, each cut was made more visible by it. Usually, when music is laid over a film *after* it is edited, all the cut points, rhythms, sensory and cerebral meanings can shift and change. In my experience, sound and music are as much part of the editor's palette as the image. One has sometimes wished that the film be left to a sound expert to complete after the edit is done, but alas.

Working with student editors and filmmakers is a reminder of this intrinsic connection between image, time, sound all the time. Viewing a twenty-second shot without sound, its interminable time is felt. Add a low ambience, and the perception of duration halves. Put in a bird chirp in the middle of the shot, and the sense of duration alters again. Rhythm and pace, the very core of cinema, do not withstand a mathematical analysis. Twenty seconds can feel like forty, or ten... depending on the interaction between several elements. This rhythm is at times distinctly apparent and sometimes inconspicuous, but regardless, the film is rooted in it.

While editing, it is clear that it is not just about the narrative (or non-narrative) line, but how it moves in time. It is so much about moulding, playing, stretching, contracting time. For those of us who have edited for many years, these insights sort of pickle their way in, as does the short-sightedness of the view that editing is about how many accomplished cuts can be made in a film.[3] It is so much about feeling the pulse of the movement of time, connecting with rhythm in different dimensions, and about discovering how sometimes a saturated moment can express the most complex meanings.

In the student film *Sudhamayee* (*Laced with the Nectar of Life*, 2019),[4] when two people sit at a table and a lull in the conversation occurs, the cameraperson-filmmaker, responding to the hiatus, lets it expand and continues filming. Her mother and her sister share a silence. Seen on the edit

Figure 10.1 *Sudhamayee* (*Laced with the Nectar of Life*, 2019) by Megha Acharya (student film from the course Creative Documentary, New Delhi). Picture courtesy of author.

table, the shot yields no meaning at first. There is no *action*, and almost no dialogue.

Spatial and temporal continuity and the creative use of discontinuity is always discussed when studying editing, but how do we explore the continuity of time, even in a pause? Interestingly, we find that the opposite of action – stillness – and the opposite of sound – silence – can start to be felt and speak aloud, as it is here, where the connection with the image occurs precisely because it is not trying to say or do anything. The breathing space facilitates a reconnection. Freed from *doing*, the filmed and the person filming flow in and out of the scene.

Rhythm and structure

Sometimes, while immersed in editing, it is only possible to respond and create rhythm in the minutiae. Each cut holds a moment and punctuates a rhythm; rhythms that are grounded in the movement of time, its resonance and evocations, and the thought, emotion, gesture, movement, or stillness. Often, one finds that the larger rhythm of the film arises from within this weave.

Rhythm emanates. It is found while working, and so is the point at which to cut. The exact same cut point on a shot (almost to the frame) has uncannily been arrived at after having been away from an edit for weeks, uncovering a latent relationship between internal rhythms and the rhythm matrix of the film – visual, aural and temporal. It follows that one needs to be completely present to be able to edit sensibly at all. The work of editing has to be done, ideally, with the editor in an `alright' state, mentally or physically not too stressed; not sleep-deprived, or too tired, or hungry, or cold – any factor that could potentially throw off a person from themselves.

I am sometimes reminded of the deep dream world of a cat, within which it is simultaneously on full alert, ready to spring into action with a calm and instinctive intelligence that is enviable. While editing, I would aspire to be as observant and present as that eternally inward, deep-breathing cat: keeping alive the unlearned, the spontaneous, yet also retaining a sharp awareness, attentive to all lurking significance. Director and editor inhabit and distil all this as they view, assimilate and organise, working with a rigorously planned edit script that usually goes through several mutations. The shape of the film starts to appear, responding to, answering and completing the intentions contained within the rushes.

But in some documentary edits, another framework imposes itself on the material, a prefabricated one. In the rhetorical mode that sometimes uses the enemy's language, the kind of thinking that is being contested is replicated, to counter it. The argument spins around itself, tires itself out. The viewer does not have to do much thinking, the case is over, the truth is told.

What Hito Steyerl writes is very pertinent here:

> Superficially, or on the content level, many documentary articulations seemed to erode or even attack unfair power structures. But on the level of form, by relying on authoritative truth procedures, the conventional documentaries have intensified the aura of the court room, the penitentiary or the laboratory within a field of art, which was already quite saturated with these mechanisms […] As is well known, documentary production has taken on forensic duties for a long time, and has functioned in the service of a large-scale epistemological enterprise that is closely linked with the project of Western colonialism. Reporting the so-called truth about remote people and locations has been closely linked to their domination. Not only mainstream documentary truth procedures, but even the features of the photographic technology, based as they are on military technology, testify to this historical link (Steyerl 2007, 5–6).

And so it comes to be that the language of the aggressor's propaganda and of the voice who speaks for the victim become similar. The representation is in contradiction to the overt political stance. This seems to defeat its purpose, demeaning both the viewer and itself. Yet, documentary relentlessly borrows its manner from common expositions in journalism, and from the missionary mandate of predominant educational modes. The educational, aiming at helping the audience understand, may dumb down, sugarcoat, or over-explain. Both occasionally overlap with one another, and both alienate the audience. In this kind of work, the labours of editing result in a pre-formulated messaging, and one wonders if a machine could have done this instead, once we feed in the rushes with labels *for, against, neutral* and so on. After all, we do have AI software that is already being used for some fiction where the categories (happy, sad, intense, slow, fast and so on) enable the AI to sort the rushes and execute basic edits.

Less, and more

Explanation and conclusion do not spark interest or leave much room for a continuing search. I find that less can be more and make a genuine connection. There are several examples, but for now I refer to a segment from a film I made a while back, *Mera Apna Sheher* (*My Own City*, 2011).[5] The film works with observations in public spaces, including recurring views from a balcony that looks down on the street in a middle-class residential area. The camera sits there and does not move to frame anything, just quietly witnessing the passing everydayness – the women and girls moving about only with a purpose, the men and boys being able to loiter, hang around, have a peaceful smoke and so on. One day, there was a small accident on this road, which triggered insults being hurled at the person driving one of the cars, a hired driver.

The framing is off centre, and we miss seeing some part of the action. This stimulated curiosity; the viewer was straining to see and hear, absorbing more than if the camera had panned to show more than what was visible in the originally set frame. There are no explanations or details – no close-ups, cut-aways or cut-ins – and you get involved without the cameraperson's volition being present. Much of the visual sense in the film was about being still, like a pebble on the side of the road, observing all, manifesting what is rendered obscure by predominant modes of observation, to allow a space to understand that many experiences have remained unacknowledged, lurking under the surface. Not revealing fully, letting the

Figure 10.2 The accident filmed from a balcony in *Mera Apna Sheher* (2011). Picture courtesy of author.

impressions from the film seep through the tiny crevices of the everyday into the textures of the viewer's lives.

I will mention a quite dissimilar instance here, from *A Quiet Little Entry* (2010) by Uma Chakravarti.[6] I am only describing a small part here from a film that reflects the interior world of a woman through diary entries, objects carefully saved away in a trunk, women's voices, song and music.

An actor evokes the protagonist Subbalakshmi. As she writes in her diary, her dark head is framed against the grills of a window from which she looks out, into greenery outside. Seeing the back of the woman's head allows an entry to her interior world actively, perhaps much more than looking at an emotive face would, at this point in the film. Then a voice speaks: 'One day, Subbalakshmi wrote only two lines, from one of Tagore's poems, perhaps. When shall my heart find its haven of rest. When shall my heart find repose'. The pages of the diary turn as we trace Subbalakshmi's journey.

Less often becomes more; in fact, most obviously in a device well-known in fiction – suspense. Surprising connections surface between a

Figure 10.3 Still from *A Quiet Little Entry* (2010) by Uma Chakravarti. Picture courtesy of author.

fairly conventional technique and an aspect of form employed by someone as radical and rigorous as Robert Bresson.[7]

I am sharing here the oft-quoted and always helpful example of editing to reveal rather than explain, as described by Bresson in *Notes on the Cinematographer* (1975, 54):[8] 'Let the cause follow the effect, not accompany it or precede it'.

> The other day I was walking through the gardens by Notre-Dame and saw approaching a man whose eyes caught something behind me, which I could not see: at once they lit up. If, at the same time as I saw the man, I had perceived the young woman and the child towards whom he now began running, that happy face of his would not have struck me so; indeed, I might not have noticed it (54).

Another example comes to mind: it is from a fiction film, but I will cite it anyway, as it is so relevant to non-fiction as well. It is from Bela Tarr's *Turin Horse* (2011).[9] The film is permeated with the unexpected, despite its depiction of the repetitive everyday, and the smallness of its canvas. In a sequence about an hour into the film, the father is seen chopping wood, and then the camera slowly starts to pull out, showing the daughter washing clothes. As the movement continues, it further reveals the father putting up a clothesline, painstakingly knotting the rope with his one able hand. By then, she has completed her washing and starts to hang the clothes on the line. It is one shot, about four minutes long, ending with a close-up of the texture of a wet cloth on the line. The mise-en-scène, the sensorial quality in image and sound and the carefully paced movement, make each detail in these lives an event, a revelation, imbued with a sense of the quality of life and labour. A whole world comes to be contained in these mundane acts. There are many such disclosures and complexities in the film, making the portrayal larger than just the meaning of what the action is. These evoke a quality of keen expectation, and the viewer may be found holding their breath in a film where hardly anything *happens*.

It is interesting to see how this kind of relationship between cause and effect is valuable in documentary and fiction: technically, to keep interest going and potentials alive, not presenting closed storylines; ethically, as a way of including the viewer, stimulating receptiveness; aesthetically, imbuing the movement of time with openness and exploration; and philosophically, creating a space which is uncharted, rather than fixing and limiting meaning. This allows the non-linear, the poetic, even the disjunctive, a place.

Yet, while working I have sometimes felt an invisible pull, a reluctant kinship with a kind of mainstream way of editing non-fiction, whether it be the issue-based documentary, or the character-driven one. In this mode, the visual and aural can largely become a support to a primarily textual logic. The image then is either used for its indexical value (this is real, this is information) or as an embellishment (attractive/spectacular/beautiful/ evocative), rather than as an essential cinematic factor. Editing with this default approach, one wonders how much the viewer becomes involved, how much thinking or feeling they do.

Constructing an experience

In the context of construction, I would like to share the experience of a lecture that I happened to attend in 2018. It was a talk by David Shulman,[10] in New Delhi. Here are excerpts from a description of the talk, from the text circulated by the organisers:

> In the lecture, Prof. Shulman explored aspects of human wickedness as seen, first, in a sixteenth-century south Indian text and then in the field, in Israeli-occupied Palestinian territories in the South Hebron hills. […] The tale of Nigamaśarma, a seemingly incorrigible rogue who turns out to be capable of becoming a human being. This transformation speaks to a transition within a person from ruthless egoism to a capability of feeling love – a mysterious transformation, perhaps meant to model facets of the human mind as understood in early-modern south India. […] Beginning with this suggestive story, […] he moved on to the speaker's first-hand experiences of wickedness enacted by Israeli settlers, soldiers, and policemen in the occupied West Bank. Wickedness can involve acts of overt, sadistic cruelty, but more often, it is a subtle movement in the self, one that involves what can only be called a choice. Concrete examples of such moments illustrate the argument and speak to questions of universal moral choices. All of us face such decisions, seemingly minor but possibly heavy with consequence, every day. Unlike 'evil', a term suggesting a somewhat abstract and impersonal force, wickedness comes from the whole person and bears the marks of her or his character.
>   What determines the direction an individual chooses for his or her actions? How are we to understand the inner decision to inflict gratuitous cruelty on innocents? (Shulman 2018)

As described by this summary, the talk moved between Nigamaśarma's tale and the occupied West Bank. It was absorbing, and the time passed rapidly. The talk energised and expanded, instilling a feeling that many transformations are possible; so much had been opened up in just about an hour.

Every time Shulman read excerpts from the sixteenth-century South Indian Tamil text (translated into English), he would indicate that he was doing so, by using a Koodiyattam-like hand gesture. This gesture was a marker of the shift, each time. A simple, indicative, unlaboured transition between parallel narratives that illuminated each other, building a composite. I will not try to describe the substance of this parallel cutting, nor attempt to encapsulate the talk, which I will surely fail badly at, particularly in the face of his easy, deep eloquence. It was only in retrospect that I realised why the talk may be particularly engaging for a film editor.

Even while discussing the ethical, and despite his intensely political concerns, David Shulman did not speak didactically. The audience entered the terrain with him, the routineness of violence and wickedness, and the madness that seemed to possess everyone. The transmission was strong, communicating two facets simultaneously – the necessity for courage to confront injustice and wickedness, and the necessity for a pervasive compassion. His approach gave the audience the liberty to draw their own conclusions. We became active participants, weaving our own narratives along with those that Shulman spoke about. This is what guided the structure of the talk, which was really a performance, a quiet one.

At some point, he started to project some images behind him – of the people and the landscape. The images did not illustrate the arguments that he was making. He was not using a pointer; he was not helping us see something in them. They just went on changing in the background (eventually in a loop), and as we received them, they kept varying in affect and meaning, resonating with the movement of our own thoughts. The audience worked with the images, inside themselves. This was the opposite of an illustrated lecture. Simply and unassumingly, the template was sidestepped, to great effect. To see how this was achieved is to look at a felt need to communicate. Given the speaker's commitment to activism and conversation, it should be no surprise that he did not use any pre-existing formats. A new form was found.

I recall another expression where the very construction enabled the viewer to receive. *No Home Movie* (2015),[11] Chantal Akerman's last film, stimulates thoughts about how form can be arrived at, and what it could be driven by. Here, too, in a different historical context, there are echoes of conflict, violence and pain. The director's mother is a survivor of Auschwitz. The film is imbued with a tenderness and melancholy that can only come from love. Akerman films her mother, often using long-duration shots. This is a character-driven film with a difference. The person and her various facets are not *action* to help determine cutting points, but punctuations that inhabit the temporal landscape and imbue it with its own particular rhythm.

It comes easily, to call some of the lengthy shots (particularly the tracking shots in a desert landscape) meditative. Yet, that somehow reduces and obfuscates what they do. The shots are energised and saturated with thought and feeling, hence time is felt and read in a certain way. The shots absorb, the person watching enters their own interiority and comes back. The image and sound become permeated with oneself, the viewer makes the cinema their own and has an almost palpable sensation of it, a kind of mirroring. *Meditative* usually suggests that the work is slow and deliberate, maybe even *poetic*. But that is not it; there is much more going on here. The duration is like a vehicle for getting under the skin of the film. The rhythm and pace take their cue from the shot material to define the movement of the film. The editing is precise, meticulous. It is clear that long duration cannot be confused with excess or laziness!

The politics of representation

> … the political importance of documentary forms
> does not primarily reside in their subject matter,
> but in the ways in which they are organised.
> It resides in articulations.
> (Steyerl 2007, 6)

While editing, one cannot but engage with these organisations, in the process complicating and destabilising conventional non-fiction narrative, navigating the politics of representation and initiating the emergence of new articulations. In student work, these negotiations are interesting to see. When working freely, willing to be lost, uncertain, vulnerable, experimenting, exploring, researching, all sorts of breakthroughs come about. Several cases in point: what began as journalistic investigation into river pollution comes to be imbued with enquiries around the Anthropocene and visions of past and future; a denunciation of the ruling Right starts to listen attentively and find meaning in casual conversations permeated with searing critique at a small-town café; an exploration of same-sex love eschews the interview format and connects with Urdu poetry, Sufi song at local shrines and women in caves writing letters of desire. Naturally, the edits are challenging and adventurous, unlikely to want or be able to follow any given moulds.

It is exciting to see how the relationship between form and content plays out in different situations, and how much the work ends up speaking about intentions. There is the portrayal which, even while claiming to empathise with poverty, creates a pornography of it, and the one which, even while claiming to condemn violence against women, titillates in its depiction of the violence, and so many more... the exoticisation of the other, the stereotyping, homogenisation and the patronising portrayal. While editing, one glimpses this again and again: the space between the purported purpose and the actual experience of the cinema. This space asserts its presence in creating meaning and makes visible the relationship between the ethical and the aesthetic.

At the micro-level of editing detail, the communication shifts and changes when alerted to aesthetic nuance, and these shifts can transform the import of the depiction. I will share an example again from *A Quiet Little Entry* (2011). Having done a rough cut, we did the right thing and took a break for a few days, so as to return to the film with renewed eyes and ears. The film uses music and song based on Subramania Bharatiyar's poetry. About fifteen minutes into the film, emerging from Subbalakshmi's diary, there comes a song, against images of a full moon seen through the dark silhouette of a tree: 'Bewitching my entire being. Oh moon! How captivating is your light! How can I describe you, Oh moon!' (*A Quiet Little Entry*, 2011).

Quite intuitively, the director felt that something was amiss about the audio level at which the song was playing in the rough sound mix. It was creating a meaning, an emphasis that was not right for the film. She suggested that the volume be lowered a little. I did so, and we watched that section of the film again. Lo and behold! The problem was solved. At a certain decibel level, the song had become a proclamation, and when the level was dipped, the song went into a deeper, more internal space that sat more comfortably with the moon in the branches. Only a slight change in the volume altered affect and meaning at that point in the film.

Much of this sort of thinking occurs only in retrospect. You touch upon a possibility; the reasoning comes later. At the time, even if in a nebulous way, one knows in a flash, somehow subliminally, if the thing is working right or not. It is very clear. The editing decisions embed themselves in the body of the film, becoming imperceptible in themselves.

Which image is useful? Or, the politics of selection

I find the activity of creation and selection intriguing. There is a dizzying profusion of images around us, and we keep creating more. The speed of production and consumption leaves little time to consider the nature of construction and what kind of meaning images yield. Some are readily accepted and validated by documentary and its close cousin, journalism:

such as handheld shots and restless edits, speaking with the urgency of an exposé; vox pop, supposedly the voice of the people; investigation, which is most often quick analysis and taking of positions; and also the exotic beauty and/or tragic circumstance of the *other* human being, the animal, the environment.

How does one understand the image, and how is it to be evaluated?

Working on an alternative edit of an already existing film can become interesting in this respect. Editing *Immoral Daughters* (2012)[12] with Nakul Sawhney, we found ourselves discovering aspects in the material that surprised us.

Sifting through rushes, non-speaking and non-action parts are the first to be removed. Also, the shots that are less perfect – due to soft focus, under- or over-exposed, oddly framed, where not enough action occurred, where the person being interviewed did not speak with confidence or fluidity. Going through the rushes again, we brought in out-takes, parts of sentences, hesitations and silences that carried the terrible weight that people were carrying, the tragedy and injustice that they were dealing with in their lives. We also looked again at the environs, as well as the barely concealed violence that was being perpetrated in those landscapes. Re-reading the material and excavating it naturally influenced how the new edit would come together.

The evaluation of rushes is a critical stage of work, yet often this is steered by what was to be, not what is. That shot was meant to pan or tilt, or the character spoke for too short a duration or too long, or the shot is overexposed… and so on. When I am guided by these judgements, many meanings pass me by, and the material may be lost forever, buried under the weight of my own habit and an inability to actually see. But the material is there; it is alive now, an entity, and regardless of the expectations from it before or as it was being shot, it has an existence.

Another trajectory begins if the fragments of time are rescued, brought back to life and speak what they may be trying to say. They sometimes yield a new recognition and help to access or touch a core that then resonates through the film. Looks like nothing is ever worthless, nothing can be labelled waste and thrown away. Remember the dance of the lens cap in *The Gleaners and I* (2000)?[13] There's a politics, too, in this respect for the imperfect, in not casting it aside.

A matter regarding the appraisal of shot material is worth recounting. It is to do with a student film, *Nazara* (2017).[14] In a series of unfortunate events, a large part of the rushes of the film were lost, due to a hardware malfunction. As we know, rushes cannot ever really be replicated, particularly not in non-fiction. Suddenly, the very existence of the film was in question. The student had been filming during the research period, some rough shooting that he did not take seriously. It was more like jottings in preparation for the final work, designated to be of no use for the film. Given the problem, that material was looked at again. And it was found that the directorial presence was very strong in those rushes. In fact, since the filming had been done as casual note-taking, he had shot with freedom and given himself into it, letting himself flow with 'no one watching'. Yes, there were errors and technical mistakes, such as a lot of image gain in some shots, soft focus, movements not quite perfect and so on – the kind of mistakes we would make in a sketchbook and not on a final canvas. But these sketches contained a most sincere, un-self-conscious interpretation, with a strong taste of reality. We would have thrown away pearls, not knowing their worth, as no one had validated them for us.

Thus began the editing with this material, looking at it closely, again. Which are the moments that are significant? What can develop from these moments? What do these new impressions say about the student's particular interest in these thematics? In some shots, even the focus adjustment became usable. The person and his context were accentuated by the shift focus, in a shot that meanders 'incorrectly'. By some yardsticks, the shot would be an outtake. But these judgments turned right around as the story formed.

The main character's very presence threatened the entire social fabric, even though he was doing nothing wrong, just selling cigarettes with his face painted white. Unbelievably, the locals in the area warned: 'Be careful, he's a strange man'. People on the margins seemed drawn to this space, such as a trans-person, people drinking alcohol in a car, a tipsy bunch of young men. All this became important as the film is exploring ideas around masculinity and deviations from the 'normal' that are subjected to scrutiny and even ridicule.

It is while logging the rushes (a much-underestimated job) that cues to structure can sometimes arise. I find that the plodding mechanics of the activity and the listing that it entails is a freedom from having to make sense or be creative. This archiving, with careful attention to each aspect of image and sound and the painstaking noting of time-codes occupy active energy and facilitate a much-needed headspace. Paradoxically, being bound by the procedure, committed to the steps to be followed, permits openness, a place where form may be glimpsed.

It was this process that had some shots make their way into the film *Mera Apna Sheher* (2011). Here, the logging was akin to going through a chronicle of everyday indignities in public spaces. Among other aspects of the film was an experiment. A woman about the city did 'invisible' enactments that we filmed – reclining in a public park, eating alone at a roadside eatery, loitering at a shop where only men loiter and so on. She moved around with a small camera fixed in her handbag. Looking at the rushes, we found that this camera was giving us 'nothing'. A burnt-out sky, the crooked line of a tree, the edge of a pavement, the woman's arm... Shaky, out of focus, pixelated, unframed images, splotches of colour, light and shade, that appeared to be of no use. Yet, something else emerged as the material was looked at afresh. The small camera with its weak, unclear image was surveying the everyday through its quiet lens, disclosing no secrets, showing what was already in the public eye, hidden from no one, yet making the subterranean visible and felt. As the edit progressed, the image started to indicate the woman's presence, her own gaze.

Each edit opens so many questions, as does each interaction in mentorship. As soon as there is a movement towards a position that is less eager to explain or educate and less reliant on the truth claim, new possibilities in the aesthetics of the documentary form emerge.

The experience and practice of editing is hard to describe, for it is not only about the negotiation of the skill of editing, but also about how it has shifted one's self. It is about the intangibles that one carries from one edit to the next and what one traverses in life, on the way. New understandings occur, many intuitive, not understood even by oneself. The journey is somewhat like travelling through a landscape for long stretches, with changing sights and perspectives, and there is really a lot I have not written about here. There would be also much to say about dense, packed structures, strongly textual nonfiction cinema, fast cutting and speaking out loud.

Notes

1 *A Season Outside* (dir. Amar Kanwar, 1997, 30 minutes). Synopsis: There is perhaps no border outpost in the world quite like Wagah, the border between India and Pakistan, where this film begins its exploration. An outpost, where every evening people are drawn to a thin white line... and probably anyone in the eye of a conflict could find themselves here.
2 Susmit Sen composed a track quite inspired by Takemitsu Toru: a sparse track, notes and sounds defining the spaces between them, interacting with the image and time.
3 As students, we were perplexed by the teacher who thought Miklós Jancsó's work not worth analysing, as it had too few cuts, and for whom the shower scene in *Psycho* remained the ideal study for an editor. What would have happened, had we studied the precision of start and end points in the long-take form?

4 *Sudhamayee* (*Laced with the Nectar of Life*, dir. Megha Acharya, 2019, 21 minutes). Synopsis: A woman's life filled with events that happen tediously often, even as she battles a chronic disease. She lives on, drawn along by the nectar of life.
5 *Mera Apna Sheher* (*My Own City*, 2011, 56 minutes). Synopsis: The experience of a gendered urban landscape, where the gaze, the voice and the body are under surveillance at all times. What if the multiple surveillances were to be turned upon themselves, to observe what is contained in the everyday? The film explores whether there is a sense of ownership, of belonging to the city. Can a woman in the city, as she continuously negotiates the polarities of anxiety and comfort, be free?
6 *A Quiet Little Entry* (dir. Uma Chakravarti, 2010). Synopsis: The Film is about an unknown woman, Subbalakshmi, who lived between the salt pans and thousands of other places in her mind and left behind a trunk, a diary and scraps of paper. Like many others, she had participated in the movement for independence in the 1920s and 1930s, but circumstances forced her to withdraw from active participation. It is a film about the choices that are denied to women, who then struggle to find other ways of expressing their resistance. The film was shot on location in South India and uses archival material from both the public and the family archive. It experiments with form by evoking the protagonist through suggestion; it uses photographs, camerawork, music and a voice-over to tell the story of Subbalakshmi. Prof. Uma Chakravarti is an Indian historian and a leading scholar of women's and feminist history-writing on the subcontinent.
7 Robert Bresson (25 September 1901 – 18 December 1999) was a French film director.
8 *Notes on Cinematography* (1975) collects Bresson's reflections on cinema, written as short aphorisms.
9 *The Turin Horse* (dir. Béla Tarr and Ágnes Hranitzky, 2011) is a Hungarian philosophical drama film. It recalls the whipping of a horse in the Italian city of Turin, which is rumoured to have caused the mental breakdown of philosopher Friedrich Nietzsche. The black-and-white film is shot in only thirty long takes and depicts the repetitive daily lives of the horse-owner and his daughter.
10 David Dean Shulman is an Israeli Indologist, poet and peace activist, known for his work on the history of religion in South India, Indian poetics, Tamil Islam, Dravidian linguistics and Carnatic music. Shulman is a peace activist and founding member of the joint Israeli-Palestinian movement *Ta'ayush*.
11 *No Home Movie* (dir. Chantal Akerman, 2015) is a French-Belgian documentary film focusing on conversations between the filmmaker and her mother Natalia Akerman, just months before her death. Her mother was a Polish immigrant and survivor of Auschwitz.
12 *Izzatnagari Ki Asabhya Betiyaan* (*Immoral Daughters in the Land of Honour*, dir. Nakul Singh Sawhney, 2012, 93 minutes). Synopsis: The film traces the resistance of young women against honour killings and diktats of clan councils called Khap Panchayats in North India. It explores caste, class and gender intersectionality in contemporary India. This version of the same film, *Immoral Daughters*, has been screened at several international film festivals.
13 *The Gleaners and I* (dir. Agnes Varda, 2000) features various kinds of gleaning. For example, in one scene, Varda forgot to turn off her camera, and as the camera hung at her side, it filmed the shifting ground and the dangling lens cap. Varda chose to put

this footage in the finished film, against a jazz music background, calling it 'The Dance of the Lens Cap'.
14 In *Nazara* (dir. Gagandeep Singh, 2017, 23 minutes). Synopsis: A man sits by a busy road, his face painted white. Passers-by gaze at him, as he is difficult to ignore. The film explores these different experiences and interactions, the vulnerabilities that perhaps we all carry in a public space.

Works Cited

Bresson, R. (1975). *Notes on cinematography*. New York: Urizen Books.
Shulman, D. D. (2018). 'Thinking about wickedness: From Nigamaśarma to the Palestinian West Bank'. Annual Ila Dalmia Memorial Lecture. FICA, in collaboration with the India International Centre (IIC).
Steyerl, H. 2007. Documentary Uncertainty. *The Long Distance Runner: The Production Unit Archive*, 72, 1–8.

Films Cited

A Quiet Little Entry. Dir. Uma Chakravarti. 2011.
A Season Outside. Dir. Amar Kanwar. PSBT. 1997.
Immoral Daughters. Dir. Nakul Singh Sawhney. Magic Lantern Movies & Newsclick. 2012.
Mera Apna Sheher. Dir. Sameera Jain. PSBT. 2011.
Nazara. Dir. Gagandeep Singh. CDC, SACAC. 2017.
Sudhamayee. Dir. Megha Acharya. CDC, SACAC. 2019.

11

Cultural documentary: Dialogues between aesthetics and society

Ein Lall

I must confess that I have never had any intention of portraying Indian art and culture. I leave that to Cultural Anthropologists. I make films on Indian artists because I live in India, as do the artists whom I have filmed. If I have focused almost exclusively on the work of women artists, it is because, on the one hand, I identified with them and, on the other, their work intrigued me. Moreover, in the 1990s, when I first made these films, I felt women artists were under-represented in the media.

The documentary film is fundamentally a socio-political animal. John Grierson, considered the father of the documentary form, was a socialist-activist, who promoted the documentary as a creative means to set right the socio-political imbalances rampant in films produced by the capitalist world. The 'Cultural Documentary', if limited to 'Art Films', would seem to be taking a sort of side-step as against the forward-march of the earliest documentaries, such as those by Robert J. Flaherty, Basil Wright and the like, which formed the basis on which Grierson was able to claim a separate space for making films on real people and real-life situations, as an art in its own right.

However, the earliest documentaries on the arts were focused on the art object – paintings, sculpture, architecture – and considered primarily as an educational tool, with educating, informing and inspiring its viewers as their fundamental purpose. Here, the filmmaker usually worked in tandem with the art historian, and their role was to provide audio-visual support to the art historian's task of interpretation. Art historians, from Ernst Gombrich to John Berger, had great insights and expressed themselves with remarkable fluency. Their writings are brilliant and have changed the way in which we look at art. But their films followed a pedagogical format where what was spoken (the commentary) dictated what we saw and how we saw it.

Several revolutions have taken place in both art and technology since Grierson coined the term 'documentary' and John Berger made *Ways of Seeing* (1972). In my own approach to making documentaries on artists and their artworks, I try as Grierson advised, to go beyond the surface-value of the subject and explosively reveal the reality of it. And my eternal hope is to understand and give expression to Berger's credo that the artist not only makes something observed visible to others, but also accompanies something invisible to its incalculable destination.

I started making documentaries on artists in the 1990s. The artists, dancers, architects I chose to work with had not yet transitioned to Conceptual Art, Net Art, or Post Art. There was, in their work, a central concern with people, with humanity, with an inbuilt critique of social and economic imbalances in Indian society. Arpita Singh and Nalini Malani are fundamentally figurative painters, although Malani also creates video works. They still rejoiced in the materiality of paint, paper, canvas; in the craft of creating stories using their skill at drawing and painting. As dancer-choreographers, both Chandralekha and Leela Samson articulated their fundamental concern about how dance affects not only the dancer's body but their self-perception in relation to the world around them. Architect Revathi Sekhar's passion was to restore the human scale to architecture. Shekhar went back to using the human body as the scale by which she measured her buildings and used mud as her preferred building material.

If I am drawn to an artwork, I find myself intrigued by a series of paintings by the same artist and become keen to understand the connection between the paintings and the painter; then I follow the example of the art student. Like the student, I locate works on the internet and copy them; I paint the same picture using different colours. I stick prints on my studio walls so that I can internalise them. Often, I intuit that there is something unique about the work to which I respond but cannot explain why. I feel gazing at the work somehow completes me, but I do not really know how to convey that very personally internalised feeling to anyone else. This is the challenge that I enjoy taking on. Can I make a film that resonates with the same intensity that I feel the paintings to have? Can I find my own expression for how these paintings affect me?

Yoking of heterogeneous elements

There is a certain irony attached to films made on paintings, for like the painter, the filmmaker also creates meaning mainly through form, colour and the juxtaposition of images. But unlike the painter who remains rooted to the confines of their canvas, even while bringing the entire world into it, the filmmaker has been freed to roam the world. The camera is their brush, while their canvas is location-free. When making a film about paintings, the filmmaker must restrain themselves to the very limitations from which they have been freed. Their camera must now stay within the framing of the canvas and focus only on the strokes of the brush. The soundtrack, that added dimension to their filmed images, has to now find a reason for existing. The obvious answer is, of course, the authoritative commentary; the interview with the artist; and musical accompaniment when the commentary and interview fall silent.

I wanted to free myself from this format. But If I could not rely on a commentary or an interview, how was I to express my own thinking, feeling, reacting to an artist and the artwork? How was I to express what I felt was so special about it? The breakthrough came when I decided to trust in my intuition that, if film could give an added dimension to a painting, then so could music and dance.

My film on Arpita Singh, *The Colour Blue*, is a good case in point. It was made in the 1990s. Arpita Singh was already a well-known artist, but until that time most critics spoke of her as an artist who delighted in her femininity; her love for children, home and kitchen. The consensus was that there was a certain charm in the naïveté of her images, which reflected the influence of Paul Klee and Marc Chagall; and that her folk images stamped her as Bengali to the core.

I did not quite agree with this analysis. It seemed to me that, while Arpita Singh used all of the above to draw viewers into her paintings, there was a subtext woven into the surface naïveté and playfulness – a subtext which exploded with violence and was subversive to the core. Around this time, I met with Estella, a dancer who had studied Butoh, the Japanese dance form which had come into being after the Holocaust. As I watched her move, it seemed to me that the controlled, exquisitely slowed-down movements of Butoh had the same quality of a surface playfulness, suppressed violence and deeply felt anguish that I thought I saw in the work of Arpita Singh's (hereafter referred to as Arpita).

I introduced Estella to Arpita. Estella and Arpita accepted each other immediately. During the two to three months of writing a proposal and waiting for funding, Estella woke up every morning to prints of Arpita's work that she had pinned up on her walls. And she practiced her Butoh movements having internalised those images. During the shoot of Estella dancing in Arpita's studio, the artist and the dancer came together so naturally, so easily, that it took me by surprise. I give full credit to cinematographer Dilip Verma for that. What I think I achieved by bringing a dancer into Arpita's studio was that the dancer was able to suggest an embodied equivalent to Arpita's verbally articulated claim that the act of painting took her on a journey to an unknown place – a sort of secret, dangerous space, which she entered with great trepidation.

The gun held pointed, as if ready to shoot, is a constantly recurring image in Arpita's paintings of that period. By positioning the dancer as the victim of that calculated threat, I was able to highlight the constant interplay of fear and aggression in Arpita's paintings. I believe it was in my film that Arpita articulated most clearly and emphatically that the series of paintings which had hitherto been interpreted as a mother-and-child series was actually an attempt to convey her own self as split into two – the smaller self being contained, as it were, within the bigger outer self. I think that this explanation was the result of Arpita's own dismissal of the possibility that the dancer might be mistakenly interpreted as her alter ego. Finally, I believe that bringing a dancer into her studio helped to deflect the oppressive attention that every sensitive artist feels when constantly watched and questioned by a committed documentarist.

I have often been asked why I chose Chopin's Nocturnes Nos 1, 7 and 12 to accompany a Butoh dancer in a film about a Bengali artist. All I can say is that it worked for me. Samuel Johnson, when analysing Metaphysical Poetry, wrote that the Imagination works through 'the yoking of heterogeneous elements by violence together' (Johnson 1779). I firmly concur with this statement. But thinking it over now, I believe that it was also an attempt to free Arpita's paintings from always being identified only with the regionalism of Bengaliness... and the rather condescending attitude to her as a female artist. I believed that her paintings had a universal relevance. I saw her being drawn to the modernism of both Klee and Chagall, not only for reasons of form and colour, but also because both artists resorted to subterfuge. Klee's seemingly childlike drawings and Chagall's Russian folksiness charmed viewers but, having drawn their viewers into their work, they gave them a glimpse of the explosive realities through which they had lived. For both artists had fled the terrors of the Nazi regime. Both had experienced more than their fair share of grief and violence. I hoped that my film would help those who stayed with Arpita's paintings to cut through the subterfuge and find themselves moving towards her artworks' incalculable destination.

When making the film *The Flowering Tree* on dancer, teacher and choreographer Leela Samson (hereafter referred to as Leela), I once again resorted to going outside of dance to explore Leela's career as a dancer and teacher. Since my daughter was her student, I had the good fortune to watch Leela not only perform but also teach as well as prepare her students for performances. Over the years, I began to sense not only the demanding work, but also the emotional strain that went into readying a dancer to be a performing artist. I used A. K. Ramanujan's translation of the South Indian folk-story *The Flowering Tree*, not danced but enacted, as a means to understand the constant shifting between the multiple roles to which a guru (teacher) who is also a performing artist has to resort in order to keep her equilibrium.

The story tells of two sisters who, reduced to poverty, resort to a desperate strategy to make a living. One sister becomes a flowering tree so that the other can collect her flowers and sell them. Before sitting down to do the *tapasya* (deep meditation) that will convert her into a tree, she (the tree to be) tells her sister to collect as many flowers as she wants, but to be careful because, if she broke a twig or snapped a branch, it would be her body that would break and tear.

I used the story of the two sisters as a metaphor to suggest the difficulties that a dancer in Leela's position was constantly facing. On the one hand, there was the commitment to give all of herself to her art, to her audiences, as well as to her students. On the other hand, the petty jealousies and rivalries that all dancers living and performing in Delhi faced were also taking their toll. There was moreover the constant awareness that living and teaching in twenty-first-century Delhi in no way equipped her to match the training that she herself had received while embedded in Rukmini Devi's Kalakshetra (dance institution). Above all, there was the constant awareness that old standards of loyalty and fidelity on which the *Guru-Shishya parampara* (teacher-disciple lineage) was built no longer held good.

I felt that it was vitally important that my documentary should include the multiple contradictions that plagued Leela, even while she was acknowledged as one of India's best Bharatanatyam dancers and teachers. It seemed to me that, as a sensitive performer and committed teacher, Leela and the eternal caution and watchfulness that she imposed on herself, even while giving her all to her students and audiences, matched that of the split functions that the sisters in the fable of *The Flowering Tree* took on themselves. But while the symbol of the flowering tree was brought in to mark the shifts in her career as a dancer, performer, teacher, choreographer, I also avoided using dance when Leela was introspectively reflecting on her life as a single woman who had devoted herself entirely to her career. Separating Leela from her Bharatanatyam, where she is all verve and joyous vitality, and showing her totally absorbed in a martial art form which allows for slow meditative movement helped me to delve further into the contradictory streams of consciousness by which she lived her life.

Here, as the camera captures her through an open window following her Tai Chi instructor Raashid's slow deliberate movements, we hear her telling us in a soul-searching voice-over that, although she has been alone for most of her life, she has never been lonely. In the background, the haunting music of 'The Serpent's Egg' by the Australian band Dead Can Dance takes us a world away from the classical music and rhythms of Bharatanatyam. I was lucky to have Dilip Verma and Amar Kanwar participate in this film as cinematographer and editor.

Cohabitation of identities

The films on Arpita Singh and Leela Samson were two units in what was to be a group or series of six women artists. The series was commissioned by Jai Chandiram, who then was the director of DD3, a newly conceived channel in Doordarshan that was devoted to the arts.[1] We zeroed in on two painters, Arpita Singh and Nalini Malani; two dancers, Chandralekha and Leela Samson; and architect Revathi Sekhar and singer Shubha Mudgal. I managed to complete four of the above before Jai Chandiram gave up the job and the arts channel closed. Fortunately, Public Service Broadcasting Trust (PSBT) was set up around this time, and I was able to complete the series, making the films on Chandralekha and Nalini Malani under the PSBT banner.

We have to accept, however reluctantly, that the world of art and artists need support. When funding by the state or by corporations dries up, artists can carry on regardless – especially if they work alone and the materials they choose to work with are inexpensive, or if they are well-known and their talent is recognized and supported overseas. The average documentary filmmaker, making films on the arts, does not have that choice.

In the newly freed India of the 1950s and 1960s, the artists of Shantiniketan – Nandalal Bose, Benode Behari Mukherjee, Ramkinker Baij – were practicing artists who exulted in their national identity. Nandalal Bose researched and drew inspiration from the murals in Ajanta Ellora. Ramkinker's sculptures celebrated the Santhal tribals; Benode Behari Mukherjee painted his mural *Medieval Indian Saints* on the walls of Hindi Bhavan, in Shantiniketan. When still under British rule, actively encouraged by both Mahatma Gandhi and Rabindranath Tagore, they participated in designing and decorating the structures in which the Indian Congress held their sessions. They identified their personal freedom with the newly won political freedom of the Indian state; in turn, the newly established Indian state acknowledged them as front-runners of Modern Indian Art and commissioned them to work on the most important public projects.

At the same time when Kala Bhavan, the Art Department in Shantiniketan, was thriving under the care of Nandalal Bose, the J. J. School of Art in Mumbai (Bombay) made its own very individual mark on Modern Indian Art, primarily through the Progressive Artists Group which was held together by Souza, Raza, Hussain and others. They challenged the Tagore family's insistence on finding roots in Indian and Oriental traditional art practices and gladly availed themselves of opportunities offered by liberal western countries to study art in colleges in the UK, France and the USA. These artists, too, while representing a whole different stream of art in India, were acknowledged as front-runners of Modern Art in India and were given support and encouragement by the newly independent Indian state.

From its inception, the Indian state – backed by the idealism of Tagore, Gandhi and Rukmini Devi – recognized that the Visual and Performing Arts needed monetary support to survive and thrive and that it should be the state rather than business corporates that should undertake that responsibility. Consequently, a budget was created for the arts, and the documentaries that were made on them, too, were funded by the Films Division, which was a state corporation. Many great documentaries on the arts were made by Satyajit Ray, Mani Kaul, Kumar Shahani and other filmmakers.

Cut to contemporary India, and we find that a sea change has taken place in the intervening years, both in the attitude of the state towards artists' freedom of expression, as well as in the stance taken by the artists towards the state's guardianship of the arts. Between the 1970s and 2000, the failure of the Indian state's economic policies, rampant corruption, the Emergency (1975), the lawlessness that followed the assassination of Indira Gandhi (1984), the Centre's capitulation to thuggery and the RSS ideology, typified by threats to artists (whether in the visual or performing arts), the murder of Safdar Hashmi (1989), the destruction of M. F. Hussain's works by vandals (1998) – these all contributed to the swift deterioration of relations between the state and artist communities.[2]

However, the retreat of the state from the active promotion of the Modern and Contemporary arts did not mean that Modern Indian artists ceased to recognize their roots; ceased to care for home, city, region, country; ceased to express their personal and political concerns vis-à-vis the nation state. Here, I have to return to my opening statement that I was not concerned about portraying Indian art and culture and clarify that, while my concern was with getting to the heart of women artists through their work, their concerns were closely related to their social and political realities.

I can speak of my own experience with the artists I interviewed and filmed in the year 2000: Tyeb Mehta, Atul Dodiya and Nalini Malani, who represented three generations of artists who had graduated from the J. J. School of Art in Mumbai. All three spent brief periods abroad and had access to first-hand acquaintance with the Modern Movement in European and American art. However, they continued to live in Mumbai, and I found that they were as passionate about their identity as Indians as their predecessors had been. Let me quote from those interviews in which I had asked how their art may have been affected by their experience of living in Mumbai:

> Tyeb Mehta: 'I am very keen … to find something that is true to us, rather than just fitting ourselves into the history of Western Painting. I am not for that. I want somehow or the other to come to terms with the place and time in which I am living. And that is India, you know, that is not Mumbai alone'.
> Nalini Malani: 'Living in Mumbai? Well, it is like asking what a fish feels like swimming in its waters. For me, it is like a skin which has been there as long as I can remember… Mumbai is my city. And the fact that I have had my studio in Lohar Chawl, which is in the heart of commercial Mumbai since the last twenty-five years, and very concertedly I have tried to bring Lohar Chawl into my artwork… I made thirty books with thirty-two pages each, over a period of two years, on Lohar Chawl. And Lohar Chawl keeps coming up in every possible way… '
> Atul Dodiya: 'Definitely! I feel that the city of Mumbai plays a major role in my work. When I see my oeuvre in the last twenty years – it is a major influence, I would say… One feels sad at the way people live and struggle… It takes a lot. Often, I feel like running away, but at the same time there is something compelling that nourishes my total being, my creative process… ' (personal interviews, Mumbai, 2000)

The artists quoted above, even while asserting a profound connection to their city and their country, were deeply critical of the state. Big dams, the nuclear bomb and the growing Hindutva extremism were deep concerns that were profoundly troubling, and they were unafraid to articulate their disagreement with the positions taken by the state on these subjects. When I set out to interview and film their work in 2000, I knew that it would be difficult to get Doordarshan or the Lalit Kala Academy to fund my project.

I did it on my own, and those films remained unfinished for twenty-one years!

Since 2014, the gap that existed between the Indian government's art and culture offices and India's artists has ballooned into a great void. The present government's attitude towards the arts is guided by the RSS, with its values based on returning to a Sanskritised past.[3] The Ministry of Culture seems to have turned its entire attention and considerable funds to enable colossal architectural and sculptured projects that are RSS-sponsored, rather than made through initiatives taken by artists.

Perhaps it is this political reality which is responsible for the paucity of documentary films produced on the arts today?

Notes

1 DD3 was state broadcaster Doordarshan's more intellectual, cultural channel, initiated in 1995.
2 RSS or Rashtriya Swayamsevak Sangh, founded in the 1920s, is the all-male paramilitary wing of the Hindu Right in India.
3 The Sanskritised past draws on the ideas espoused by Professor M. N. Srinivas, referring to a process in which people belonging to the lower castes imitate and adopt the culture, ideals, practices and rituals of those from the upper castes, usually Brahmins, in order to improve their caste status.

Works cited

Johnson, S. (1779). *Prefaces, biographical and critical, to the works of the English poets, vol. 1*. London: Bathurst et al.

Films Cited

The Colour Blue. Dir. Ein Lall. Doordarshan. 2014.
The Flowering Tree. Dir. Ein Lall. Doordarshan. 1996.

12

The politics of image-making

R. V. Ramani

Self-reflective camera

Representation in cinema often lies between what is shown and not shown, or what is seen and unseen. What you try to represent can become a misrepresentation or escape representation, or it might represent something else or something contrary to your intention. Meanings change in the passage of time; they fossilise, rupture and create new layers. The concept of a composition, the element of the fourth wall, even the choice of lens and microphones often deal with the vexations of what is to be included or excluded or what cannot be included, alluding to the perspectives and aesthetics of the time.

Every new technology in photography and cinematography has brought its own aesthetic values as to what is appropriate. When I joined the Film and Television Institute of India (FTII) in 1982 to study filmmaking, 35mm celluloid was the dominant format, the BNC Mitchel 35mm camera was the demigod, and Eastman Kodak films were the ultimate. At FTII, I had a classmate, Shoba Sadgopan, who happened to be the niece of the incredible cinematographer K. K. Mahajan. During bromide printing in the dark room, she would print an image from a negative, which was high in contrast or a deliberately under-exposed or over-processed image. When I tried to 'correct', she would insist that this was the kind of image she wanted. The printed image lacked 'appropriate' tonalities, a bit harsh, a bit violent. This approach made sense to me only many years later, when I made friends with artists and painters in Cholamandal Artists's Village, Chennai, and started making films with some of the artists who were experimenting with image-making. I realised that one can question the process of meaning formations, the consumptive quality of an image, and alternatives can be proposed using different kinds of material, moving away from hierarchy in the quest for an original expression. I realised only then that Shoba Sadgopan was rebelling against a certain idea of aesthetics.

Sometimes, a transgression arrives at an abrupt end, a 'Cut', or a collapse of a narrative or, sometimes, the birth of a new narrative. The eyes crossing across the lens axis with ease or stumbling and looking into the lens revealing the fourth wall can be a ploy or a mistake or an accident. Argumentative politics of good and bad, values pitted one against the other, often perpetuates sediments and blocks in cinema, distorting perspectives unknown to the makers. Cinema – whether it is commercial, propagandist, promotional, or leaning towards a sensual, provocative, attractive, seductive, emotional plotting – often reinforces clichés and establishes an aesthetics of class and caste.

So, what is the basis of representation when things are so intangible and in flux? Can one escape plot, in the plot? Can a characterisation free the character or the characterisation? Can an argument free the argument? Can discourse free itself from the values and hierarchies in its construction? Can I construct a layer which is transparent or allows transparency or create layers which live independently or coexist?

Moving away from the clichés of representative politics, in my first film, *Saa* (1991), I searched for my own rhythm, in the flux of rural and urban rhythms. Sticking to my concerns, immersive in nature, I tried to free myself from the narrative itself, seeking my own space within. Nothing said, argued, postured, postulated, but just experienced, internalised, experiencing possibilities of free interpretations – a notion of the abstract in cinema, through the figurative, but as self-reflective camera work and image-making.

High art in low resolution

My sojourn with artists started much earlier, in a rather unconscious way. As a school boy in Mumbai, I used to sit, mesmerised, looking at a painting in my neighbour's house. It was a drawing which for me was haunting and magnetic. The painting was just hanging on one of the walls with which none in the house seemed to make any connection. It was a painting by the artist K. Ramanujam, the younger brother of my neighbour Vedha Mami. Ramanujam had gifted her the painting when he had visited Mumbai much earlier. Vedha Mami's sons and daughters were all around my age, so I would often spend time in their house, and every time I went there,

I would keep staring and immerse myself in this painting. They would even joke: 'Ramani seems to like that painting a lot and perhaps comes here only for that'. In a way, it was true. Ramanujam, so I later found out, had committed suicide at a very young age. The family played hush-hush, feeling upset, even suspecting foul play in his death.

One of the areas which I frequently visited during my college days was Flora Fountain in South Mumbai. A habit started to form: stopping outside an art gallery called Pundole and also visiting the Jehangir Art Gallery. I remember seeing the paintings of the artist J. Swaminathan displayed in Pundole. I would freeze in front of his paintings, seen through the glass doors. The experience of watching Ramanujam's painting in my neighbour's house and watching J. Swaminathan's paintings had a similar impact on me, mesmerising, even though they were completely different.

After the FTII course, when it became inevitable for me to move to Chennai around 1988–89, one of the first things I did was to visit Cholamandal Artists's Village, where Ramanujam used to live. It was also here that he committed suicide in 1972, when he was just thirty-two years old. Most of Ramanujam's paintings were done on found paper and easily perishable scrap paper. But his output and expression were phenomenal. His works sold well. Visitors would pick up his works at a cheap rate: high art in low-resolution bandwidth. The base was fragile, as paper could fade, disintegrate. Initially, when I desired to work on a film based on K. Ramanujam's work and life, in the mid-1990s, I wanted to do it in the best format of those times, in 35mm celluloid. But I could not generate the resources to make the film then. Hence, like Ramanujam, over the years I kept working on whatever format one could access at any given point of time. Ramanujam's images live in a surreal space, in an imaginary space, physically and mentally challenged as he was in the world's eye, aspiring to live in a dream world, where things are different, where he has a space for himself, where he is adored, where he feels comfortable, where he finds his solace. The film intends to give him that space, maybe visit him or just be with him from this space to that space.

Beyond technological horizons

Image-making in cinema is related to technology and formats, which are often linked to attitudes and values. Sometime in the mid-1990s, the Director of the Max Mueller Bhavan (MMB) invited me to a dinner party at one of the posh clubs in Chennai. The club, a residue of the colonial hang-over, maintained values in terms of its clientele and memberships. I reached the venue on my two-wheeler. The director of MMB was waiting outside in the parking lot, with a big cloth bag. He looked at my feet and then said: 'You need to wear shoes. Slippers are not allowed in this club'. He took out different-sized shoes and asked me to wear one pair. I tried, but none of them fit me. They were tight. Since shoes were compulsory to enter, he asked me to manage. I crossed the main entrance and removed the shoes, then walked barefoot, carrying them in my hand, through the club corridors to sit at the table where all invitees had gathered. I had a great time at this party. Once the dinner was over, I exited the place barefoot, the shoes in my hands. This dress code and hierarchy exist in the formats of filmmaking today.

At the MAMI (Mumbai Academy of Moving Image) Film Festival held in Mumbai in 2019, one of the few film festivals where documentaries and feature films are treated equally, my film *Oh That's Bhanu* was premiered. The film was shot in many formats, low-res, hi-res, mobile footage, HDV, MP4, edited and mastered as a .mov file and then converted as DCP 2K resolution for theatre release. The film looked fabulous on the big cinema screen at a wonderful theatre in Bandra, with an audio-mix in stereo. No one could argue about the image quality or sound or the screening experience. The film worked completely as a large-screen projection. The response from the audience was fabulous. One could easily sense that this film could have had a fantastic theatre release, but those gates and restrictions put by the commercial and political market do not allow a feature documentary to enter that arena. Because we do not wear shoes.

A year ago, during the ongoing pandemic, an artist friend who also makes short documentaries called me to seek my suggestion on a camera model that she wanted to purchase. I asked her about the purpose of the filming. She wanted to do documentaries as well as attempt a fiction narrative with a small crew. Then she insisted that the camera recording needed to be compatible with telecast requirements on the OTT platforms. I said: 'Any image can be broadcast on Television and OTT platforms and even in cinema theatres'. She did not believe what I said, and I continued: 'You can also make a feature film with a pinhole camera'. She laughed at my suggestion. But recently a student of mine, in her attempt to make a pinhole camera, ended up converting her entire bedroom into a dark space, creating a pin hole on one side, to receive an image on a screen, which she managed to shoot with her mobile phone camera. It was fabulous. Today, the OTT platforms which have captured a major market-share have set up minimum standards of formats, even specifying models of cameras to use. A leading cinematographer advertises on social media as 'OTT-approved camera'. He is their brand ambassador. The recent Olympics in Japan were broadcast live in 8K format, raising all benchmarks. Now I wonder what Paris will do, as one has to set new records in the Olympics.

On one level, technology excludes, but often technology has opened up ease of access to everyone. But at the same time, market forces equalise, bring back the status quo of political, national, or corporate hierarchy. After a range of formats such as U-matic, Betacam and S-VHS in the late 1990s and the beginning of the 2000s, we saw the arrival of the MiniDV format, small and compact, which revolutionised video acquisition. Many filmmakers emerged, breaking away from the shackles of hierarchy. It was one of my favourite formats. It was around the same time that one entrepreneur from Bangalore, G. R. Gopinath, had started Air Deccan, a low-cost airline to provide access to air travel for everyone. To travel in his airlines, you did not need to be rich; there was no expected dress code. One was not required to wear shoes. You just needed the desire to travel by air. He mentioned that it was not the elite that he considered as customers, but also the humble cleaning women in his office, auto-drivers and other such people to whom he wanted to cater. He wanted them to dream that they too could fly and make that dream possible.

In 2006, when cinema theatres started converting from film projection to digital projection, the hierarchy of the formats suddenly could be broken in distribution, too. I was the cinematographer of a documentary film shot in MiniDV format, a film on a musician, directed by my friend Prasanna Ramaswamy. We arranged to explore morning screenings of the film at the Prestigious Satyam Cinema Complex, Chennai, as a ticketed morning show. The theatre had just made a shift from film projection to digital projection. The newly installed digital projector was amazing. The projectionist was still figuring out the new technology. Some days before the screening, I tested the MiniDV Master at this newly installed hi-tech 2K projection system. The DV master was played on my MiniDV player, through an S-video connector to the projector. It worked, even to the delight of the projectionist. The experience of projection completely convinced me that the MiniDV format was totally compatible for large-screen projection. All tonal reproductions came true. The sound was fabulous. The experience of the cinema was fabulous for the audience. But this experience was short-lived. Soon thereafter, a clause was brought in, with one nodal control for all films/videos to be released in theatres. It stated that all films shot on film or video for theatre releases had to pass through Qube conversion, where they would provide the code for use in theatres with digital projections while also ensuring Censor Certification. Playing through separate video players was banned. Once again, big-time players dominated image-marketing, just like it existed in celluloid. Thus, it was back to hard-core business through narratives, heroes, the star system, selling and marketing. Coincidentally, Air Deccan, too, had its wonderful times, termed as one of the friendliest airlines, with the renowned cartoonist R. K. Lakshman's cartoon of the common man as its logo. This aspiration lasted for almost a decade, eventually losing out to the market forces around the same time as MiniDV as a format started waning when the tapeless mechanisms started to arrive. It is an irony that my documentary *Oh That's Bhanu* made in all available formats, produced by myself, and the hero-based Tamil feature film *Soorarai Pottru* (2020), based on the life of the founder of Air Deccan, Captain Gopinath, were both awarded at the 68th National Film Awards.

One of the films that I made in the MiniDV format was *My Camera and Tsunami* (2011). The film was about my relationship with my MiniDVCAM camera, as well as my partner, who perished in the tsunami.

Figure 12.1 Still from *My Camera and Tsunami* (2011). Picture courtesy of author.

It was an evocation of partnership in meaning-making between me and my camera; negotiating imagery, trying to engage, reflect, heal oneself, expressing the inexpressible. What is being expressed is not even that important. The film allows a journey of self-reflectivity in image-making itself. The notion of construct is being questioned, going beyond proving or establishing or justifying. As the film itself was based on the idea of an experience of filming the tsunami, the footage of which does not exist, along with a deeply displaced experience emerging from the tsunami, I decided to work on the borders of reality where meaning-making goes through a black-hole-like spasm washing itself of all meanings. The notion of reality is denied in presenting the reality and in its construction. What I say is not what it is. What it is is not what I can say, and what it is, is not what it is. I even went to the extent of constructing an absence of image in its various shades of image-making: the inability to film an image that erupts outside of its construction without showing it; a non-consumptive mode of cinema.

In *Santhal Family to Mill Recall* (2017), I played with perspectives, juxtaposing meaning formations, re-interpreting the re-interpretations, again with an accent of self-reflection. The film was based on a collaborative installation and performative work on the life and works of the artist Ramkinkar Baij. As installation artist Vivan Sundaram and his team re-imagined the artist Ramkinkar Baij in the contemporary political times and as I, as a filmmaker, created a prismatic approach looking at all the artists, I re-deciphered their processes and also those of the artist Ramkinkar Baij, in a way freeing him as well as others involved in interpreting, from the narrative. It does create a strange experience watching the film.

Formats dissolving time

The Covid pandemic has stirred up the notion of a linearity of time. As the cloud layers of a rather strange global phenomenon seem to thin slowly, for me the days seem to go too fast; the past looks collapsed, the future looks like the present, the present seems like a vapour. A project that I had started three decades ago with the contemporary experimental theatre group Koothu-p-pattarai, as a parallel to my own journey in cinema, to make sense of history, a linear diary, an assertion, an aspiration, suddenly makes reality and linearity irrelevant, offering multiple reflective challenges. It is no coincidence that recently I saw a television series on an OTT platform, a marathon nine-part serial which was produced by the OTT platform itself.

I started watching it at 10 pm, and it went on until 6 am in the morning, non-stop, just like the experience of witnessing a Therukkoothu folk theatre performance in terms of duration.

Although Koothu-p-pattarai is a contemporary experimental theatre group, it was inspired by Tamil folk theatre, Therukkoothu. I have witnessed this folk theatre over many nights. The performance starts around 10 pm and ends in the morning, as the sun rises. Moreover, the protagonist of this OTT show that I watched all night is 'a common man', from the middle class, reminding me of R. K. Lakshman's cartoon of the 'common man' and Captain Gopinath's attraction to it as a logo. But in this serial the protagonist is not just 'a common man'; he is the man who carries the hyper-nationalism of the country on his shoulders, secretly, like a brain-washed schoolboy. The all-encompassing seductive aesthetics of film-making restores the essentially glossy and promotional, consumptive film manual of the advertising world. As the OTT platforms dictate the technical requirements and also the content, the film on Koothu-p-pattarai, a work that I started thirty years ago, is almost like a history of Video – ranging across Hi Band, Betacam, V8, Hi8, SVHS, VHS, MiniDV, DVCAM, MP4, HD, 2K and 4K – but it does not fulfil any criteria of the present technical qualifying parameters of the OTT content realtors, non-conforming to the dominant aesthetics, stirring the combustion of real time and film time, moving on to an experience which can challenge your real-time experience of watching the film.

Films Cited

My Camera and Tsunami. Dir. R. V. Ramani. PSBT. 2011.
Oh That's Bhanu. Dir. R. V. Ramani. 2019/20.
Saa. Dir. R. V. Ramani. 1991.
Santhal Family to Mill Recall. Dir. R. V. Ramani. 2017.

13

Two starting points: The sonic in my films

Yashaswini

In 2009, the construction of the Bangalore Metro Rail Corporation Limited (BMRCL) was in full swing. They were building two lines: the East-West Corridor (the Purple Line) and the North-South Corridor (the Green Line). The entire city faced excavators, bulldozers, cranes and crushers. They were rapidly mowing down new and old buildings, and trees that shaped the streets. Schools, playgrounds, local shops, clinics, pubs, hospitals and the livelihoods of people were displaced, disregarded, barely ever compensated for the Metro to be installed. It continues to be one of the city's most expensive, painfully illegal and highly controversial projects. Many students, environmentalists, activists and locals gathered and protested. Some days we managed to stop the work, other days we were pushed away by the police. When the work stopped, several construction workers from different parts of the country, freshly employed by BMRCL, watched the protestor's frustration with perplexity. The opposition of their gaze in contrast to us protestors was a fact. To embrace a moment of doubt is always a good starting point.

We crossed the road and started a different conversation. However, things were far more complex. It was the first time that many of the workers had travelled down to South India for work. They had started forming a newer relationship with the city. My friends and I spent the next five years creating a film-based project titled *Behind the Tin Sheets*.[1] Through this project, we formed relationships with workers, who formed a natural affinity with the camera. We moved from one worker's colony to another, making sense of the scale of migration and the multitudes of lives that existed in these transitory make-shift homes.

The construction sites possessed a time in the future of a city, while the construction workers lived in a continuous state of movement and uncertainty. We filmed many interviews, usually on the last days of their work, as they were often transported from one site to another – to build another metro station, a mall, an apartment, a highway, a bridge, or a dam. This temporariness, in contrast to the fixed pillars, created an unfair, strange disjunction in the city.

It is our privilege that allowed us into the labour colonies. We had started to form relationships which changed the ways in which we used to associate with the city. The workers were happy to share their thoughts, discussing their desires, fears, dreams, their exhaustion, travel, work and home in their after-hours. With a minimal budget, we put together three short and succinct films: *Presence, Distance,* and *In_Transience* – these stitched-together stories of ghosts, love and labour against the backdrop of this mutating city.

Unsynchronous soundscapes

Perhaps it was the first time I recognized, more closely, how the essential elements of film – image, sound and voice – when subtracted from each other and inter-mingled, could start to reflect the atmosphere of the narrative more convincingly. To use a low-hum sound against an image of a rapidly digging excavator, to use an interview of a dream against a skinny metal shaft, or to mute the sound against the visual of a moving train as opposed to sync sound – these all unexpectedly extended the feeling of alienation. The metro worker's inner lives often seemed estranged from home and the city while continuously adapting to newer and transient spaces, such as the construction sites or the tin-sheet colonies. We wanted to connect the spectator with this psychological state of the workers on-screen, by re-designing the relationship between image and sound and the story interviewed.

Sound lent itself more idiosyncratically to destabilising time than the visual for our work with the project *Behind the Tin Sheets*. It seemed capable of pushing the documentary form into a more unpredictable state. You could fix your camera on-site and, by using non-diegetic sound design, drift the audience's attention to something else. I shifted my work from the visual medium to the sonic for a few years. It gave me liberty to experiment and re-think how narratives were constructed; or, more pressingly, what dominates our decision-making while creating a story. And I had the urge to break away from the predictable or normative as it seemed to continuously retell from the perspective of hegemony. To start telling a story as though you are listening would then automatically break the instructive pattern of 'now, let me tell you a story'. The eye and the ear are two organs on which we seem to rely the most to make meaning; they are closely interwoven but not necessarily synchronised. This got me thinking of a new method where we can find a way to picturise sound that would then steer us away from filming based on the eye's decisions and perceptions and immediacies. As in the opening scene of the film *The Swamp* (2001) by Lucrecia Martel, the audience are immediately introduced to the characters and their disturbing reality of power by the scraping, scratching sounds of the chair against the floor of a swimming pool; or, even in her later film *Zama* (2017), we are exposed to this turmoil with high elongated sound, resulting in a beguiling cinematic experience unique to Martel. Somehow the ear prepares us more than what the eye is viewing. How we listen could automatically make us far more present. For example, during my Master's studies in London, I was exposed to the anechoic chamber, a place without sounds. When you enter this odd-looking place filled with inverted triangles and material that can absorb all sounds, your ear withdraws inwards. Initially, out of panic, it creates its own clicking sound. After a good fifteen to twenty minutes, you begin to listen to the next-loudest thing in your body, your heartbeat, and after about thirty to forty minutes, your ear can tune in and listen to the sound of the blood flowing within you, like a river.

My friend, Jackie, with whom I made several sound recordings and tracks, and I used the anechoic chamber to make recordings of soft objects and things barely audible to the human ear, such as the layers inside a mushroom or the thin fibre of an orange or of the sound that is produced by plucking an eyelash. These recordings provided a provocation for finding a newer approach to my documentary film-making practice. How can I record a space layer by layer, from the lowest hum to the loudest sounds, and what clues can that provide to a story or the film? This process has allowed me to imagine narrative structures which are unusual in their concern, form, gaze and experiment.

Put your eye to the ear and the ear to the toy

In 2016, I bought a set of toys from a toy-seller at the Ulsoor market in Bangalore. I had these toys as a child, but this time I bought them out of curiosity about their material and loudness. On a large bamboo pole, toy-sellers hang balloons, plastic masks, plastic binoculars, plastic whistles of different sizes, *chorki* or windmills and *kyatketi* or rattlers (as referred to in Bengali). This glistening red *kyatketi* had a clamorous sound emanating from its spine as it flipped against 35mm Bollywood and Tollywood film cut-ups, which we followed and eventually included in *That Cloud Never Left* (2019).

Across the large lake in Murshidabad, toy-makers are often busy cutting reels and reels of film found in the garbage dump-yards of Calcutta. Each film-can is roughly available for Rs. 120, out of which at least 10,000 *kyatketis* can be made and sold. Two blocks of wood, one smaller than the other, are placed on top of each other and punctured with two long nails. Two cuts are made on either side of the film reel to separate the sprockets from its skin. The 35mm film is placed between the blocks and pulled through by the whole family, and within minutes it is ripped apart. From here, the film takes its re-birth in the form of a sounding device, a rattler. The image on the film, along with its other elements, is dipped into pellucid pink paint and made to beat against a cane-stick, leaving sharp scratches on its body.

Film here is used only for its flexibility, forgetting its previous avatar as an image from the movies. The more the toys spin, the more of the

Figure 13.1 Still frame of a 35mm celluloid film strip used to make *kyatketi*s, from *That Cloud Never Left* (2019). Picture courtesy of author.

image evaporates – transforming itself into a spirited sound. There is a belief among toy-makers that, 'if a toy rotates in one's hand for less than five seconds, then the Earth we are standing on rotates for thousands of kilometres a day, which means we are all meant to move. The land is for the dead and not the living. We are meant to move'. Murshidabad is close to the border, and people here have had to rebuild their economy after the Partition, which forced them to move away from their jute-based income. They have found new ways and invented their own anarchic, haphazard, small-scale cottage industries that produce everything from beedis to fake Nikes, Adidas, Pepsi, Coca-Cola, CDs and DVDs, as well as other plastics from China. They bring a heady inventiveness to their work and sustenance, which needs constant innovation and enterprise. The toy-makers agreed to work with us on the film and built into it the same appetite for experimentation within the cinematic form.

In *That Cloud Never Left* (2019), the camera was an imagined toy that could be spun, rotated and moved. It could be dressed in filters or glazed paper, and its ISO setting allowed it to be way beyond 1600. We did not mind grains of dust or pixels showering our image. We documented most things that moved in circles in the village, to exaggerate the toy's movement and their philosophy. This decision also allowed us to be loose with our structure. We could enable the different stories of the toy-makers to come in and exist fluidly. Our only rule was to make a film within twenty days, before the arrival of the longest lunar eclipse. We decided to take a bunch of prompts that would naturally unfold as a set of stories and converge on the night of the eclipse. This film was the first time for me to have chosen a subject that had sound embedded in its inception. We allowed ourselves to freely use the ability of surround-sound, which would navigate us from one narrative to another, creating a distinct sense of scale and physicality for the viewer. In the film, we see the toy-makers making a toy with a specific rhythm to its work; we extended that very sound to the sequences of the two brothers constructing a large orb-ladder, which we later learn to be a platform for viewing the eclipse. Similarly, we see the scans of the 35mm film-frames superimposed onto the rotating boat, layered with the recordings from the pond intermingled with the retrieved sounds from the 35mm frames – enlarging and compressing all the small and significant details.

When the toy rotated, it produced sound. We literally emulated the toy's movement by rotating the camera, which led to a distinctive style/form for the film. This is perhaps the most obvious example of what I mean by picturing sound. Another example from *That Cloud Never Left* (2019) is the use of film dialogues and songs against the images of the toy-makers watching television. My editor, Abhro Banerjee, and I were interested in taking time with this scene and keeping it long, as the sound design was created based on what people listened to in their homes while they worked on cutting the film frames of perhaps the same films for their livelihoods.

Abhro has a very acute sense for sound design, too. He is able to fuse very disparate tropes within the film's narrative and give it a similar atmosphere by using sound. He often distorts speed, uses VFX and adds effects to images and gets them to react to the sound. For example, in *Presence*, the second film of the project *Behind the Tin Sheets*, he plays with still and moving images against the sound of a barking dog, which increases the sense of tension and ghostliness in the film. In *That Cloud Never Left* (2019), he created an incredible flow of images moving from the rotating boats to the rotating planets, by dissolving the sound of insects with noise. Bigyna Dahal, our sound designer, pushed its galactic potential by expanding its scope and sculpting it within 5.1.

I made *That Cloud Never Left* in 2018, and it was released in 2019. Since then, much has changed; film reels are no longer available, toy-makers are not on the streets due to pandemic rules, and many of them have shifted to work on the construction sites of Delhi, Hyderabad and Bangalore. The film's two brothers (Chickoo and Baban) are now working on the Koramangala Metro construction site. The BMRCL labour colonies are sealed and have private security guards who prevent anyone from entering. During the first lockdown in 2020, the workers protested for their previous month's payments to be made. They insisted on trains being released before imposing a lockdown at a four-hour notice by Prime Minister Narendra Modi. There were plenty of images to prove the distances that needed to be covered. Many toy-sellers from Bangalore partly walked and partly hitchhiked their way home, 2,070 kilometres away.

We once again returned to make films with the protesting Metroworkers. We are yet to release it, as the supervisors from the BMRCL and the police threatened to file lawsuits against us and the workers whose Aadhaar numbers they had collected.[2] Much of the footage is shot by the workers, and some sent back videos of their train ride. For many this is their first time outside of the general compartment.

The second starting point

I recently heard a friend say that she knows her neighbours only through the walls and has never seen them. In her mind, they were a family of two with a cat. She often can hear the whistle of the pressure cooker, the squeaking of the cat and the singing of an old man. Her increased loneliness drove her to knock on the wall during the pandemic. She has not heard them ever since. I asked her whether she felt as if she had jinxed it? She said no; that her brain had the powers to imagine them.

Notes

1 *Behind the Tin Sheets* is a film-based project initiated in 2009 by Ekta Mittal, Paromita Dhar and myself, on the construction of the Bangalore Metro. More information can be found at www.tinsheets.in.
2 Aadhar is the name of the Universal Identification Number based on biometric and demographic data, allocated to Indian citizens and foreign residents who meet statutory requirements. It is mandatory to access many public welfare schemes.

Films Cited

That Cloud Never Left. Dir. Yashaswini. 2019.

14

Conversations, confusions, confessions: Living with and working in cinema

Anupama Srinivasan

Our film teacher would tell us: 'When you are editing, go through the scenes that you have put together and see which of them are there only to advance the plot. Remove them! The purpose and power of cinema is much more'. This was Dušan Makavejev, the Serbian director known for his unconventional and provocative films. When the clamour of voices – to fall in line, to stick to the story, to make the film accessible – grows loud all around, these words come back, their sparkle intact after more than two and a half decades.

Who decides what films get made? Do we succumb to the market? How do we resist? These are some of the key questions I have been pondering. At the risk of stating the obvious, when we are professional free-lance filmmakers, we usually need to earn a living by making films. This means that we must convince someone else to invest in our vision. While trying to raise money for your film, a sense of powerlessness may creep in, and it often does – presenting your film idea to people who mostly have no clue about cinema, but who have been given the authority to judge a film's and filmmaker's potential, their power derived from the country from which they may be operating, and/or the institution or company that they represent. In this essay, I reflect on the questions and tensions that have organised the shape of my practice as a filmmaker, film educator and festival curator, to the extent that the form of these practices is a response to my working through these questions.

The central issue is, of course, that there is zero funding for documentaries or documentary infrastructure in India. The Public Service Broadcasting Trust (PSBT) functioned for twenty-one years, but has, for all practical purposes, closed down. While they funded many documentaries, launching and helping to sustain the careers of several filmmakers, the funds offered were extremely limited, restricting the kind of films that could be made. Hiring a full crew and making fair payments to all the crew members was almost impossible, unless you planned for ten to twelve days of shooting. Imagining documentaries that needed more time to explore, more resources in terms of the kinds of cameras or sound equipment was rarely possible, unless the director tripled up as cinematographer and editor and had other means of support to pay their rent and basic expenses. Having said that, I want to emphasise that, while budgets are a severe constraint, it is not the only issue at play. Equally or more important is creative freedom. And with PSBT, there was aplenty. Feedback from the evaluators was not binding, and many of us did feel that we had the chance to make the film we wanted to make. In terms of form, some of the films that they supported would never have received funding from international funds or broadcasters, because they do not fit into the widely accepted rules of storytelling.

Filmmaking

For my own work as a filmmaker, after resisting for many years, I took the plunge into the international market in 2017. I participated in pitching forums and wrote numerous grant applications and was moderately successful. However, I have not reconciled myself to the obsession with characters and a rather reduced understanding of storytelling that I encounter at most of the international forums. The expectation is to present every film fitted into a three-act structure, with one or two (at the most three) main characters. This comes largely from European broadcasters and their understanding of story-telling and what would be palatable to their audience. However, this has not remained limited to this group but become a formula imposed on filmmakers, even by funds or organisations that claim to support artistic films. It is as if the role of the documentary filmmaker is to latch on to an interesting character and hope that his or her life will make the film for you. In grant applications, we are asked to give the narrative structure when we have barely started shooting, predicting what will happen with plot points and dramatic highs and lows. It seems that the goal is a typical fiction experience but with real-life characters. If the lives of the chosen characters did not quite play out in an interesting enough way, there would be no harm in staging and creating situations of conflict. Nobody says this openly, but it seems to be implied and freely practised. The fundamental problem, apart from the obvious ethical issues, is that it leads to a homogenisation that stifles filmmakers, limits audience experience and growth, and finally works actively towards making cinema a poorer, weaker and duller medium. For me, it goes against everything I find exciting about the documentary: the revelling in the unexpected, not being tied to a character-driven story, innovating with form, bringing in various strands, because as a filmmaker you want to touch on broader themes and nuances.

I have heard one statement quite often: 'If you want to make a film for an international audience…' Of course, this means European or North American; I do not think anybody is thinking about people in Ghana, the Philippines, or Chile, when they speak about an international audience. The reduction of a whole continent of people into a single monolith is in itself problematic, but even if we, for the sake of argument, were to assume that all or most Europeans receive film in the same way, what about films that take inspiration from forms of expression that are rooted in other cultures? Should they not get made? Form is a political choice, and any attempts to control form have to be seen for what they are – cultural domination. Again, it comes to the fact that those who have the money to fund the films and run the reputed film festivals call the shots. Hence, a country like India is seen as a source of interesting stories, but the message is that filmmakers from here had better rein themselves in and make films to suit the 'international' audience. If we see ourselves as filmmakers who do not want to cater to a demand in the market, but want to make films of our choice, about topics about which we care, and work with forms that do not fit into the norm, what are we to do?

In such a climate, I often wonder what is the 'right' approach to take when I am in the role of a teacher or mentor. I recently participated in in a session of R. V. Ramani's online filmmaking course, and I screened an excerpt from Sergei Parajanov's *Shadows of Forgotten Ancestors* (1965). A participant responded by saying: 'This is ok for the masters to do, but if we attempt something like this, isn't it likely that we end up making something self-indulgent?' I answered with a bit more confidence than I was feeling: 'If we attempt something keeping the market in mind, and then fail, how is that any better than attempting to find your own cinematic voice through a film and failing? Do we have to feel proud of ourselves for trying to pander to some vague notion of the popular, and feel ashamed of making a sincere attempt at cinematic exploration?'

Film education

In 2006, I had the opportunity to conduct a filmmaking workshop with children under the aegis of Katha, a Delhi-based NGO working in community development, child welfare and literature. I said that I would guide the children to make short films in eight days; no prior knowledge of cameras or filmmaking was necessary. Oh, the possibilities of digital technology – simple, cheap, fuss-free! The idea was not to train children to become filmmakers, but to open up a space for them to explore film as a medium and develop their own relationship with it to interpret the world around them.

Subsequently, I conducted many workshops with children and young people, always quite amazed by the enthusiasm with which they, especially children, embraced the idea of careful observation, expressing themselves with spontaneous fluid movements of the camera and unrehearsed conversations with those whom they encountered while filming. It has often been a humbling experience to see how quickly they 'figure out' the digital camera, not just to record, but to create. In the first meeting, their intention is always to make a fiction film in which they themselves will act, mainstream films and television being the only exposure they have had so far. Documentary is usually an unheard word, or at best a hugely misunderstood one. However, in just a couple of days, there is a transformation. When they hold the camera and take a single shot of something out there, not staged or set up, and we see it together as a class and analyse it – the duration of the shot, the composition, the light, what is happening within the shot, does it sustain? – most of the children get drawn into the magic of creating and experiencing an image in time. Because it is a documentary, they have no references from which to 'copy', and soon enough, we all get aligned to the journey of free and fearless exploration.

With film students, the process has always been more stressful because of the weight of expectations and too much knowledge. For me, the workshop space is more precious, because we have the freedom to fail, because there are no financial stakes. If something does not work at all, no one but the ten to twelve participants in the workshop need to know! While it is exhilarating, teaching is also a quite delicate affair. How can we be ourselves as teachers, but not let our own tastes and understanding limit the students? How can we let them grow and have their own trajectories, rather than make them fall in line with our notions? The need is to create a space where dissent is possible, not to project ourselves as the ultimate authority who knows everything and whose approval is the be all and end

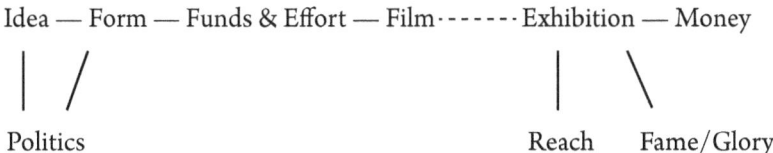

Figure 14.1 A rough attempt at a diagrammatic representation of the filmmaking and exhibition process.

all, but to acknowledge that we are all co-travellers. If I make everyone follow my way, all I would do is to make sorry clones of myself. Then there is not much difference between that and training students to fit into the industry, in fixed, pre-conceived roles; it is probably much worse. Further, when students go out into the real world, will they be ready to face the challenges, or would they be unable to cope after being in a protected and idealised space?

As filmmakers, we find ourselves at the receiving end, our worth being judged regularly, facing rejections more often than we can bear. Perhaps to restore a sense of balance in my life, I have whole-heartedly accepted opportunities for conducting film appreciation workshops, curating films, influencing viewing culture in whatever way possible, with nothing short of a missionary zeal.

Film curation

In my curatorial work, emphasis is on finding films with an originality of voice, sincerity of intent and cinematic rigor rather than any notion of technical competence or finesse, the idea being that film festivals are spaces that should welcome experimentation and brave attempts, rather than fête 'excellence'. Moreover, festivals with which I was associated, such as the IAWRT Asian Women's Film Festival and PeaceBuilders International Film Festival, being non-competitive, allowed for a true celebration and camaraderie rather than tense competition. There was no hierarchy of best film or best cinematography; films were considered in their totality as cinema enmeshed in politics and philosophy. At the Asian Women's Fest, the effort pointedly was to not allow women's films to be ghettoised in any way, restricted to certain so-called women-centric issues. We tried to include a diversity of themes, forms and ways of expression, and we sought the female gaze in all its wide and vibrant splendour. We showed documentaries, animation, short fiction, and in 2012 we opened it up to feature fiction as well; in fact, no form, duration, or genre was forbidden.

This vision owes much to Jai Chandiram who started the film festival in 2005. In 2008, for example, when I was not yet part of the festival's organising committee, she and her team selected my short film *Everyday* (2006) as the opening film. It was shown right after the chief guest had made an inspiring speech about feminism. The film was a quirky six-minute piece on a couple of pigeons outside my seventh-floor apartment window. It left the audience perplexed, people wondering why it was the opening film, and what the feminist message in it was. When I asked Jai why she had selected it, she said she liked the meditative quality in the film.

Thinking back, I cannot remember making a single 'populist' decision when I was the festival director. It was not that we did not want a big audience or a packed hall. We managed both at many times, through reaching out to educational institutions, doing curtain-raisers in colleges where we showed short films and excerpts from previous editions and had discussions with students. The way I saw it, our purpose was to give a space to films that may not have been shown at other festivals, may not have been made by well-known filmmakers, but have a spark. Backing your selection and creating an audience for it is crucial. I am quite disturbed by the tendency of festivals to put together films that have been shown at the 'famous' festivals in the world. Is that not just herd-mentality? Just as each filmmaker has their own unique perspective and cinematic voice, should not curators have the vision, will and courage to actually watch films and make a selection by which they can stand? In the festivals in which I have been part of as organiser, there has been no corporate or state sponsorship – that is, we worked with extremely limited budgets. Once again, small budgets allowed us more artistic freedom and to be our own bosses rather than having to answer to some funder. Organisations such as the Goethe Institut, the India International Centre and cultural centres of other countries did support us, but their support came without any strings attached.

As censorship started tightening its noose around film festivals, we had to reframe some of the screenings. There was once a film about Kashmir that we showed, featuring it as part of a presentation and not as a film. We also managed to show a film on Tibet without the authorities objecting. The film *The Women of Tibet: A Quiet Revolution* (2008) by Rosemary Rawcliffe show-cased the struggle of 15,000 unarmed Tibetan women who in 1959 took to the streets of Lhasa to oppose the violent Communist Chinese occupation of their country. The festival being held at the India International Centre in the heart of Central Delhi meant that all events were directly under the gaze of the government. Nation, religion, gender, caste and sexuality are some of the axes along which works are 'judged', screenings stopped, screening venues vandalised, people dragged to court. 'We don't want to get into trouble' may be the sentiment of many filmmakers and film festival organisers. One cannot be too naïve about it, but merely succumbing may also not be the only option. Maybe we can first keep our connection with our understanding of the truth intact before we begin to think of the repercussions of putting something potentially controversial in a film or including a film in a programme.

In 2004, as part of the anti-censorship Films for Freedom initiative in Delhi we organised a two-day seminar on experiences with form, called *Multiplicities*. Here we were looking at self-censorship of form. The need to be accepted, accessible – how much does it affect the way in which we express ourselves? One could ask, why are you making a film if you do not want to communicate, if you do not care whether your audience is able to slip into and experience the world you have created? Then it comes back to the question of which audience? Who are you going to keep in mind? Also, should not our role as artists be to push the envelope and create forms that audiences may not have seen before, instead of doling out seemingly different narratives in the same format? The issue of political censorship has been predominant in our minds, especially in recent years. Now the situation within the country has become dire, with anything considered remotely controversial coming under the radar of the state machinery. In informal discussions with film festival organisers such as R. P. Amudhan and Sanjay Joshi, who have done stellar work in regularly having film festivals in small towns and villages, I learnt that the only way to carry on may be by being even more low-profile, allowing films to be shown in small gatherings and classrooms rather than any fancy-looking festivals.

There is a prominent festival in India called Jio MAMI (Mumbai Academy of Moving Image) funded by the Reliance Company. It is known to be well-curated; when a film is selected for it, it comes as a validation for both the film and the filmmaker. However, at most other forums, the same filmmakers who show their films proudly at this festival would vehemently oppose corporates, especially the particular company in question. How do we reconcile this ethical dilemma? Most of us are creatures who seek approval from reputable institutions or individuals. Will we be happy if our film is shown in ten to fifteen schools in Bihar, Uttarakhand, or Tamil Nadu, and not at high-profile festivals?

I do not have answers to many of the questions posed here. As I stand steeped in the world of international fund-raising for my filmmaking work, I remember the scepticism and trepidation I initially felt because I feared that one would be hurled onto the path of being in constant selling-mode.

We have to start selling before we have made anything and continue to sell while we are making the film and after we have made it. I was not totally wrong. But as I go along, I think about what the alternative way of evaluating might be. When there is such an enormous number of projects from around the world, how does anyone choose? What could be another process? As people from this part of the world, we are at a severe disadvantage, because we cannot raise any money from within the country, leaving us with no bargaining power, often forcing us into situations that are clearly exploitative.

Within this landscape, there fortunately are exceptions. It takes a bit of time to get to them, and also a will to not bend over and blindly kow-tow to the self-proclaimed masters. There could be a simple rule: work only with people who respect you as an artist. This is easier said than done, especially in the case of filmmakers who are at an early stage of their career and struggling to establish themselves; But for others, too, because the need for acceptance and validation sometimes clouds our mind. Can we play the game, negotiating with the existing rules and creating some of our own, resisting the push towards the creation of homogenised, pre-formatted, over-mentored films that have lost the power of authenticity and authorial voice?

Films Cited

Everyday. Dir. Anupama Srinivasan. 2006.
Shadows of Forgotten Ancestors. Dir. Sergei Parajanov. 1965.
The Women of Tibet: A Quiet Revolution. Dir. Rosemary Rawcliffe. 2008.

15
About critique: Indian media and documentary cinema

Kunal Ray and Mochish K. S.

The mainstream Indian media's dwindling interest in matters of art and culture has been a cause of long-standing alarm. Since the introduction of economic liberalisation in the 1990s, the media ecosystem in India has witnessed a perceptive shift. Here it must be stated for reasons of clarity that, even during the pre-liberalisation days, the media did not play a very encouraging role in the promotion of art and culture. Art- and culture-related writing was usually reserved for weekend supplements. Defining the idea of Indian culture in a very narrow and homogenous way, these features largely extolled the cultural heritage of the country by featuring interviews with classical dancers, musicians and painters. The emergence of a market-driven, lifestyle-based journalism in the 1990s led to an increasingly compromised media ecosystem which began to look away from pressing economic and social issues existing in the country, at the cost of embracing a neo-liberal economy.

Changes in the ownership pattern of the Indian media with direct links to political parties and increasing corporatisation and profit maximisation began to drive and shape its operations. Reflecting on the nature of the post-liberalisation Indian media, P. Sainath (Franklin et al. 2014, 305) observed: 'Today we have multiple schools of thought in journalism. You have broadly two kinds of journalism: journalism and stenography. Much of what is called journalism, or what passes for journalism today, is essentially stenography to power, to the powerful, increasingly to corporate power'. As an immediate consequence of the changing attitude of the Indian media, its focus on social welfare gradually began to disappear from the post-liberalisation Indian media, and its approach to issues of the working classes, farmers, rights of artists and various marginalised sections of society changed drastically.

The enthusiasm among media houses to welcome the policies of economic liberalisation further revealed their aspirations to market capitalism. Sonwalkar (2002, 827) argues:

> The face of Indian media as a whole changed during the 1990s, structurally, professionally, and technologically. This also led to changes in editorial practices, particularly after the introduction of a corporate perspective to journalism. The evolution of a corporate culture that gives an overriding primacy to 'marketing' rather than 'editorial' is seen to have distanced the press from its social obligations (Gupta 2005; Rao and Mudgal 2015; Thakurtha 2013; Nanjundaiah 1995; Ram 2011; Thussu 2007).

The aggressive marketing strategies used by various Indian media such as *The Times of India* since 1990 for maximising profits is an indicator of the new media culture in India.

Prior to liberalisation, especially the broadcast media environment in India was highly regulated by the government. The government-run television network Doordarshan was the sole operator in the field until the early 1990s, when a bouquet of private television channels was launched, changing the Indian broadcast media landscape permanently. While newspapers did enjoy a certain degree of freedom during this period, ownership remained in the hands of a few feudal families and business groups; today, thirty years after liberalisation, very little has changed in the pattern of newspaper ownership in India.

Owing to the growing commercialisation of the media ecosystem in the country, conversations about the serious arts began to disappear from its coverage. Entertainment and lifestyle-based features soon emerged as substitutes for art-based news programmes and writing. In such a climate, discussions on documentary films perceived to be critical of social hierarchies or probing societal structures were abandoned by the media, to such an extent that a news feature on a documentary film became a rarity. After all, discussions on documentary cinema would not help to sustain the goals of a neo-liberal Indian media. This chapter will therefore attempt to understand and analyse a major shortcoming of the Indian media – its ignorance and lack of interest in documentary cinema and its attempts to invisibilise an important film practice.

The marginalisation of documentary cinema in Indian media

Several media practitioners are of the opinion that the absence of documentary films from India's mainstream media is reflective of the regular film-goer's lack of interest in the subject. This attitude, however, has to be historically analysed. According to Meenakshi Shedde, India and South Asia Delegate at the Berlin Film Festival, as well as independent film curator, ...

> Most documentaries in India were initially produced and distributed by the government's Film Division (established in 1948), as Soviet-style propaganda, with mostly short, twenty-minute newsreels initially promoting nation-building activities, that were compulsorily screened before the main feature in cinemas nationwide. In my childhood, I remember it as a time when men went out for a smoke and families took their kids to get wafers or to pee. The Chanda Committee report of 1966 commented on the poor quality of the documentaries, and resistance of Indian cinema theatres to the mandatory screening, for which they also had to pay a service fee (Shedde 2021).

These documentaries prejudiced the Indian viewer who began to associate documentary cinema with a drab aesthetic. The choice of the subject-matter for these films did not help either. Some viewers found it too academic for their interest. The voice-over-based narration in these films also failed to engage the viewer who found it didactic and instructional. Shedde further adds:

> The extreme contrast of the deathly boring documentaries on dams or crops with the entertaining features that followed right after with glamorous stars, high drama and song and dance, as well as the mandatory nature of the screenings, created a deep-rooted public resistance to documentaries whose hangover has unfortunately lingered for decades. It poisoned the ground for talented, creative, courageous documentaries that followed, and till date there are relatively limited opportunities for regular public screening or even appreciation of documentaries (Shedde 2021).

Funding and distribution of documentary films in India were controlled by the government until about early 2000. The government funding agencies encouraged a certain kind of documentary cinema, which largely helped to unfold the art and culture aspect of the country, explored livelihoods and urban issues. Very few of these films directly addressed political issues or concerns related to social hierarchies. The kind of documentaries shown on public platforms created among the audiences a certain perception about documentary films made in India and further isolated the viewers from these films. Mainstream media largely overlooked this aspect of television programming. Indian viewers were also unaware of the different kinds of documentaries that were being made in the country. They were only familiar with voice-over films, thus thinking that documentaries ought to have a voice-over. Many viewers perhaps looked away from documentary cinema, without even considering its other narrative possibilities which the films chosen for funding or screened on Doordarshan failed to highlight. Besides, little discussion about international documentary films or experiments in documentary cinema ever made it to the mainstream press.

Historically, popular fiction cinema has dominated art and culture coverage in the Indian media, thereby marginalising all other prevalent art forms and the traditional arts. Instead of focusing on the diversity of Indian arts and cultural heritage, the media took the easy route of writing about mainstream fiction cinema which enjoys enormous popularity in the country. Commenting on the decline in arts journalism in the post-liberalisation age, noted critic and former arts editor of *The Economic Times* (ET), Sadanand Menon (2019) observes:

> So, if the art pages had to continue, they would have to dumb down and become more like an 'entertainment' page – going to popular culture, mainstream cinema, Bollywood, etc. Even the excellent science and education pages in ET were deemed to be redundant and, one by one, they started pruning these. The management was very clear that the focus had to be entertainment, whereas we, who were producing the pages, were very clear that it had to be serious and engaging with social issues and so on. This tussle lasted roughly a year before the interference became so much that I decided to move out.

Writing about popular cinema soon replaced all forms of art and culture writing or discussion in the mainstream Indian media. Occasionally, film coverage would include a report or mention of a documentary film which dealt with a famous Indian personality or a major episode in the country's historical past. Or else, a documentary film had to court its share of controversy to invite the attention of the mainstream Indian media. For instance, several of Anand Patwardhan and Rakesh Sharma's documentary films were discussed in the popular media for the controversies that they created. Films like *Ram Ke Naam* (1992; see The New Indian Express 2021) and *Final Solution* (2014; see The Hindu 2019) still continue to be written about for their political content, which make them relevant to contemporary occurrences in the country.

Several factors regarding the apathy of the mainstream Indian media can be traced back to the nature of journalism training in Indian educational institutions. There is a distinct lack of emphasis on art and culture sensitisation that might prepare aspiring journalists to tackle these subjects and write sensitively about these issues. We rarely see a course that focuses on diverse Indian art and cultural forms that will prepare journalists for writing about these issues. This lack of training therefore leads to a superficial understanding of art and culture which is reflected through reportage on music, dance and theatre, among other areas. Fiction films, however, dominate this coverage, owing to their popularity and the enormous markets involved. Lest we forget, many of the film campaigns are also paid promotions through the media. Furthermore, the advent of film journalism with its focus on gossip, 'Page 3' parties and paid reviews has compromised the seriousness of conversations about cinema. Therefore, anything with a serious topic is not deemed worthy of being featured in the mainstream press. Even a cursory glance through mainstream media reveals that interest in fiction film is confined to film releases, the box office, celebrity interviews and promotions with almost no space devoted to any serious discussion or review of cinema. This has led to a near exclusion of serious artistic efforts, such as documentary films, from mainstream art and culture discourses.

While funding for classical music and dance concerts which are also believed to be representative of Indian culture or Hindu heritage increased in neo-liberal India, the same cannot be said about the other arts, especially documentary cinema. Classical music and dance concerts are also perceived as largely recreational activities promising refined entertainment for the cultural urban elite. These events also took care of the aspirations of the newly formed middle and upper-middle classes, the by-products of a neo-liberal society. Furthermore, private capital was wonderfully comfortable with the Indian classical arts which made references to spirituality and the divine without questioning or probing the social hierarchies so deeply entrenched in Indian society. Unsurprisingly, private capital and media have continued to support classical arts in the country on a large scale.

The selective representation of Indian documentary film practice

Films such as *Ram ke Naam* (1992) and *Final Solution* (2014) are rarely discussed in the Indian media for their artistic or aesthetic properties, or for the people who made them. It is the political nature of films that keeps them alive in the mainstream media space. This representation further highlights the ignorance of the popular Indian media about documentary cinema as an artistic expression. A film critic and one of the very few journalists who regularly write about documentary films, Nandini Ramnath explains:

> For decades, documentaries were considered extensions of our school textbooks – a chore that we had to suffer through because they were meant to be good for us. Despite a bunch of Films Division (FD) titles that have been recently celebrated for their storytelling imagination and visual excellence – the films by Jean Bhownagary, S. N. S. Sastry, S. Sukhdev, Pramod Pati – the fact remains that on the whole FD films were dull and preachy, had a voice-of-God complex, and were meant purely to aid nation-building rather than be an art form in themselves. A few generations of Indians watched these films on Doordarshan, which meant they could walk away from them, or in the movie halls before the main features, which meant they could ignore them. Arguably, it is with the rise of the independent documentary movement, initially rooted in activism and questioning the state (the early films of Anand Patwardhan, for example) that we began seeing the formal possibilities (Ramnath 2021).

This begs the question, by selectively featuring a handful of films and film-makers to suit their sensationalist journalism and political project, does the popular Indian media then do a huge disservice to the cause of documentary cinema? The films usually featured or discussed in the media share common features, such as an international award. For example, Shaunak Sen's *All That Breathes* (2022) or Rintu Thomas and Sushmit Ghosh's *Writing with Fire* (2021) have recently garnered mainstream media attention for winning laurels overseas. Films are also featured when directly linked to a controversy such as the recent event at Ravenshaw University in Odisha, where the screening of two documentary films, *Gay India Matrimony* (2020) and *Had Anhad* (2007), had to be dropped from a campus festival after objections from right-wing groups. Moreover, there is barely any writing in the popular media about documentary filmmakers and their creative practice. This absence is significant because it prohibits the creation of awareness about the diversity of the artform, its expressive possibilities and its social impact. In a conversation with Arvind Rajagopal, documentary filmmaker and writer Paromita Vohra (2012) puts this succinctly:

> Whether in film criticism, film schools or, to a lesser degree, the film community's contextualisation of itself, there is little sense of documentary history – almost a refusal of it. In other words, how do you discuss practice, when the history of the documentary as an aesthetic or arts practice is constantly obscured and the significance of a documentary is often judged by its relationship to political ideology? (16)

Documentary cinema more than political communication

For many decades, documentary cinema has been chiefly understood as political cinema, despite the evolution of the documentary form with the entry of various practitioners into the field from a range of social and cultural backgrounds and art practices. Due to experimentation and the diversity of voices, the traditional focus on social and political realism is no longer its defining feature. This shift has caused some confusion among Indian critics with a conservative understanding of documentary cinema. Paromita Vohra addresses this confusion thusly:

> For instance there have been protracted arguments within the documentary film community along the lines of 'we are activists, not artists' in the 1990s – an ongoing argument that seems to have arrived at some sort of uneasy resolution. In initial interviews with people who have served on juries and selection committees, there also seems to be some discomfort with decisions about films that do not conform to a more familiar convention of realism (and activism). What are the concerns and reservations of those who are uncomfortable with more individualistic forms – and is there something that binds these reservations? (Rajagopal and Vohra 2012, 13)

The confusion indicated by Vohra also applies to the Indian media that understands documentary as a watertight category. A filmmaker or their work is therefore positioned in the context of a political event or ideology. There is seldom a profile of a documentary filmmaker featured in popular media without linking it to a contemporary event. Clarifying the process of selecting documentary films to discuss in her columns, Ramnath explains:

> I pick documentaries the way I pick features – topicality first. Is it new or newish? Will it be premiered or screened at an upcoming festival? So, I try and follow the Indian documentary festival calendars as much as possible to see what catches my interest. As for what does, that depends. I like to focus on feature-length or slightly longer films because there is more to unpack here. I do a mix of reviews and interview-based previews, but I feel that we simply do not hear enough of the voices behind the films. I also look for an interesting narrative or formalistic device. This is not always the case, but sometimes a film in an established category – say, the personal documentary, or the social message film – will deploy an unusual filmmaking language. A few examples off the top of my head include Reena Mohan's *Kamalabai*, which challenges and enriches the biographical documentary, and Shaan Khatau's *The Dark I Must Not Name*, which I have seen but is unfortunately not available anywhere. The latter film looks at the aftermath of the Bhopal gas tragedy in a whole new and imaginative way. Deepa Dhanraj's *Something Like a War* brings urgency

and ferocity to an exposé of the Indian family planning programme. *An Old Dog's Diary*, Shai Heredia and Shumona Goel's film on F. N. Souza, is similarly a beautiful new way of examining a small chapter from an artist's rich life. Another of my favourite films is *Amir Khan* by S. N. S. Sastry – a short film that captures the essence of its subject purely through performance and a few other images (Ramnath 2021).

While Ramnath strives to discover formalistic ingenuity in documentary film practice and thereby enrich the conversation by writing about a variety of documentary features, only a handful of her counterparts look for diversity while reporting about documentary films.

Insufficient media coverage for documentary film festivals

The partisan and selective attitude of the popular Indian media is further on display during their coverage of film festivals held in various parts of the country. In comparison to fiction film festivals, the coverage for well-known documentary film festivals in the country, such as the Mumbai International Film Festival (MIFF) and the International Documentary and Short Film Festival of Kerala (IDSFFK), is negligible. This kind of coverage could also be discerned as a direct representation of the economic power and influence of fiction cinema in comparison with documentary cinema. An increasingly corporatised media naturally affiliates with fiction cinema, as opposed to the social critique championed by documentary films. Reportage about the prominent film festivals in India revolve around fiction films, thereby ignoring the occasional documentary section that most of them comprise. For instance, surveying news reports published in mainstream print media – such as *The Times of India*, *The Hindustan Times* and *The Indian Express*, among other publications – during and after the recently held International Film Festival of India (IFFI), Goa (2022) reveals that the focus of these reports remains on the fiction films screened, interviews with visiting dignitaries, opening and closing ceremonies, and Bollywood representation at the event. Even the documentary sections, like their fiction counterparts, bring diverse voices from around the world. The mainstream media's negligible attention to these films and their makers also results in depriving the audiences of an opportunity to watch international documentaries which are not easily accessible in the country. The corporatisation of fiction filmmaking in India and its proximity to market capitalism has transformed the cultural industry in the last two decades in the country. Documentary cinema, on the contrary, continues to raise tough questions and critique fiction film's growing obsession with market capitalism.

Corroborating this attitude of the Indian media, Gargi Sen – a writer, filmmaker and curator – states:

> There is an invisibility about the documentary in the mainstream media. It is perceived to be boring, socially relevant cinema. There is no serious attempt to understand the documentary with very few exceptions. There is also a great degree of media sensitisation that is necessary in this area. While running the Magic Lantern Foundation, we used to reach out to journalists and ask them to write about various films, and some of them did. In my opinion, the urban English media is not so interested but, to some extent, the regional print media is. For example, Marathi, Hindi, Bengali and definitely Malayalam press have written about documentary films (Sen 2021).

This writing, however, is limited in its scope. As stated above, these features or articles treat the film as news, to the extent that little or no commentary about the form, method, or structure of these films is mentioned. Writing about documentary film is either reduced to an interview with the director or offers a quick summary of the film, with some quotes from the crew thrown in. The track-record of Indian-language media is no different in this regard. They, too, gravitate towards documentary cinema when it is newsworthy or involved in a controversy.

Documentary cinema as alternative media

For a vibrant democracy, a free and independent media is of great importance. It is well-known that the media play the role of a watchdog in a liberal democracy. According to Jacobs and Johnson (2007), 'there is a general understanding both among the researchers, media practitioners, and the people from the political spectrum that media assumes a focal part in articulating interests and debates in a liberal society; specifically, how thoughts develop, diffuse and influence systems' (128). For decades, documentary films in India have played the critical role of questioning the powers that be about any attempts to deviate from the secular fabric of our democracy. Furthermore, many of these films also serve as a constant reminder about the rights of the marginalised. Documentary films in India also offered the biggest and most relevant critique against majoritarianism, communal polarisation and oppressive gender and caste hierarchies. Filmmakers Anjali Monteiro and K. P. Jayasankar (2016) argue that films such as

Deepa Dhanraj's *Kya Hua Iss Shaher Ko?* (1986), Anand Patwardhan's *Ram Ke Nam* (1991), *Father Son and Holy War* (1995), *War and Peace* (2002), Lalith Vachani's *The Boy in the Branch* (1993), *Men in the Three* (2002) and Rakesh Sharma's *Final Solution* (2003) engage in important memory work, keeping alive within the public sphere debates around the ruthless suppression of various others, and also problematise the violence at the heart of nation-building. Documentaries have the breadth and scope for offering constructive criticism on several issues, while the popular mainstream media's attention and coverage is time-bound, short-lived and guided by vested political and economic interests.

The issues that documentary films highlight remain captured or recorded for posterity, whereas a news report can often be lost or difficult to redeem. An issue such as climate change which is of great concern all over the world is rather well-demonstrated through documentaries as opposed to media reports and coverage. Documentaries often offer diverse and marginal perspectives and deeper analysis of issues when compared to news reports. Various social movements in India, such as the *Narmada Bachao Andolan* (NBA) or the recent farmers' movement, extensively used documentaries to share information and their voice. Filmmakers like Amar Kanwar have made films that take us deep inside Odisha to unmask the tribal protests against the illegal land-grabbing of mining corporates. In many such places, the documentary film is perhaps the only recorded evidence of the events as they transpired in the field. These films have been successfully used for political mobilisation, alongside other campaign methods such as public speeches.

Documentary films can act as an alternative to mainstream journalism, by addressing the issues of the marginalised sections of society. Alternative journalism offers a critique of the attitude of mainstream media which ignores the concerns of the vast majority by selectively focusing on the interests of the urban elite. Political documentaries are also critical of the establishment by closely examining state policies, gender and caste hierarchies, as well as religious fundamentalism. Historically, such films have been used to voice dissent and express anguish about the ruling forces. The increasing interference and indirect control by government agencies of the private media in India make it further difficult for the mainstream media to feature or discuss documentary films if they are critical of the ruling establishment.

At a time when the media's credibility is under serious scrutiny, documentary films have an even bigger role to play in order to sustain the ideals of a democracy. It is characteristic of the popular Indian media to divert attention from serious social issues at hand by focusing on inconsequential issues. Former Press Council of India Chairman Justice Markandey Katju (2015) argues that 'the most important issues for the country are our massive poverty, unemployment, casteism, communalism, malnutrition, and healthcare etc., but our media usually highlights issues of relatively lesser importance, or even trivial ones, and diverts attention from the more important ones'). It is understood and well-known that popular fiction cinema often becomes an ally in such a process, through its escapist entertainment which distracts the audiences from reality through song-and-dance routines. This could also explain the recent spate of Hindi fiction films which, in particular, aim to valorise India's past through stories of freedom fighters and other national heroes while diverting attention from contemporary challenges facing the country.

Digital media have most certainly diversified India's media landscape. Documentary films are featured on these platforms such as *Scroll*, *The Wire*, *Quint* and others. However, this is far from adequate since their reach is not as wide as that of the mainstream media. The target audience of the digital media platforms largely consists of English-speaking urban elites, and the circulation is therefore limited to specific cohorts. Moreover, the documentaries chosen for reporting are current affair-based films serving as a corollary of news or an extension of current issue-based news analysis. In this context, we draw attention to the work of PARI (People's Archive of Rural India) which captures rural realities through short documentaries available on its website. Even as these short films work as an extension of the featured reports, the expressive visuals not only illustrate but imaginatively depict the context and settings of the narratives, a sharp contrast to the short, documentary-like features available on other digital news platforms in India.

Final thoughts

In an increasingly corporatised media system that relies entirely on revenue via advertisement, there is minimal space for documentary films which may not generate any revenue for the media organisation. The eminent journalist P. Sainath argues that 'corporate ownership destroys diversity; it stifles smaller but important voices. It destroys journalist's freedom by converting the job market of a journalist into contracts, where earlier they have very solid tenured jobs' (Agarwal 2018). Indian media is controlled by urban, upper-caste elites who also dictate the issues to be covered by the media. Most recently, an Oxfam (2019) study on caste in Indian media pointed out the caste realities which exist in the media landscape. According to the report, 'Indian media is an upper-caste fortress. Out of 212 leadership positions surveyed in newsrooms, none are held by those belonging to Scheduled castes and Scheduled tribes' (Oxfam 2019, 6). This media system hesitates to engage with issues related to gender and caste oppression and other hierarchies that are ingrained in the system; it is therefore not surprising that documentary films which address these issues struggle to find a space in this media landscape.

To a considerable extent, the public discourse on documentary films in India is organised by academics, by means of books, academic papers, public talks and other allied events. Documentary films are regularly screened in academic spaces, as part of curricular and extracurricular activities. Nevertheless, even in the area of Film Studies, the attention paid to documentary films is far below that granted to popular fiction films. Largely, Film Studies in India and those writing about Indian cinema overseas usually engage with Hindi and other popular fiction film cultures. Having said that, it is perhaps academia alone which discusses documentary cinema with some seriousness, but owing to the nature of academic discourse, which is exclusive to a chosen few, this discussion fails to reach beyond certain scholarly circles. Therefore, academic writing cannot be an alternative to conversations about documentary cinema in the popular media, but it can certainly offer support to the cause of dissemination of such cinema and the filmmakers involved in such a practice. These divergences and disparities perhaps indicate that academia, journalists and documentary practitioners must develop shared goals and modes of cooperation towards developing a critical documentary agenda.

Alternatives to counter the silence of the mainstream media about documentary cinema in India could look towards initiatives like Gargi Sen's now defunct publication, the quarterly *Alternative Media Time*, which ran on a subscription model. Each issue carried filmmaker interviews and reviews of documentary films and was also translated into Indian languages such as Marathi, Hindi and Bengali. While this was a praiseworthy effort, it struggled to sustain itself, owing to a lack of funds, but the digital medium offers various possibilities. Online blogs, digital newsletters and podcasts can be used to create similar initiatives. Filmmakers can play an active role in this regard, through newsletters and blog posts, as well as training programmes, such as the pioneering work of filmmaker and media activist Amudhan R. P. who travels across the country to organise short documentary festivals in educational institutions and media and journalism schools. These activities create awareness and encourage young minds to think about the documentary as a serious art form.

Questions remain about the effectiveness and reach of alternative platforms; therefore, disengaging from mainstream media is not an option. Now, the constructive use of digital platforms can lead to improved media engagement and critical public interest in documentary cinema. While the recent Academy Award for the Indian documentary film *The Elephant Whisperers* (2022) has caused a sudden albeit expected spurt of interest in documentary cinema among the Indian public, this momentum can translate into affirmative action only through sustained media engagement and public participation. This is an opportunity that the Indian media should seize unequivocally to compensate for its long silence.

Works cited

Agarwal, C. (2018) Journalism has been reduced largely to a revenue system, says P. Sainath. *Newslaundry*. https://www.newslaundry.com/2018/06/25/corporatisation-of-media-journalism-revenue-ownership-self-censorship-sainath [accessed 20 December 2021].

Franklin, C. G., Shankar, S., and Sainath, P. (2014). Against stenography for the powerful: An interview with P. Sainath. *Biography: An Interdisciplinary Quarterly*, 37, 300–19.

Gupta, S. (2005). Post-liberalisation India: How free is the media? *South Asia: Journal of South Asian Studies*, 28(2), 283–300.

Herman, S., and McChesney, R. (1997). *The global media: New missionaries of global capitalism*. London: Cassell.

Jacobs, S., and Johnson, K. (2007). Media, social movements and the state: Competing images of HIV/AIDA in South Africa. *African Studies Quarterly*, 9(4), 127–55.

Jayasankar, K. P., and Monteiro, A. (1996). *A fly in the curry: Independent documentary film in India*. New Delhi: Sage.

Katju, M. (2015). The Indian media's got its priorities wrong and need to introspect if it wants to be respected. *Newslaundry*. https://www.newslaundry.com/2015/12/22/the-indian-media-has-got-its-priorities-all-wrong-and-needs-to-introspect-if-it-wants-to-be-respected [accessed 5 January 2022].

Menon, S. (2019). The demise of arts journalism in India and the democratic deficit. *Lilainteractions*. https://lilainteractions.in/theoretical-imagi-nations-towards-bridging-the-arts-in-india/ [accessed 10 December 2022].

Nanjundaiah, S. (1995). Deregulation of television broadcast in India: Cultural and informational impacts. *Asian Journal of Communication*, 5(17), 71–87.

Oxfam India (2019). Who tells our stories matters: Representation of marginalised caste groups in Indian newsrooms. *Oxfam India*. https://drive.google.com/file/d/1BsyiTPDIBh9mFArtvPnNSKMoZ-Kjlcp6/view [accessed 3 March 2022].

Prasad, K. (2008). The false promise of media liberalisation in India. In C. George (ed.), *Free markets, free media? Reflections on the political economy of the press in Asia*, 171–92. Singapore: Asian Media and Communication Centre (AMIC).

Ram, N. (2011). Sectional president's address: The changing role of the news media in contemporary India. *Proceedings of the Indian History Congress, 72*, 1289–1310.

Ramnath, N. (2021). Personal interview.

Rajagopal, A., and Vohra, P. (2012). On the aesthetics and ideology of the Indian documentary film: A conversation. *BioScope: South Asian Screen Studies, 3*(1), 7–20.

Rao, S., and Mudgal, V. (2015). Democracy, civil society and journalism in India. *Journalism Studies, 16*(5), 615–23.

Sen, G. (2021). Personal interview.

Shedde, M. (2021). Personal interview.

Sonwalkar, P. (2002). 'Murdochization' of the Indian press: From by-line to bottom-line. *Media, Culture and Society, 24*, 821–34.

Thakurta, P. (2013). Curbing media monopolies. *Economic and Political Weekly, 48*(16), 10–14.

The Hindu (2019). 'Final Solution', documenting events in Gujarat in 02-03 is free to view once more. *The Hindu.* https://www.thehindu.com/entertainment/movies/final-solution-documenting-events-in-gujarat-in-02-03-is-free-to-view-once-more/article26810321.ece [accessed 18 November 2023].

The New Indian Express (2021). JNU administration advises students union to cancel unauthorised screening of Ram Ke Nam. *The New Indian Express.* https://www.newindianexpress.com/cities/delhi/2021/dec/04/jnu-administration-advises-students-union-to-cancel-unauthorised-screening-of-ram-ke-naam-2391837.html [accessed 18 November 2023].

Thussu, D. K. (2007). The 'Murdochization' of news: The case of Star TV in India. *Media, Culture and Society, 29*(4), 593–611.

Epilogue

On building documentary cultures of resistance

An interview with K. P. Jayasankar and Anjali Monteiro

Anjali Monteiro and K. P. Jayasankar are leading documentary filmmakers, thinkers and writers based in Mumbai, India. Professional and life partners, they have made forty films together since 1987; films that question hegemonic concepts surrounding identity, modernity, nationalism, gender and development. They are actively involved in movements against censorship and founder-members of Vikalp, a collective of documentary filmmakers campaigning for freedom of expression.[1] Together, they have mentored more than a hundred student and fellowship documentary film projects.

Monteiro and Jayasankar's professional location as former Professors of Media and Cultural Studies within a prominent institution of the social sciences (the Tata Institute of Social Sciences, Mumbai) opens a standpoint to reflectively evaluate the fundamental effects of institutional categories on documentary concepts, culture and practice. Neither generalising documentary as a discourse of sobriety, nor as a specific formal artefact, their approach is cognizant of the multiplicities of people, vocabularies and functions that inhabit documentary, and integral to its capacities for resistance. Drawing on their practice grounded in ethics and reflection, they offer vital considerations and methods for bringing together documentary scholarship, practice and education.

Shweta Kishore: You inhabit many roles in the field of documentary culture in India. What do you think at this point are the strengths and weaknesses of the conditions in which independent documentary practitioners work in India?

K. P. Jayasankar: The growth of documentary in India is, as you know, rhizomatic, with no particular aesthetic coherence. It has always been informed by multiplicities, and that is one of its strengths. The strengths and weaknesses of the genre arise from the same set of conditions; for instance, a lack of patronage or funding opportunities from the state and an absence of mainstream media distribution networks for a very long time. The latter, perhaps, is now changing. There might be some limited funding, but not as much as it should receive. The existence of a very strong fiction film industry – when you say film in India, that's always linked to a fiction film culture – has meant that documentary has always been relegated to a second place.

The initial relationship that documentary film had with the state, through the Films Division with its agenda of propaganda and a hypodermic, top-down developmental model, tended to position the genre as a prophylactic, against the undesirable influence of fiction film. So that also set a tone to the genre of documentary film in India.

And, of course, in contemporary times, the presence of formal and informal censorship. Censorship in India comes in many flavours – firstly, the censorship of the state, secondly of the market, which excludes documentary films from its distribution networks. And thirdly, of course, vigilante censorship that happens on the street, even after it clears censorship procedures of the state.

But one of the major aspects is its links to social movements and processes. Documentary film has been linked to many social movements right from its inception.

Anjali Monteiro: So, looking at these conditions, the lack of patronage and funding, the interface with social movements, the strong commercial film industry and then censorship, I would say that these factors have been both the strengths and the weaknesses of documentary film in India. For instance, the lack of funding opportunities has made documentaries much more diverse and hybrid in their forms than in many other countries, where it has been closely tied up with television markets. The range of films and the kinds of audiences which they reach is so diverse. And there is a strong strand of resistance to the power of the state and of dominant social groups.

And because of this kind of relative informality and the space that documentary occupies, it has invited practitioners from very diverse backgrounds, and not all with film school education. A lot of the time film school graduates, particularly from the main film schools, tend to gravitate towards the feature-film industry and towards specialised functions as editors, directors, sound recorders and so on. But for most documentary filmmakers making a documentary is a labour of love because it often comes with very limited monetary benefits and often with a lot of costs.

The lack of commercial funding and distribution has helped to create networks for informal funding, distribution and circulation. The fact that independent documentary has often contested the narratives of the state makes either state or market sponsorship difficult because the market doesn't want to touch content that might offend the state. So, in the final analysis, it has been these informal networks for funding and circulation and even for production, where filmmakers rely on others to help them, sometimes pro bono, or at certainly much below market rates, that has made possible a lot of the documentary film work in India.

K. P. Jayasankar: The weaknesses also stem from the same set of conditions. The lack of funding and commercial distribution possibilities has also led to a lack of visibility and a secondary status for documentary film. In the present times, state institutions such as Films Division that produced documentaries and supported some independent documentary work have been shut down. This has also had implications for non-governmental institutions such as PSBT (Public Service Broadcasting Trust), which was able to support independent documentary through its funding from Films Division and other government institutions. With the government crackdown on grant agencies such as the Ford Foundation, most local sources of funding for independent documentary have dried up.

Shweta Kishore: Recently, after Shaunak Sen's film All That Breathes *received international attention, there has been a fair amount of media coverage and popular writing about documentary. Do you feel this popular media attention may translate into greater support for documentary, and institutions may consider documentary in India worth supporting, worth nurturing? Could this be a turning point?*

Anjali Monteiro: I think that films like *All That Breathes* or Rintu Thomas and Sushmit Ghosh's *Writing with Fire* are exceptions in terms of their content, and the fact that they reached the Oscars is amazing. I mean, what tends to reach the Oscars is more films like *Smile, Pinki,* or *The Elephant Whisperers,* feel-good films that don't really question relationships of power.

Documentaries on OTT platforms are similarly circumscribed. Recently, we were having a conversation with some filmmakers who have done some work with the OTT platforms, and they were saying how they were not ethically or even aesthetically comfortable with these templates. Some have even walked out of film projects because they felt that this was just not something they were able to do. So, sure, there might be more space for documentaries, but what kinds of documentaries? Will these be documentaries that speak of the rights of marginalised groups or talk about what's wrong with India today? I think not.

K. P. Jayasankar: In fact, it is interesting that there are some conversations around the idea of documentary now, with the Oscar nominations and international awards and the attention that ensued. But I doubt that it's going to translate into any growth for the genre itself, because ultimately, it's not OTT platforms or other transnational networks that are going to provide documentary with growth, because it depends largely on more open-ended, local funding processes.

Anjali Monteiro: For it to translate into any growth, documentary must have access to public networks, to more open-ended funding, and that funding is becoming increasingly scarce. PSBT used to provide such funding, having worked with them ourselves. They supported some important and interesting films, but now PSBT has most of its sources of funding curtailed. Possibilities for domestic funding other than crowdfunding are minimal.

On the other hand, the conditions under which documentary filmmakers work are getting harsher in terms of violence on the ground, through vigilante censorship and the general clamp-down on any dissent in this country. Despite that, and in fact very often because of that, censorship makes documentary film much more visible.

Shweta Kishore: You are highly prolific in areas of both scholarship and documentary practice whilst located in an educational institution. How did you navigate this context, and how did it implicate your practice and your artistic development? For example, did institutional mandates or missions feature in how you organised your practice in production or ethics?

Anjali Monteiro: We both started off as academics, working in diverse areas. Jayasankar's work is in the Humanities. He has a Master's [degree] in German studies and a PhD in Humanities and Social Sciences. I have a Master's [degree] in Economics and a PhD in Sociology. We've been working in the areas of Humanities, Media and Cultural Studies, and with a passion for art and social activism. And subsequently we strayed into documentary practice, without any formal training in documentary production. Our diverse backgrounds perhaps helped us make connections between the ethics and politics of representation, which were a part of our intellectual concerns, and became embedded in our film practice. So, for instance, we were always acutely aware of our relationship with our subjects and wanted to explore it in ways that would be meaningful both for ourselves and them. We were never in a hurry to capture images of them. It was about building a relationship and the film emerging out of that relationship. I think this helped us to look at ourselves as filmmakers and our narratives more critically.

Many of these individuals and groups we worked with were marginalised in different ways. And they were also often involved in creative practice, be it poetry, storytelling, or music. As fellow practitioners, we saw this as a wonderful opportunity for creative collaboration between two sets of artists that could be life-affirming for both of us.

K. P. Jayasankar: The other aspect that informed our work was that we were both affiliated with an institution for social work, which had a commitment to social justice and rights-based community practice. So, this horizon informed and nourished our work. Working within an academic institution where we were 'marginal' to the main thrust of the institution helped us. In a film school, it would have been different. Of course, it also meant that we had a very small budget. But that also gave us a certain amount of freedom and leeway to try out new things, without compunctions of the market or sponsorship, because we did not spend too much money. It helped us to develop a style of working where we did almost everything. So even today, when we work, except for sound recording, we practically do everything ourselves.

Anjali Monteiro: Over time, most of our work was self-initiated and not project-driven, which allowed us to pursue themes that interested us and [that] were related to our philosophical and ethical concerns. Reflecting and writing about our practice also helped us understand our own creative processes and concerns, which are often intuitive and always not deliberate or thought out. It's not that a concern always fed into the work, but they always stayed side by side, nourishing each other.

Shweta Kishore: Your practice is quite different from, say, television documentary production or commissioned documentaries. For example, you work with communities and individuals over a long period of time, sometimes decades, and sometimes come back years later to edit the material. The process is not determined by deadlines or industry formats. In some ways, it resembles an ethnographic practice because you are closely associated with the communities with which you work. Ethnographic film practice has certain debates about the ethics of the relationship between filmmakers or the researcher and subjects. How did these debates feature in the way in which you organise your practice, or how you positioned yourselves as filmmakers often working with marginalised or vulnerable communities?

Anjali Monteiro: Basically, reflexivity and self-reflexivity are very important to us, even before we knew those words, or we had read about them. We tried to embed our own process and ourselves into our films, but probably very differently in different films. So, for instance, in *Naata* [dir. K. P. Jayasankar and Anjali Monteiro, 2003] we have segments that are talking about our stories. In some of the Kutch films, we have subjects who are talking about us and what us documenting them has meant to them. So, there are different ways in which we sought to mark our presence in our subjects' lives, and in most cases it's been an ongoing relationship. They became more than just protagonists of our films, they became people that were important in our lives, and we learned a lot from each other.

K. P. Jayasankar: We have written at length about this relationship that we have with our communities and our own filmmaking practices and the significance of the concept of reflexivity for us. So, we won't go there now. But it is our biggest take-away from the ethnographic filmmaking practice. We are not making a film about 'them', but also using it as an occasion to interrogate our own social location and the kind of subject-position we represent – as urban educated university professionals and filmmakers. We found the debates within the ethnographic practice fascinating, and we tried to engage with them in our work, both in our writing as well as in our filmmaking practice.

Anjali Monteiro: So we wouldn't know whether we are ethnographic filmmakers. We have never formally studied ethnographic filmmaking, but those debates have always been a part of our thinking process, and they have also helped us grow as filmmakers.

Shweta Kishore: Often, we find that filmmakers or practitioners and scholars tend to exist in silos, and practitioners are focused on navigating the complexities of the industry, and scholars are focused on research and engaging with other scholars. So, I'm interested in understanding the effect of these professional silos on both entities. How could there be a more fruitful dialogue or a circular knowledge flow between the groups who are essentially adjacent to each other?

Anjali Monteiro: It has been our own experience that most documentary filmmakers have been happy to talk about their work, whenever we have approached them as scholars writing about documentary. And we have also met many scholars who would be glad for the opportunity to engage with filmmakers, whether through workshops or informal interaction. I think the silos are perhaps because of the nature of education in the field that tends to compartmentalise theory and practice.

In our work as filmmakers, as educators and as researchers, we have actively attempted to undermine these silos. So, for instance, the credo of the MA programme that we helped create is: 'thinking doers and doing thinkers'. There are some universities in India that are attempting to engage with both theory and practice in their pedagogy; apart from our own programme at the School of Media and Cultural Studies at TISS, Mumbai, we have the Communication programme at the University of Hyderabad, or even MCRC at Jamia Millia Islamia. These are examples of spaces that bring film scholars and filmmakers together and create opportunities for engagement between these two groups. These programmes have a flavour different from traditional film schools where the programmes are more compartmentalised, skill-oriented and geared towards the media industries.

More and more scholars are moving out of their comfort zones and engaging with filmmakers in workshops or seminars, in educational institutions, or through informal networks such as those offered by movements and campaigns. One area where this seems to have worked well is within the feminist movement, where we see fruitful engagements and warm relationships between those who write about films and those who make films. When there is a common sense of purpose, it makes it easier for scholars and filmmakers to come together and learn from each other.

Shweta Kishore: Yes, silos often occur at the level of film school departments where film and documentary practice and education or studies are separated. How did your experience of practice influence the way in which you taught film in the classroom, or how you conceptualised film education more broadly?

K. P. Jayasankar: There is a mutual mistrust often between practitioners and scholars. It is as if there is a division between social sciences and social work, and both mistrust each other to some extent. Therefore, combining both practice and theory became one of our concerns through media education. Through this critical media education work, we were actively countering the dominant common-sense approach that privileged a censorship model, which sought to see media in terms of 'impact' and 'effects'. This posited that there are 'less powerful others', particularly young people, who needed to be guarded against undesirable media effects. That was also the time of changes in the media environment, including the arrival of transnational networks in the Indian skies. We emphasised critical engagement and media use as an opportunity to empower audiences to actively read media artifacts, rather than acting as a patriarchal filter.

Anjali Monteiro: Our first experience teaching media was with the critical media education work that we did with students of social work, at TISS in the early 1990s. That then developed into workshops that we offered to a range of other groups, from social activists and parents to school students. The broad purpose of this initial work was to get the participants to actively engage with the media to understand how relationships of power – be they of gender, class, caste, or race – are articulated within various media texts, thus providing a space to critique both the relationships of power and media representations.

The creation of the Master's programme in Media and Cultural Studies at TISS gave us an opportunity to bring together theory and practice in innovative ways with a committed group of faculty that collaborated in designing the programme. Among other things, the programme was involved in engagement with media, culture and film theory, including documentary film and the production of documentaries as a part of the curriculum over the two years, and the emphasis was on group work, on learning from each other, as we had a very diverse group of students with different disciplinary and social backgrounds. They were not all from the social sciences; we had people who might be from an IT background and even Physics post-graduates. And in terms of social backgrounds, people from villages, from small towns, from large metros speaking different languages, whose competence of English also was quite different, and this very diverse group of young people had they their own ways of engaging with the field and their own strengths.

K. P. Jayasankar: The way we structured our curriculum, we made the documentary film a site where students could bring together the insights and learnings from both theory and practice-based courses in the programme, and not just the film theory or the Film Studies courses, but various other courses. All of them contributed to enriching the students' perspectives as they went out in the community and engaged with subjects. And that gave them a much broader perspective than what they might have been working on with specific protagonists or themes. The horizon was always larger, and this grounded students not only in Film Studies, but in broader critical humanities, and a social science framework did help to do this. In other words, documentary, as part of this programme, became a site for engagement with various ideas, bringing together research, community-based work and theoretical concepts. It became a site to actualise many of these learnings, even within the confines of an academic institution. We've been asked this question: 'But why documentary, it's so marginal, and you can't make a living out of this. Why teach documentary?' So, the answer lies in the fact that documentary becomes that occasion for bringing together various social and intellectual commitments. Yes, the answer lies in that direction.

Anjali Monteiro: If I were to look back at our work with students, the strength of our programme has been social engagement and its attempt to provide opportunities to students to understand the spaces they live in through their practice. We focus on the politics and ethics of their relationship with their subject, and this makes their work more mindful of community dynamics and processes. For instance, we always insist that our students take their films back to their subjects before finalising them, and we also invite all the subjects to the public premiere of the films. Over the years, this has resulted in an ongoing relationship with several neighbourhoods in Mumbai.

Shweta Kishore: It's exciting to think of documentary as a space for intersecting interests, and for bringing different knowledge forms together, rather than as a codified aesthetic form. And as you were speaking, I was thinking about a politics of access, or the decolonisation of knowledge, in ways that challenges a hierarchy of categories that are imposed by curriculums within an institution and to make it available to those who do not have the kinds of capital that is required to succeed in a film school. In this endeavour, were there any needs that you felt when teaching media or film, besides the Eurocentric bodies of knowledge that dominate Film Studies?

K. P. Jayasankar: Now there is a larger body of work on Indian feature films, but when we first started teaching, we felt an acute shortage of material relating to documentary film in India, except for an odd dissertation or two and a few journal articles and interviews with filmmakers, which probably motivated us to write our book *A Fly in the Curry*. Since then, of course, there has been other significant writings on the Indian documentary, such as your book, but by and large there was scant attention paid to the large body of path-breaking documentary work in India, which has grown exponentially over time. So, we feel that there could be much more writing and scholarship about documentary in India.

Anjali Monteiro: We've been using standard documentary texts that are somewhat Eurocentric, whether it is the work of Bill Nichols, Stella Bruzzi, David MacDougall, Brian Winston, but also Trinh Minh-Ha, and we have drawn on the writings of filmmakers and film scholars who worked in India. I mean your work, and others like Shohini Ghosh, Sabeena Gadihoke, Paromita Vohra, who has written a fair amount; Anne Rutherford has written about our work and about Amar Kanwar's work. Then Nicole Wolfe, Ravi Vasudevan, Julia Battaglia, Anuja Jain. We get our students to engage with a wide range of cinematic texts as well as all these writings.

When it came to the films that they were making, we followed a different process. For instance, we created several web archives combining the work of our students and the fellows whom we worked with as a spine. These web archives contain crowd-sourced films, research material, paper clippings and a lot of other resources. The archives are a part of what we called DiverCity, to evoke alternative narratives of the city of Mumbai and provide space to marginalised histories, voices and visions.[2] In a city like Mumbai, both geographies and histories are constantly being rewritten, erased, or excluded.

K. P. Jayasankar: Every year for the entire DiverCity series, we would choose a theme in consultation with the students and curate a set of texts around that theme for them to read. So, for instance, one year it was Remembering 1992, on the 1992 ethnic violence in Mumbai; another year it was looking at issues around the textile mills and what happened to the mill workers once the mills shut down. We worked on waste in the city, on migrants, on caste, on the street, who has rights to the street, on housing rights… In each of these cases, we would curate a set of readings around these themes: from newspaper articles to citizens' reports, to scholarly writing. We also set up conversations and invited resource persons to speak to the students – activists, researchers and filmmakers who had worked on that theme. We expected them to think about all of that, along with their experience of going out in the field and then decide what specific aspect of that theme they would want to address.

It was quite a rich experience for students to engage with so many different texts and not only Film Studies writing, but many other kinds of writing that helped them deepen their relationship with the spaces around them.

Shweta Kishore: It is a wonderfully interdisciplinary curriculum that connects documentary to many other socio/cultural bodies of knowledge and thinking with a social purpose. We have come to the last question, which returns to practice and audience. As scholars and filmmakers who have screened your films over a period of several decades, do you see a shift in the way in which people perceive documentary? Are there any broad trends in terms of taste or film literacy?

K. P. Jayasankar: With the opening of online spaces and exposure to a wide range of non-fiction work, even if it is a YouTube video or any other artifact, there is an engagement with the non-fiction mode, which makes the audience a little more open to documentary work. Earlier, the questions that came up after a film screening invariably included: What is it that you wanted to say in the film? What is the message of your film? What is its impact? What solution do you have now? All pointing to very simplistic ideas of documentary as an instrumental tool aimed at bringing about behaviour change; a text which is under the filmmaker's control.

Anjali Monteiro: Sometimes, people still ask those kinds of questions, but I would say that over time audiences have become more diverse and more dispersed. And their expectation of the documentary genre is correspondingly more varied and complex. So, for instance, the fact that a lot of young people have experience of making their own content or curating content makes them much more film-savvy and much more cognizant of cinematic language. And as Jayasankar said, there is more of a culture of making non-fiction narratives of various kinds, not just documentaries.

But also, one notices that attention spans have shrunk, and not all audiences are interested in engaging with films that require active involvement, interpretation and discussion. Online audiences tend to become a little impatient with something that's a little slow. I was suddenly thinking of our students. A video where our students made, making fun of our *So Heddan So Hoddan* [2011, dir. K. P. Jayasankar and Anjali Monteiro, Public Service

Broadcasting Trust]. They made a video called *Slow Heddan Slow Hoddan* which was a spoof; it's quite funny!

K. P. Jayasankar: But access to technologies and image-making is something that has also changed people's attitude. Earlier, when we started making films, it was an exclusive domain of the experts and professionals. Access to even the lowest-end video camera was so skewed, but today everybody has that kind of equipment – there is a surfeit of images, and that changes one's relationship with the medium itself.

Then there has been another interesting development. I think, in India since the 2000s, there has been a proliferation of local film festivals and dedicated screening spaces for documentaries across the country. These spaces and festivals and curated screenings of films have certainly helped in the development of audiences who are interested in watching and discussing documentary films. They may be few and far between in relation to the size of the country and the number of people. But I certainly think that they are significant, and they have managed to create a documentary viewing culture.

Anjali Monteiro: I would say that now we have various kinds of audiences, but overall audiences have the wherewithal to become more cognizant. They have the space to become documentary film aficionados, which earlier would have been much more difficult, when the technology did not make that easily possible. So, there is hope that all these changes will translate into some support for documentary film production, teaching and scholarship in India.

Notes

1 Vikalp Films for Freedom was born as a parallel film festival in 2004, in response to censorship imposed on the Mumbai International Film Festival.
2 DiverCity [http://divercity.tiss.edu] is a web-based audio-visual archive that brings together work done at the School of Media and Cultural Studies, at the Tata Institute of Social Sciences, Mumbai. Students and faculty engage with diverse communities and spaces within Mumbai, seeking to celebrate the unrecognized subaltern energies that have contributed to the city.

Films Cited

Access details are provided where available.

A Cry in the Dark. Dir. Haobam Paban Kumar. 2006.
A Quiet Little Entry. Dir. Uma Chakravarti. 2011. https://vimeo.com/160158058
A Season Outside. Dir. Amar Kanwar. PSBT, 1997. https://www.youtube.com/watch?v=r5WllkBLG7o&t=476s
AFSPA 1958. Dir. Haobam Paban Kumar. 2005.
An Insignificant Man. Dir. Khushboo Ranka and Vinay Shukla. 2016.
Angels of Troubled Paradise. Dir. Raja Shabir Khan. The Asian Pitch. 2011. https://vimeo.com/21901485 (Password: whitemoon)
Cities of Sleep. Dir. Shaunak Sen. Films Division, 2015.
Dr. B. R. Ambedkar: Now and Then. Dir. Jyoti Nisha. 2023
Dragonfly and Snake. Dir. Lipika Singh Darai. 2014.
Everyday. Dir. Anupama Srinivasan. 2006.
Final Solution. Dir. Rakesh Sharma. 2004. https://www.youtube.com/watch?v=tLQA8zJhogU
Forest. Dir. Ranbir Kaleka. 2009. https://vimeo.com/568366965
Had Anhad: Journeys with Ram and Kabir. Dir. Shabnam Virmani. The Kabir Project. 2008. https://www.youtube.com/watch?v=Dr83axn1IbM
Immoral Daughters. Dir. Nakul Singh Sawhney. Magic Lantern Movies and Newsclick. 2012. https://youtu.be/6GUEqNIlWco
Jari Mari. Dir. Surabhi Sharma. 2001. https://vimeo.com/435262962
Kahankar: Ahankar. Dir. Anjali Monteiro and K. P. Jayasankar. SMCS, TISS, 1995. https://www.monteiro-jayasankar.com/films/filmography/kahankar-ahankar/
Lady of the Lake. Dir. Haobam Paban Kumar. Oli Pictures. 2016.
Lynch Nation. Dir. Shaheen Ahmed and Asfaque E. J. 2018. https://www.youtube.com/watch?reload=9&v=c3qcGLSVPsI
Mera Apna Sheher. Dir. Sameera Jain. PSBT. 2011. https://vimeo.com/455409032
Mr. India. Dir. Haobam Paban Kumar. 2009.

My Camera and Tsunami. Dir. R. V. Ramani. PSBT. 2011. https://www.youtube.com/watch?v=_NTkW8UnLHw

Naata: The Bond. Dir. Anjali Monteiro and K. P. Jayasankar. SMCS, TISS. 2003. https://www.monteiro-jayasankar.com/films/filmography/naata-the-bond/

Nazara. Dir. Gagandeep Singh. CDC, SACAC. 2017. https://www.youtube.com/watch?v=_oPbhorAwgM

Oh That's Bhanu. Dir. R. V. Ramani. 2019/20. http://www.ramanifilms.com/?page_id=6

Our Family. Dir. Anjali Monteiro and K. P. Jayasankar. SMCS, TISS. 2007. https://www.monteiro-jayasankar.com/films/filmography/our-family/

Pariah Dog. Dir. Jesse Alk. 2019.

Phum Shang. Dir. Haobam Paban Kumar. Films Division, 2014.

Ram ke Naam. Dir. Anand Patwardhan. 1992. https://vimeo.com/88518769

Saa. Dir. R. V. Ramani. 1991. http://www.ramanifilms.com/?page_id=6

Saacha. Dir. Anjali Monteiro and K. P. Jayasankar. SMCS, TISS. 2001. https://www.monteiro-jayasankar.com/films/filmography/saacha-the-loom/

Santhal Family to Mill Recall. Dir. R. V. Ramani. 2017. http://www.ramanifilms.com/?page_id=6

Shepherds of Paradise. Dir. Raja Shabir Khan. The Asian Pitch. 2013. https://youtu.be/zLui8SaFLqs

Some Stories Around Witches. Dir. Lipika Singh Darai. PSBT. 2016. https://youtu.be/UgDK-tI8y8w

Sudhamayee. Dir. Megha Acharya. CDC, SACAC. 2019. https://drive.google.com/file/d/1Dfzu5oYwi_qFtPFfzx6_XLMwrakv1-on/view?usp=share_link

That Cloud Never Left. Dir. Yashaswini. 2019. https://vimeo.com/thefilms/thatcloud

The Colour Blue. Dir. Ein Lall. Doordarshan. 2014. https://www.einlall.com/the-color-blue

The First Leap. Dir. Haobam Paban Kumar. Doordarshan. 2008.

The Flowering Tree. Dir. Ein Lall. Doordarshan. 1996. https://www.einlall.com/the-flowering-tree

The Garden of Forgotten Snow. Dir. Avijit Mukul Kishore. 2017. https://vimeo.com/328907967/9f359b6ab2

The Last Adieu. Dir. Shabnam Sukhdev. Films Division. 2014. https://vimeo.com/114551630

YCP 1997. Dir. Anjali Monteiro and K. P. Jayasankar. SMCS, TISS. 1997. https://www.monteiro-jayasankar.com/films/filmography/ycp-1997/

Index

Note: Figures are shown with a page reference in *italics*. Notes are indicated with an n.

Acharya, Megha, *Sudhamayee*, 150–1, *150*
Adorno, Theodor, 5
aesthetics
    aestheticisation of Indian cities, 36
    as a critical space, 5–6
    of documentary practice, 13, 131
    embodied social aesthetics, 29–30, 32
    of feminist filmmaking, 10–11
    Griersonian aesthetics of state-produced
        film, 8, 9, 89
    technology and, 174
Akerman, Chantal, *No Home Movie*, 157–8
Ali, Agha Shahid, 135
Alk, Jesse, 53; *see also Pariah Dog* (Alk)
Ambedkar, Dr Bhimrao, 117, 118, 120–1
animals
    the anthropomorphic gaze, 49, 56
    in Baudelaire's work, 50, 56
    canine spaces in early silent films, 50
    The Elephant Whisperers (Gonsalves), 16,
        47–8, 124n, 209, 213
    embodied agentic animals, 48
    ethical responsiveness to animal deaths, 61
    in Indian documentary films, 47–8
    in liminal urban spaces, 51, 60, 62
    in realist documentary, 48, 53
    scholarship on animal documentaries, 48–9
    viewer relationships with, 48–9
    zoomorphic lens, 49
    see also Pariah Dog (Alk)
Arluke, A., 59–60
arts
    in early cultural documentary, 165, 171

    embodied interpretations of art, 167–8
    in the Indian media, 197, 198, 200–1
    K. Ramanujam's art, 175–6
    Modern Art in India, 171–2
    in 1950/60s India, 170–1
    Progressive Artists Group, 171
    state funding for, 171–3
    see also cultural documentary; Lall, Ein
Atema, A., 59–60
audiences/viewers
    affective engagement, 31, 70
    circulation approaches of independent film,
        13–14, 213
    the citizen viewer, 4
    construction of the spectator experience,
        156–8
    contexts of reception and production, 73
    engagement with non-fiction film, 221–2
    informal distribution networks, 213
    narrative reliability/unreliability and
        spectatorial engagement, 29, 41–3
    perceptions of Films Division
        documentaries, 178, 199–200
    public engagement in documentary
        exhibition, 127, 136–7
    responses to animals in realist
        documentaries, 48–9
    spectatorial engagement in *Cities of Sleep*,
        29
    spectatorial engagement with the subject,
        70
    see also editing
Avikunthak, Ashish, 85

Baudelaire, Charles, 50, 56
Benjamin, Walter, 14, 28
Berger, John, 165, 166
Bhownagary, Jean, 85, 86, 131
body, the
    body-environment relationship, 30–2, 42, 43
    the environmental conditions of the homeless body, 29, 37–8, 42, 43–4
    the filmic face, 36–7
    homeless bodies in movement, 38–9
    as a sensory node, 32
    spatial politics of urban settings, 27, 32
    see also embodiment
Bresson, Robert, 155

caste
    anti-caste movements, 117, 118
    Bahujan spectatorship, 119
    as a form of othering, 115
    lack of cultural representations of the Scheduled Caste, 114, 115, 116–17
    in the media landscape, 207–8
    in *Natchathiram Nagargiradhu* (Ranjith), 115–16
    Oppositional Bahujan Agency, 115, 118, 120
    stereotypes, 115, 117, 120
censorship
    anti-censorship Films for Freedom initiative, 195
    censor certificates, 14
    Cinematograph (Amendment) Bill 2021, 14
    in contemporary India, 212
    digital content filtering practices, 15
    impact of film festivals, 194–5
    in the 1960s, 85
    public protest actions, 14
    self-censorship of form, 195
    vigilante censorship, 212, 214
Chakravarti, Uma, *A Quiet Little Entry*, 154, 154, 159
Chalchitra Abhiyan, 20n
Chandiram, Jai, 170, 194
Chandralekha (dancer), 166, 170
Cities of Sleep (Sen)
    affective power of the face, 36–7
    embodied social aesthetics, 29–30, 32
    embodied social practices, 30, 39–40
    the environmental conditions of the homeless body, 29, 37–8, 42, 43–4
    homeless bodies in movement, 38–9
    intersubjectivity and viewer response, 31
    narrative reliability/unreliability, 29, 41–3
    Old and New Delhi settings, 32–4, 35–6
    sensory representation of homelessness, 28–30, 40–1
    the 'sleep cinema', 34, 40
    sleeping patterns of homeless sleepers, 33–4
    urban phantasmagoria, 28
    Yamuna Pushta area, 32–3, 34–5
colonialism
    of the *Adivasi*, 68–9
    neocolonialism within international funding regimes, 130
committed cinema
    of the 1970/80s, 8
    socio-political relations interrogated in, 9–10
    Third Cinema and, 9–10
communities
    community-based documentary practices, 215–16
    community-making function of documentaries, 4–5
    marginalised communities in popular culture, 119
    mohalla committees, 71, 73
    subject collaboration vs 'othering' in filmmaking practices, 10–13, 15, 70, 97–8, 106–7
Corner, John, 5
cultural documentary
    The Colour Blue, 167
    in contemporary practice, 166
    cross-genre practices, 167–8
    early forms, 165, 171
    The Flowering Tree, 168–70
    funding struggles, 170, 172–3
    Lall's series on Indian women artists, 165, 166–70, 172–3
    parallels with painting, 166–7
    soundtracks to, 167, 168
culture
    challenges of cross-cultural and trans-locational translation, 139–42
    cultural producer/consumer relationships, 10–13, 15, 70, 97–8, 106–7

cultural representations of the Scheduled Caste, 114, 115, 116–17
as a field of struggle, 5
impact of economic liberalisation, 11, 13, 15
in the Indian media, 197, 198, 200–1
India's traditional culture in a global world, 128–9
marginalised communities in popular culture, 119
multi-disciplinary creative practices in film, 131–2

curation
collaborative curatorial practice, 129
cross-genre curatorial practice, 127, 132–3, 193–4
curatorial practice and translation, 139–42
of educational texts, 220–1
of film festivals, 121
Loss and Transience, Hong-gah Museum, 127–8, 132–3, 140–1, *141*
Srinivasan's curatorial practice, 193–6
sutradhar as curator-director, 66, 77, 78

Darai, Lipika Singh
Adivasi identity, 92, 93, 96–9
Dragonfly and Snake, 93, 94
multi-tasking, 94–5
in the Odia Film and TV industry, 92–3, 94–5, 96
Some Stories Around Witches, 95–7
studies in audiography and filmmaking, 92, 93
subject collaboration vs 'othering' in filmmaking practices, 97–8
The Waterfall, 98
works in Odia, 93–4

Datta, Madhusree, 12
Dewan, Saba, 11, 12
Dharwadker, A. B., 67, 78

digital technologies
audience engagements with non-fiction film, 222
in *Cities of Sleep* (Sen), 28
contemporary documentary practices, 1–3, 207, 208–9
Information Technology Rules 2021, 14–15
OTT platforms, 177–8, 180–1, 213–14
in the social and political domains, 2–3
streaming video on demand (SVOD), 15–16

workshops with children and young people, 192

documentary exhibitions/festivals
censorship and, 194–5
challenges of cross-cultural and trans-locational translation, 139–42
cross-genre curatorial practice, 127, 132–3, 193–4
diagrammatic representation of the filmmaking and exhibition process, *193*
Forest (Kaleka), 137–9, *138*
The Garden of Forgotten Snow (Kishore), 133–7, 140
insufficient media coverage, 204–5
JIO MAMI (Mumbai Academy of Moving Image), 195
local film festivals, 222
Loss and Transience, Hong-gah Museum, 128, 132–3, 140–1, *141*
Mumbai International Film Festival (MIFF), 15, 102, 204
public engagement with, 127, 136–7
Vikalp Film Festival, 15, 211
VisionMix, 127, 129–30

documentary film
as alternative media, 205–7
alternative political voices in, 2, 3, 4, 5, 14
artisanal modes of production, 13
circulation approaches, 13–14, 213
death on screen, 61
definition, 131
functions of, 1, 4–5, 13, 152, 201–2
funding challenges, 2, 189–90, 195–6, 201, 212–13, 214
genre, 211–12
historical development of in India, 1, 7–8, 9–10
India's tradition of, 1, 77–8, 121–2, 131, 199–200
international awards, 213–14
international funding regimes, 15–17
marginalisation of in the Indian media, 198–201, 212
as a performative act, 31
personal cinema, 86–9, 122
politics in, 5–6, 7, 152, 165, 203–4
role of the cultural producer, 12–13
scholarship on, 208, 220–1
streaming video on demand (SVOD), 15–16
see also committed cinema; Films Division

documentary practice
  aesthetics of, 13, 131
  community-based documentary practices, 215–16
  within contemporary digital practices, 1–3, 13, 14–15
  digital technologies and, 1–3, 207, 208–9
  Griersonian legacy of documentary practice, 8, 9, 90
  practices of resistance, 1–2, 4–7, 8, 12, 14
  resistance towards state hegemonic practices, 1, 4, 5, 9, 11, 15, 205, 212
  scholarship-documentary practice relationship, 214–15, 217–18
  self-reflexive and interrogatory practices, 11, 12, 216
  subject collaboration vs 'othering' in, 10–13, 15, 70, 97–8, 106–7, 117
Dodiya, Atul, 172
Doordarshan
  commercialisation of, 11
  DD3 (arts channel), 170
  English and Hindi languages, 104
  independent filmmakers and, 96, 103, 104, 172
  state monopoly, pre-deregulation, 198
Dupont, V., 33

editing
  construction of the spectator experience, 156–8
  evaluation of rushes, 160–1
  Immoral Daughter (Sawhney), 160
  Mera Apna Sheher (Jain), 152–3, 153, 161–2
  No Home Movie (Akerman), 157–8
  the politics of image selection, 159–62
  the politics of representation, 158–9
  practice of, 148, 162
  A Quiet Little Entry (Chakravarti), 154, 154, 159
  as revelation rather than explanation, 152–6, 189
  rhythm and structure, 151–2
  silence and sound in *A Season Outside* (Kanwar), 148–9
  spatial and temporal continuity, 150–1
education
  politics of access, 219–20
  scholarship on documentary film, 208, 220–1
  theory and practice in critical media education, 218–21
  training in feature filmmaking, 104–5
  workshops with children and young people, 192–3
embodiment
  of agentic animals, 48
  definition, 32
  embodied interpretations of art, 167–8
  embodied social aesthetics, 29–30, 32
  embodied social practices, 29–30, 39–40
  see also body, the
Estella (dancer), 167–8
ethics
  ethical gaze of the documentary maker, 61–2
  in *The Last Adieu* (Sukhdev), 88
  responses to animal deaths, 61

feminist filmmaking
  interrogation of documentary ethics, 10–11, 12
  in the 1970/80s, 10
  Oppositional Bahujan Agency, 120
  subjective documentary modes and aesthetics, 10–11
Films Division (FD)
  closure, 213
  didactic function, 202
  documentary films for, 78, 199–200
  independent filmmakers and, 85–6, 131, 132
  The Last Adieu (Sukhdev), 85
  practices of resistance against state-sponsored cultural production, 8–9
  as state-run, 8, 9, 85, 212
  voice-overs, 67
first-person documentary, 83, 84, 87–8
folk theatre, 66–7
Foster, Simon, 52

Gadihoke, S., 10, 220
García Espinosa, Julio, 9
gaze
  the anthropomorphic gaze, 49, 56
  Bahujan spectatorship and, 118, 119
  Bahujan woman filmmaker's gaze, 120
  the casteist gaze, 116–17, 118
  in *Cities of Sleep* (Sen), 28, 31, 43
  the colonial gaze, 69–70

ethical gaze of the documentary maker, 61–2
the orientalist gaze, avoidance of, 54
Ghosh, Shohini, 10
Ghosh, Sushmit, *Writing with Fire*, 124n, 202, 213
Gonsalves, Kartiki, *The Elephant Whisperers*, 16, 47–8, 124n, 209, 213
Grierson, John, 8, 9, 90, 165, 166

Haraway, D., 47, 59
Hoffman, Philip, 90
hooks, bell, 119–20

identity
  Adivasi identity and Odia language in Darai's works, 92, 93–4, 96–9
  cultural producer/consumer relationships, 10–13, 15, 70, 97–8, 106–7
  in documentary's practices of resistance, 7
  in *Naata* (Jayasankar & Monteiro), 71–2, 74–5, 216
  Our Family (Jayasankar & Monteiro), 75–7
  plural identities with transnational contexts, 128
  public discourse on national identity, 2
  religion-based subjectification, 71–3
  representations of marginalised communities in popular culture, 119
  of the 'revolutionary' filmmaker, 11–12
  see also caste
image-making
  linearity in, 180–1
  market control over formats, 177–80
  political representation, 174–5
  self-reflectivity, 179–80
  technology's impact on, 171, 176–80, 181
images
  image-sound-voice relationships, 183, 187–8
  the politics of image selection, 159–62

Jain, Sameera, *Mera Apna Sheher*, 152–3, *153*, 161–2; *see also* editing
Jayasankar, K. P.
  audience engagements with non-fiction film, 221–2
  community-based documentary practices, 215–16

within the field of documentary film, 211–12
Kahankar: Ahankar, 68–70
memory work of documentary film, 205–6
Naata (The Bond), 71–5, 216
Our Family, 75–7
Saacha, 70–1
scholarship-documentary practice relationship, 214–15, 217–18
self-reflexive praxis, 216
So Heddan So Hoddan, 221–2
theory and practice in critical media education, 218–21
YCP, 70, 75, 78–9
Juhasz, A., 6

Kaleka, Ranbir, *Forest*, 137–9, *138*
Kanshiram, 117
Kanwar, Amar
  Odisha in the works of, 206
  A Season Outside, 148–9
Kapur, G., 11, 132
Kashmir
  Anthem for Kashmir (Ravindranath), 15
  Each Night Put Kashmir in Your Dreams (Sheikh), 134, *134*
  filmmaking in, 110–11, 112–13
  The Garden of Forgotten Snow (Kishore), 133–7
  political violence, 109–10, 111, 135
  in Shahid Ali's poetry, 135
Katju, Markandey, 207
Kawash, S., 42
Kellett, P., 60
Khan, Raja Shabir
  Angels of Troubled Paradise, 113
  Broken, Silence, 110
  experiences of violence growing up in Kashmir, 109–10, 111
  film school in Kolkata, 110, 111
  filmmaking in Kashmir, 110–11, 112–13
  film-politics relationship, 111, 112
  Shepherds of Paradise, 111–12
Khan, Waqar, 71, 72–4, 75
King, Lucía Imaz, 129, 140
  see also documentary exhibition
Kishore, Avijit Mukul
  The Garden of Forgotten Snow, 133–7, 140
  Scribbles on Akka, 133–4
  Sundari, an Actor Prepares, 133

Kluge, A. et al., 4–5
Korde, Bhau, 71, 72–3, 74, 75
Kracauer, S., 55
Kumar, Haobam Paban
   AFSPA 1958, 100–2, *101*
   A Cry in The Dark, 102
   fiction filmmaking, 104–7
   film studies and apprenticeship, 102–3
   The First Leap, 103–4
   Manipur in film, 103–7
   Mr India, 104
   Phum Shang, 106
   subject collaboration vs 'othering' in filmmaking practices, 106–7
Kumar, Karuna, *Palasa 1978*, 117–18
Kumar, Pankaj Rishi, 87
Kundu, V. S., 86

Ladino, J., 49
Lall, Ein, documentary series on Indian women artists, 165, 166–70, 172–3; see also cultural documentary
language
   Darai's works in Odia, 93–4
   English and Hindi languages at Doordarshan, 104
   voice and sound in independent documentary, 9
Last Adieu, The (Sukhdev)
   in association with the Films Division, 85, 86
   first-person documentary form and, 83, 87–8
   as personal cinema, 86–8
   truth and ethics, 88
   see also Sukhdev, S.
Lebow, A., 6, 83, 84
Li Kuei-Pi, 140–1
lived experience
   Bahujan spectatorship, 119
   in documentary practice, 18
   of homelessness, 28–9, 43–4
   in popular culture, 119
   resistance as grounded in, 3
   see also caste; identity; subjectivity

MacDougall, David, 29, 30, 31, 32, 39, 220
Malani, Nalini, 166, 170, 172
marginalisation
   of animals, 49, 51
   of documentary film in the media, 14, 198–201, 212
   representation of marginalised communities in independent film, 1, 70, 115, 117–18, 119, 120, 122–3, 205, 206, 215, 216
   representation of marginalised communities in popular culture, 117, 119, 120
Martel, Lucrecia, 184
Max Mueller Bhavan (MMB), 176–7
Mckee, Robert, 114
McKernan, L., 50
media
   arts and culture in, 197, 198, 200–1
   caste realities of, 207–8
   commercialisation of, 207–8
   coverage of documentary film festivals, 204–5
   democratisation of media technologies, 3
   deregulation of, 2, 11, 127–8, 198
   documentary's oppositional location to, 4–5, 8, 205–7
   impact of economic liberalisation, 11, 13, 15, 127, 197–8
   journalism training, 200–1
   mainstream fiction cinema in, 200, 201, 204, 207, 121
   marginalisation of documentary film, 198–201, 212
   partial representation of the documentary genre, 201–2
   state-sponsored patriotism and nationalism in, 1, 2
   transnational influences, 128
   watchdog role, 205
   see also Films Division
Mediastorm, 10
Mehta, Tyeb, 172
Menon, Sadanand, 200
Merchant, Jabeen, 87–8
migrant workers
   Behind the Tin Sheets (Yashaswini), 182–3
   BMRCL labour colonies, 182–3, 187
   see also Cities of Sleep (Sen)
Mohan, Jag, 85, 89, 90
Monteiro, Anjali
   audience engagements with non-fiction film, 221–2
   community-based documentary practices, 215–16

within the field of documentary film, 211–12
Kahankar: Ahankar, 68–70
memory work of documentary film, 205–6
Naata (The Bond), 71–5, 216
Our Family, 75–7
Saacha, 70–1
scholarship-documentary practice relationship, 214–15, 217–18
self-reflexive praxis, 216
So Heddan So Hoddan, 221–2
theory and practice in critical media education, 218–21
YCP, 70, 75, 78–9
Moore, Michael, *Roger & Me*, 49
Mudgal, Shubha, 170
Mulay, Vijaya, 86
Mumbai International Film Festival (MIFF), 15, 102, 204

narrative
 diverse narratives and viewpoints, 67–8
 the documentary maker's subject-position, 67–9
 editing practices and, 150
 European conceptions of story-telling, 190, 191
 filmmaker as *sutradhar*, 66–7, 78–9
 Naata (Jayasankar & Monteiro), 71–5
 narrative expectations for filmmaking, 190–1
 narrative reliability/unreliability and spectatorial engagement, 29, 41–3
 non-linear story-telling in *Kahankar: Ahankar* (Jayasankar & Monteiro), 68–70
 Our Family (Jayasankar & Monteiro), 75–7
 the power of stories, 114
 Saa (Ramani), 175
 soundscape and story-telling, 183–4
 voice-overs, 9, 67, 199–200
nation
 exclusionary narratives, 12
 nation-building documentary, 1, 199, 202, 206
 religious definitions of, 71
 statist aesthetic, 1, 8, 9, 12
 'We all are one' documentary, 72–3
nationalism
 in centralised media production, 1, 2

documentary's counter-hegemonic practices, 1, 4, 8, 11
 in the state-run Films Division, 8, 9
Natya Shastra, 66
Nichols, B., 4, 30, 31, 61, 220
Nisha, Jyoti
 Bahujan spectatorship, 119
 Dr. Bhimrao Ambedkar: Now & Then, 120–1
 film school education, 114, 121
 Oppositional Bahujan Agency, 115, 118, 120
 representations of marginalised communities in popular culture, 119
 responses to the casteist gaze, 116–17, 118
 search for self-representation on screen, 114, 115
 use of the documentary film, 120–3
 witnessing, 119–20

Otway, F., 41

Pariah Dog (Alk)
 the automobile in, 55–6
 canine spaces, 49, 50–1, 55
 canine-human entanglements, 48, 49, 56–60
 cinematic influences, 53
 critical reception, 60
 ethical gaze of the documentary maker, 61–2
 Kolkata setting, 53–6
 pet dogs/stray dogs contrast, 55, 59–60
 soundscape, 53
 the stray dogs of, 52–3, 55, 60–1
 zoomorphic lens, 49
Patwardhan, Anand
 Bombay, Our City, 20n
 on the Cinematograph (Amendment) Bill 2021, 14
 in the Indian media, 200
 socio-political conflict in the works of, 9–10, 11
Philo, C., 51
Pick, A., 49
politics
 in documentary film, 5–6, 7–8, 9–10, 152, 203–4
 editing and the politics of representation, 158–9
 political techniques of documentary film, 14
 representation and image-making, 174–5

Public Service Broadcasting Trust (PSBT), 96, 170, 189–90, 213, 214

Rajabali, Anjum, 114
Ramani, R. V.
   impact of K. Ramanujam's art, 175–6
   My Camera and Tsunami, 179–80, *179*
   Oh That's Bhanu, 177, *179*
   online filmmaking course, 191
   Santhal Family to Mill Recall, 180
Ramanujam, K., 175–6
Ramnath, Nandini, 202, 203–4
Rancière, Jacques, 6
Ranjith, Pa, *Natchathiram Nagargiradhu*, 115–16
Ranka, Khushboo, *An Insignificant Man*, 121–2
Ravindranath, Sandeep, *Anthem for Kashmir*, 15
religion
   Dharavi in *Naata* (Jayasankar & Monteiro), 71–3
   religion-based subjectification, 2
resistance
   practices of in documentary film, 1–2, 4–7, 12, 14
   as social practice, 3–4, 212
   towards state hegemonic practices, 1, 4, 5, 8–9, 11, 15, 205, 212
Rushdie, Salman, 136
Rutherford, Anne, 220

Sainath, P., 197, 207
Samson, Leela, 166, 168–70
Sawhney, Rashmi Devi, 129, 140; *see also* documentary exhibition
Sekhar, Revathi, 170
Sen, A., 32
Sen, Gargi, 205, 208
Sen, Shaunak, *All That Breathes*, 47, 124n, 143n, 202, 213; *see also Cities of Sleep* (Sen)
Sharma, Pabung Aribam Syam, 102–3
Sharma, Partap, 87
Sharma, Rakesh, 200
Shedde, Meenakshi, 199
Sheikh, Nilima
   Each Night Put Kashmir in Your Dreams (Sheikh), 134, *134*
   in *The Garden of Forgotten Snow* (Kishore), 133
   Scribbles on Akka (Dutta), 133

Shukla, Vinay, *An Insignificant Man*, 121–2
Shulman, David, 156–7
Silverman, L., 32
Singh, Arpita, 166, 167–8, 170
Smaill, B., 48
Sobchack, V., 48, 61
Sonwalkar, P., 198
sound
   diegetic/non-diegetic sound design, 39–40, 183
   editing and, 149
   of Films Division documentaries, 9
   image-sound relationship, 70, 92, 136
   image-sound-voice relationships, 183, 187–8
   in independent documentary, 9
   Pariah Dog (Alk), 53
   A Quiet Little Entry (Chakravarti), 159
   A Season Outside (Kanwar), 148–9
   sound design, 85
   soundtracks to cultural documentaries, 167, 168
   story-telling, 183–4
   Sudhamayee (Acharya), 150–1, *150*
   That Cloud Never Left (Yashaswini), *185*, 186–7
   voice-overs, 9, 67, 199–200
soundscape
   film transformed into a sounding device, 184–7, *185*
   of Mumbai, 93
Stallabrass, Julian, 131
state, the
   critique function of committed cinema, 8–9
   documentary's resistance towards state hegemonic practices, 1, 4, 5, 11, 15, 205, 212
   regulation of the media, 198
   see also Films Division (FD)
Steyerl, Hito, 152, 158
subjectivity
   filmmaker as *sutradhar*, 66–7, 78–9
   of the first-person documentary form, 84
   image/object/subject indexical bond, 61
   practices of resistance, 7, 8
   social aesthetics, 29, 32
   subject collaboration vs 'othering' in filmmaking practices, 97–8, 106–7, 117

subjective documentary modes in feminist film, 10–11
subject-positionality of the cultural producer, 12–13
Sukhdev, Kanta, 84, 86
Sukhdev, S.
India 67, 85
legacy in Indian documentary film, 84, 85, 86, 90
on personal cinema, 88–9
relationship with his daughter, 83–4, 90
work in association with the Films Division, 85
see also Last Adieu, The (Sukhdev)
Sukhdev, Shabnam
Earth Crusader, 89–90
relationship with her father (S. Sukhdev), 83–4, 90
self-reflexive praxis, 89
Unfinished, 90
see also Last Adieu, The (Sukhdev)

Third Cinema, 8, 9
Thomas, Rintu, *Writing with Fire*, 124n, 202, 213
Torun, Ceyda, *Kedi*, 56
transnationalism
impact on India's traditional culture, 128–9
in the Indian context, 127–8
plural identities and, 128
trans-locationality and, 130

urban spaces
aestheticisation of Indian cities, 36
body-environment relationship, 31–2
liminal spaces inhabited by animals, 51, 60, 62
neoliberal economic reforms and, 32–3, 35–6
slums, 71
spatial politics of urban settings, 27, 32, 35–6
street-settings, 55
urban phantasmagoria, 28
see also Cities of Sleep (Sen); *Pariah Dog* (Alk)

Videotage, Hong Kong, 130
viewers *see* audiences/viewers
Vikalp Film Festival, 15, 211
VisionMix, 127, 129–30
Vohra, Paromita, 12, 16, 202, 203, 220

Waugh, T., 9
Wilbert, C., 51
women
Asian Women's Fest, 193–4
Lall's series on Indian women artists, 165, 166–70, 172–3
represented in the Odia Film and TV industry, 92–3, 94–5, 96

Yashaswini
Behind the Tin Sheets, 182–3
film transformed into a sounding device, 184–7, *185*
image-sound-voice relationships, 183, 187–8
soundscape and story-telling, 183–4
That Cloud Never Left, *185*, 186–7

EU representative:
Easy Access System Europe
Mustamäe tee 50, 10621 Tallinn, Estonia
Gpsr.requests@easproject.com

www.ingramcontent.com/pod-product-compliance
Lightning Source LLC
Chambersburg PA
CBHW051121160426
43195CB00014B/2289